LOVELY FEE

Kind words from e

'Kate Toon's book is honest, smart and genuinely helpful. This is a practical, realistic guide to building a diverse, digital product passive income business that supports your lifestyle.'

Suzi Dafnis | HerBusiness

'*Six Figures While You Sleep* aligns perfectly with the core principle I advocate as a financial advisor: elevating income is essential for wealth accumulation to become financially independent. Kate Toon offers more than inspiration; she delivers a practical guide for turning your expertise into profitable digital products. This book is a great resource for anyone aiming to find ways to elevate their income to better their financial future.'

John Cachia | Thriving Wealth

'Reading this book has made me excited about my next steps. It's also shown me that there were previous projects I attempted where I was in fact on track, but I had missed a couple of key steps and gave up too early. This book has helped me realise that I do have the skills, expertise and knowledge to create something meaningful, and to make it successful.'

Lauren Moxey | Moxey Creative

'I read this book cover to cover three times. I work in this space every day, so I know how helpful this book will be. You can go from woe to go following the simple, straightforward steps at the end of each chapter. What I really love is the unpacking of often confusing concepts and bringing them all together simply so you can make your first, or maybe even your hundredth, digital product.'

Jennifer Gale | Pink Hat Digital

'I loved it! *Six Figures While You Sleep* is the perfect guide to help me take the next step in my business. It was easy to read and followed a logical path, with clear examples, instructions and tasks. I loved the inclusion of Kate's own experiences, shared generously in her trademark fun and approachable style.'

Angela Pickett | www.angelapickett.com.au

SIX FIGURE$

— WHILE YOU —

SLEEP

How to turn your services and skills into high-profit, low-effort digital products

KATE TOON

MAJOR
STREET

For Leanne Woff.

The Thelma to my Louise – a smart, sensible human who is a fabulous friend, a firm rock, a lighthouse in dark times and just an amazing person all around. My business would not be what it is without you.

MAJOR
STREET

First published in 2024 by Major Street Publishing Pty Ltd
info@majorstreet.com.au | majorstreet.com.au

A catalogue record for this book is available
from the National Library of Australia

**NATIONAL
LIBRARY**
OF AUSTRALIA

Printed book ISBN: 978-1-923186-15-6
Ebook ISBN: 978-1-923186-16-3

Cover design by Tess McCabe
Author photo by Jade Warne
Internal design by Production Works

10 9 8 7 6 5 4 3 2 1

Disclaimer: The material in this publication is in the nature of general comment only, and neither purports nor intends to be advice. Readers should not act on the basis of any matter in this publication without considering (and if appropriate taking) professional advice with due regard to their own particular circumstances. The author and publisher expressly disclaim all and any liability to any person, whether a purchaser of this publication or not, in respect of anything and the consequences of anything done or omitted to be done by any such person in reliance, whether whole or partial, upon the whole or any part of the contents of this publication.

Contents

About the author

Okay, we're going to do this in the third person even though it's awkward.

Kate Toon is an award-winning business mentor and digital marketing coach, as well as the author of popular business book *Six Figures in School Hours: How to run a successful business and still be a good parent*.

She's an honest, down-to-earth human on a mission to demystify the realities of running a successful online business. And while she's serious about business, she doesn't take herself too seriously.

Her Stay Tooned group of companies includes the Digital Marketing Collective, The Clever Copywriting School, and The Recipe for SEO Success. Kate has helped more than 20,000 other businesses demystify digital marketing, grapple the Google beast and find their own version of success.

Kate is a renowned podcaster and speaker, and is regularly invited to speak globally about her online business and share her expertise. She was named Australia's Most Influential Small Business Businesswoman of the Year as well as Training and Education Provider of the Year, and is a resident expert on Kochie's Business Builders.

All this working from a shed in her pyjamas in her backyard on the New South Wales Central Coast, where she lives with her teenage son. She's accompanied by her very own CFO (Chief Furry Office Dog), Pomplemousse, and assisted remotely by a small team of talented humans.

Acknowledgements

This isn't my first book rodeo, so I thought climbing back in the saddle would be way easier.

Who was I kidding?

Trying to distil everything you've learned over the last 15 years of running your business is tough. And add to that the challenge of not making it a snoozefest, bloated with boasting and a million exclamation marks. It's the perfect recipe for navel-gazing and absolute angst. I'll be honest, there were times I wanted to hurl my computer out of the window. But here it is, done and dusted, and I'm immensely proud. So, who to thank? Ah, there are so many.

First up, my team Kat, Shannon, Sue, Darren, Christina, Wendy, Harman and Bruce for helping me 'do the do' each day.

My partner Tony, who is the ideal avatar for this book, so much so that he's featured throughout. Thanks for listening to me working through all the problems when we should have been watching Netflix. And for putting up with my relentless meeping (moany weeping).

To mum and dad for being my first readers, and to all my other readers:

- Bronwen Whyatt
- Lauren Moxey
- Lauren Minns
- Phaedra Pym
- Angela Pickett
- Jennifer Gale
- Nicola Filia
- Nell Frapelle.

To my guinea pigs, thanks for being so helpful, vulnerable and encouraging:

- Ingrid Fernandez
- Tony Cosentino
- Stephanie Holdsworth.

To my amazing designer and illustrator Sue Waterson from Max Gecko Design.

To my fabulous cover designer, Tess McCabe.

And of course, big shout out to the team at Major Street, my publisher Lesley and my editor Will. I appreciate you letting me push the boundaries a little further with this book baby.

Introduction

My five-year-old son and I are in the LEGO® aisle in Kmart. We spend a lot of time here, so much so that I could describe every box with my eyes closed. It's what we do on my non-working days: grab a bite to eat, go to the park and then swing by Kmart before we do the food shopping. Our little ritual.

But we're here to look, not to buy. Why? Well, financially, things are tight. A little accounting short-sightedness means my partner and I are currently on a 'money lockdown' as we try to pay back tax debt. These are lean times, but it's hard to explain that to my son.

After spending some serious time reviewing the big boxes on the bottom shelf, he holds up the second-smallest box in the aisle: a cute little set with an ice cream truck.

'This one?' he asks in his most adorable voice.

As I wearily prepare to say no, I hear it. A gentle 'ping'.

I pull my phone out of my bag and see the notification from PayPal. I've made a sale. The digital template I created this week and just popped on my site has sold – and bizarrely, for almost the exact same price as the LEGO set.

I rush my son from the store and spend my first passive income funds on a flash bottle of pinot grigio. Only joking, of course I don't. I buy him that cute little ice cream truck and much more LEGO after that. *(Our loft these days is like a bizarre Tutankhamen hoard of LEGO boxes.)*

That was the moment when the digital product adventure became real for me.

*

But in truth, it started much earlier than that.

I'd given up my hideous 'real job' several years prior – as I was 'with child' – and set up as a freelance copywriter. After that, I quickly built a successful business while juggling *(not literally)* my child – you can read all about that journey in my previous book, *Six Figures in School Hours: How to run a successful business and still be a good parent.*

Six or so years in, I was doing well, happily writing websites, ads and emails for small businesses and flashy big brands. I'd polished my processes and boosted my profile, and was in high demand despite having pushed my prices up. In fact, I was charging the tippity top of the going rate. But I was still committing the cardinal business sin: **I was exchanging my time for money.**

Why is exchanging time for money such a bad idea? Well, time is finite, and your hourly rate is often dictated not by your needs but by what the market will wear. If you stick to the time-for-money exchange, you're ultimately limiting your income. I talk more about this in Chapter 2. Even with my fancy rates, as a working mum with little time, I still wasn't seeing huge financial rewards. Oh, and on top of that, I was tired, frustrated, and wondering when my **big thing** would happen.

In the end, I discovered that my journey didn't start with one huge thigh-shudderingly awesome breakthrough. It started with a, 'Hey, I made this thing, and I find it useful. I wonder if other people might also find it useful'. My one small idea was later affirmed by that delicious PayPal ping.

But even after that, I didn't make big moves; I took a series of tiny, deliberate steps that ultimately led me to (near) complete financial freedom, future security, and the ability to build generational wealth.

As Mr Warren Buffett said, 'If you don't find a way to make money while you sleep, you will work until you die'.
I worked out how to make money while I slept, or at least while I was in Kmart.

In 2015, I took the road less travelled and started building my business empire – or, as I lovingly call it, my 'business cul de sac'. *(For the non-Brits, this is a small, cute street with a dead end.)* It began with a single digital download and progressed to creating courses, memberships, and masterminds. I quickly moved from making a six-figure revenue a year to seven figures. And I've done most of it without putting on a bra or leaving my little backyard home office.

And it wasn't even about the revenue; it was all about the profit.

With minimal staff, no commercial premises and no postage or packing, my business was leaner than a lean thing. While small business profits of 10% to 20% are considered splendid, my business's net profit stood at 50% and counting.

How did I get started?

The process was annoyingly simple:

1. I took my existing skills and services and figured out how to sell them on a one-to-many basis rather than one-to-one.
2. I created 'things' that I could sell again and again and again with relatively little effort.
3. I developed diverse income streams, so I wasn't overly reliant on any one thing, repurposing my know-how into small chunks of buyable goodness.
4. I effectively lowered the price barrier to working 'with me', allowing me to share my expertise with more people and create a totally scalable business.

If I could do it, you can too. We all have skills we dramatically under-estimate. We think to ourselves, 'Well, sure, I know this, but so does everyone else'. They don't. Perhaps you're a landscape gardener, sick of lugging bags of gravel around day after day. But you think, 'Surely everyone knows how to build a patio?' They don't. And you could help them. Or you're a lawyer, tired of working with clients one-on-one, creating the same documents repeatedly. But you think, 'Surely there isn't a market for legal templates?' There is. And people will buy them.

The secret to building a six-figure business in your sleep is not about being a next-level genius or having some mind-blowing big idea. It's about being a few steps ahead of your customer, appreciating and embracing the skills you already have and finding ways to use them that are different, innovative, and profitable.

The bad news

Of course, it wasn't all sunshine and unicorns of love and happiness. There were many stepping-on-LEGO® moments and tears. So, I share both the positives and negatives in this book.

Here are a few negatives to get us started:

· I took a big financial step back to make a giant leap forward. (I share my real financials throughout the book in relevant spots.)
· I stuffed up along the way – I had many fails, flops, and faux pas.
· My 'price it low, stack it high' approach meant it took me longer to hit my financial goals.
· It took a while for me to stop comparing myself with others and build my confidence.
· My dream was to have fewer clients, but I replaced them with thousands of customers.
· I hoped to have more time to do 'non-work things' but seemed to perpetually come up with new business ideas that kept me busy.

But I can't complain (even though I love complaining). My iterative, customer-focused, automated, passive income plan has allowed me to make millions. I've paid off all my debts and secured my future. I've also created a business (and a life) that gives me flexibility, control, creative freedom, and absolute undercarriage tingles of delight every single day.

(Psst: I even have time to write this book and will knock off early and chill out by my new swimming pool – paid for by my business, I might add. What a smug bitch I am!)

But a few home truths before we go any further...

Home truth 1: this is not a get-rich-quick scheme

I'm sorry, but if you were looking for a fast path to 'skyrocket your sales' and 'uplevel' your whatever, you've picked up the wrong book. I'm not selling fairy stories here; I'm giving you a reality-based, doable plan – one that doesn't require a rich partner, generous parents, or a massive bank loan.

This book outlines a slow, steady, low-risk approach to building streamlined, high-profit income. Why? Because that's how I did it. There was no sharp hairpin turn from service-based business to passive income mogul. Instead, it was a gradual, somewhat ungraceful arc from doing 'all the things' to focusing on fewer, high-profit adventures. I achieved all this as a risk-averse working mum and as the primary breadwinner (and eater). I had no savings to speak of, no clue about 'angel investors', and zero generational wealth to fall back on. There was no plan B. I couldn't afford to take unnecessary risks, and that made the journey a little slower.

Home truth 2: this is not your usual business book

Honestly, most business books are drier than a mouthful of stale Weet-Bix. Sure, they might get the facts across, but your eyes glaze over as you read, and a pool of tedium drool gathers in your lap. While I'm not promising slap-your-thigh, snort-your-tea giggles, I hope to bring some levity to a much-dulled-down topic. Or perhaps just a little honest humanity. *(Watch out for some odd idioms and peculiar references that my editor will have tried to remove but I'll have clung to, like Kate Winslet on that bit of wood at the end of* Titanic.*)*

In this book, I'm not promising the world or bombarding you with cheesy sales advice, marketing hacks, tricks, and clickbait. Instead, I offer genuine, sustainable, realistic ideas with a proven track record.

Home truth 3: I share the story of real-life humans

Most passive income or digital marketing books are padded out with lengthy, bombastic interviews between the author and 'best-in-breed' entrepreneurs *(just to get the word count up, I reckon)*. While I love a lofty success tale, I think if I hear the Boost Juice or Lorna Jane story one more time, I'll chew my own leg off. So, instead, *Six Figures While You Sleep* focuses on real-life humans who are perhaps not making squillions *(I mean, some are)* but are making an excellent living doing what they enjoy without sacrificing themselves on the altar of their business.

Home truth 4: any type of business human can achieve this

You might think digital products are solely the remit of marketers, entrepreneurs, and geeks. But that's just not true. Whether you're a cake maker, an accountant, an artist, or an aged care consultant, you **can** turn your service into a digital product. And I've included examples of these kinds of people in the book. So, I'm sorry to say, there are **no** excuses for not giving it a go.

The goal of this book

In this book, I share the exact roadmap for taking your existing skills and turning them into digital assets. It's not a smug, chest-beaty story of **my** success – instead, it's an honest, realistic plan for how to create **your** success. Some might call it a passive income story; I prefer to call it an automated income story. Yes, there's work involved, but it's a doable amount – especially considering the potential rewards.

By the end of this book, you'll not only be equipped with the practical knowledge of how to build your own financial freedom, but you'll also have learned some valuable lessons from my highs and woes. I hope this book is your ticket to hop on the successful 'sleeper' carriage on the express train of business awesomeness.

Automated Digital Passive Income Product (ADPIP)

I needed to invent a new term for this book that included the words 'passive income' but made it super clear that it was digital-product-based. I struggled to create something snappy or a phrase that abbreviated into a sexy little acronym. ADPIP was the best I could come up with. You'll see it repeated throughout the book.

How this book works

The book starts with an outline of my story, and then moves into six beautiful chunks of goodness:

1. **Before you begin** – all the things to do before you head down the ADPIP path.
2. **Start where you are** – working out your brand and your Big Little Idea.
3. **Choosing your ADPIP** – how to choose the right product to start with.

4. **Slippery little funnels** – understanding how to build an audience and sell.
5. **The next steps** – how to manage your launch, time, money, and common issues.
6. **Success stories** – encouraging tales of success from my Digital Marketing Collective members.

Here are a few things to look out for:

Toon Tips. Occasionally I highlight a point or share my personal expertise to really drive it home.

TL;DR (too long; didn't read). If you're tight on time *(of course you are)* and have to skip or skim sections, don't worry, I sum up the key points of each chapter in the TL;DR sections.

Over to you. I've created mini lists of actions you can take at the end of each chapter to help you dig a little deeper into the exercises. If you don't like writing in books *(I don't)* then head to SixFiguresWhileYouSleep.com to grab the free workbook.

Guinea pigs. I've included stories from some members of my membership community, the Digital Marketing Collective. I'm using these to illustrate how they could (and will) implement their digital product strategies to prove this is entirely doable.

Here are the three guinea pigs whose adventures we'll be following:

1. **Ingrid Fernandez** is a commercial lawyer turned small business founder. After several years spent working her way through courts, law firms, and in-house roles, Ingrid decided she wanted to work more directly with her clients and assist those who didn't have access to the legal advice they needed. She now works with small business owners to ensure they are legally compliant and protecting themselves in the best ways legally possible. Ingrid takes the stress out of drafting legal documents and contracts for business, making the law simple, straightforward, and easy to understand. As a wife and mother of two young boys, Ingrid keenly understands the challenges of mumming and working; to her, this means

saying no to mum guilt, making self-care a priority, and rejecting 'busyness' as the next great marker of success.

2. **Tony Cosentino** is known as 'The WordPress Guy' and has been rocking the WordPress scene since 2008, building and sprucing up websites with a personal touch. He's the go-to guy for web owners in a pickle, offering a virtual helping hand and some serious know-how. Sharing his knowledge is a passion of Tony's. He has presented at several WordPress conferences, offering useful tips and advice for website owners and developers. He's also a straight shooter when running website audits. Tony is all about giving people real, honest advice and steps on what needs fixing. Alternatively, he can do the fixes for them.

3. **Stephanie Holdsworth** is on a mission to change the way we think about eczema and allergies. Using knowledge and experience gained from her 25 years in nursing, she began reshaping perceptions and improving understanding through her online businesses, Allerchic and Adult Eczema Shop. She has been featured in both print and online media for championing the idea that 'eczema and allergy products, information and awareness don't have to be delivered in a white lab coat to be taken seriously'. She runs her online stores from the NSW Central Coast, where she lives with her family.

After you've read *Six Figures While You Sleep*

My hope is that, by the end of this book, you'll have a clear outline for your Big Little Idea and a path towards making it happen.

If you want more support, consider:

· signing up to my mastermind – Six Figures While You Sleep: The Program
· joining my membership – the Digital Marketing Collective.

You'll find both of these on my website: katetoon.com.

(Psst: Both products are literal examples of how you can turn one asset – this book – into multiple ADPIP streams.)

Get involved

If you're loving the book and want to get more involved, here are some fun ways to do so:

- **Listen to the podcast.** Search for 'Six Figures While You Sleep' to hear me offer great tips and interview other 'ADPIPers' on topics covered in the book.
- **Follow on Instagram.** Search for '@katetoon' or post your own content using the hashtags #6fwys and #ADPIP.
- **Grab the accompanying workbook.** Download it at SixFiguresWhileYouSleep.com (it's free).
- **Join the Facebook group.** Hunt for 'The Misfit Entrepreneurs' Facebook group to share your experience of reading the book.

My story

I'm not a fan of books that spend the first 800 pages telling you how awesome the author is, then giving you one tip and trying to sell you into their $20K business program. But I do feel it's important to explain what I did before we dig into what you can do. I want to reassure you that if I can do it, you can too. Then, hopefully, I can inspire you to act. Don't worry; I've kept it short and snappy.

Before I began

I didn't think I had an entrepreneurial bone in my body. Rather, I was a risk-averse, toe-the-line, follow-the-path kind of girl. At university, I did a pointless but enjoyable Arts degree with the vague idea of becoming a teacher or a writer. After college, I worked in events and then advertising.

Over the next 15 years, I climbed the corporate ladder somewhat reluctantly and landed myself a role running the digital department at a very smug advertising agency. I was even on the board. And I hated every second of it. The politics, the awful Friday night drinks, overconfident bosses and the unrelenting smell of tuna in the office fridge.

I sacked it off and got a job packing roses for a flower delivery company *(I kid you not)*. I even trained to be a masseuse but discovered that rubbing the bellies of old people wasn't my jam. So, I reluctantly returned to contracting, moving from stupidly well-paid role to stupidly well-paid role with various advertising agencies. I was financially well-off but kind of dead inside.

Then I got pregnant, and everything changed.

It had taken many years to get pregnant, and I'd almost given up on the idea of being a mum. So, when I got up the duff, I took it as a sign from the gods. I knew I didn't want to raise a human and work like a dog in an agency. So, at five months pregnant, I resigned and started my own business – as a freelance copywriter.

Over the next few years, I built up a successful six-figure copywriting business and niched into SEO copywriting and audits. Life was good. But there weren't enough hours in the day. I was stupidly busy, perma-exhausted and somehow still had very little money. You can read more about that phase of my business journey in my book, *Confessions of a Misfit Entrepreneur: How to succeed in business despite yourself.*

Repurposing my services

I slowly realised *(I'd like to say quickly, but I was too tired to do anything quickly)* that one of my biggest time sucks was finding and winning new business. It took an age to talk to clients, quote jobs and write proposals – which, of course, often didn't even result in winning the job.

So, about three years in, I decided to solve this problem – and I did this by productising my services. By this, I mean I packaged up my offering and slapped a price on it. I cover how I did this in Chapter 5. Essentially, I created a set of small business copywriting packages based on three-, five- and seven-page websites, all named after the different James Bonds. (My top package was, of course, 'The Connery'.) I think my tagline was 'Copy that's licenced to thrill' – cringe!

But these well-organised packages, with clear inclusions and firm pricing, sold like hot frogs. People would ring up asking for Pierce Brosnan with a side of Moore. *(This was pre-Daniel Craig; that copy package would have been all verbs and no adjectives.)*

Tipsy on my success, I used the same model to create productised services for blog posts, video scripts and more. I worked through the mechanics and tech to sell these directly from my website with smart tech and sexy sales pages.

Now that I had clear products to sell, my marketing became more focused, and my processes and finances were simpler to manage. Life was so much easier. It was around this time that I really felt my business was going to work out, and so I invested in building a little home office *(shed)* in my back garden called 'The Toon Cave'. It's still where I run my little global empire today.

From 'done for you' to 'done with you'

Once my services were productised and I had a formula for marketing and selling, I realised I could hit my basic income targets by only selling four of my Connery packages a month. Anything on top of that was sweet, fluffy cream.

So, with all my extra free time, I decided to start coaching. This was about four years in. I began offering one-hour sessions on some of my core skills (SEO and copywriting), charging this out at three times my 'doing rate'.

While I found coaching tiring, it really helped me build my confidence as a teacher, develop my coaching style and test out (and improve) my teaching materials. I cover all of this in Chapter 5.

From one-night stands to deeper relationships

I'd always been a 'get in and get out' kind of copywriter. I get easily bored and love to swap and change. But over time, I realised that strong relationships with my clients meant I didn't have to relentlessly hunt for work. So, I got over myself and started offering my clients retainers, where I gave them set hours a month at a given rate, and they paid me upfront. My cash flow nightmares were over – I finally had a definite income each month that I could rely on. By year five, I had no space for new clients at all.

From online to in-person

Around this time, I started running in-person workshops, partly because I was desperate to get out of the house (because of my small human). It felt amazing to put on a bra, wash my hair and interact with other adults. But turning my one-hour SEO coaching sessions into full-day workshops was a real experiment in engagement and stretched my PowerPoint skills to the max *(this was pre-Canva)*.

Most facilitators can keep people relatively interested for an hour – but how about eight? I could see when their eyes glossed over and the drool began to drip. And that helped me tweak and massage my content to ensure it really hit home. It was a great way to improve my speaking skills and see how my material landed with a range of humans.

The first product

When my son was around five (and at school), I felt my brain start to wake up – a little like a grumpy bear emerging from his winter cave. As the parenting fog cleared, I discovered I was having ideas again – my mojo was back.

I'd started a free community of copywriters to stave off the freelancer loneliness, and, having worked in advertising, I could bring a lot of insight. And templates. I'd created dozens of templates for briefs, proposals, copy decks and plans over the years. And over time, I cobbled together my own template library based on this.

My favourite template was my copy deck – a way of presenting a big blob of copy to clients (primarily for websites). I'd honed it, added in SEO elements – which, I have to say, was a touch innovative at the time – made notes for the reader and included editorial guidelines. I'd ended up with a super schmick, client-impressing mega document. I shared it with a few other copywriters, who shared it as well and then others started to ask about it.

And I thought, 'I could sell this'.

Now, this was back in 2014, when selling digital products was not really a thing. I had to learn how to add products to my website, integrate with payment platforms and set up automated emails to deliver the product. Naturally, I worried over and fiddled with my template for hours. It took weeks to perfect it and push it live. And, of course, no one bought it. I was crushed.

But then I started talking about it, mentioning it on my nascent social media accounts and dropping it into the conversation in groups. Then, I had my PayPal ping moment in Kmart.

That template ultimately became the foundation of my second online business: The Clever Copywriting School. Since then, I've added 40 or more digital downloads to that site. My digital downloads make me a comfy $70K a year now. It's not six figures, but it is, without a doubt, my highest-profit-margin product. I cover digital downloads in Chapter 10.

The big course

After running several SEO workshops, I began receiving messages from customers who said they'd love to learn but couldn't make the in-person event. And so, the idea for an online course was born. By this time, course platforms such as Udemy and Coursera existed, but I didn't like the idea of building my empire on someone else's land. So, once again, I set about learning the tech to build my course on my humble WordPress website.

I launched and sold the first round of my course, 'The Recipe for SEO Success', in February 2016, and 20 people signed up (mostly previous clients). The next round, there were 30, then 53, then 30 again, then 44, then a mournful 22. But by 2019, I was selling 80 spots in less than eight hours.

This one course and all its associated elements has now earned me over $3 million in revenue and is my second-highest-profit-margin product. I talk more about courses in Chapter 11.

The first membership

I ran the free copywriting group for a few years, and then I decided that this, too, might be something people would pay for. I set up a Facebook group and created my first membership in 2014. Again, there were few memberships back then, and the model wasn't really defined; mine evolved over the years, with more content… then less, more coaching… then less, a job board, a directory, courses and more.

I even launched a highly unprofitable conference for my membership, which ran for a few years. *(I learned the hard way that events are not passive income in any way, shape or form.)* Memberships were a true expression of the one-to-many model. My communities are what I'm most proud of and are highly lucrative. I cover memberships in Chapter 12.

The second membership

By this time, the Recipe course had over 600 graduates. The course came with 12 weeks of support, but what about after that? I realised I couldn't keep answering students' questions free of charge forever.

I didn't want to start a solely SEO-related membership. So, instead, I created the Digital Marketing Collective (initially called the Digital MasterChefs – DMC for short – to carry on the Recipe cooking analogy).

I'd learned a lot from my copywriting membership, so the DMC grew quickly at a higher price point. It's now my core offering and my favourite digital product.

Masterminds

Masterminds come in many forms; they're generally high-price small groups where business owners chat with each other under the guidance of a mentor. Alternatively, they can be more involved, with training included, one-on-one sessions and experts coming in to chat.

I've run two masterminds and found the format pretty intense. I'm an over-giver, so I ate into my profit by helping my mentees too much. I'll try masterminds again, but next with more solid boundaries. I cover masterminds in Chapter 13.

The rest

I've also sold a myriad of mini courses, workshops, in-person group events and retreats – with varying degrees of success. But it's clear to me that my most lucrative and most passive digital products fall into four camps:

1. digital downloads
2. courses
3. memberships
4. masterminds.

And that's why I'm covering these four in this book. But don't worry, I've slipped in a few extra ideas in Chapter 14.

Figure 0.1: My timeline

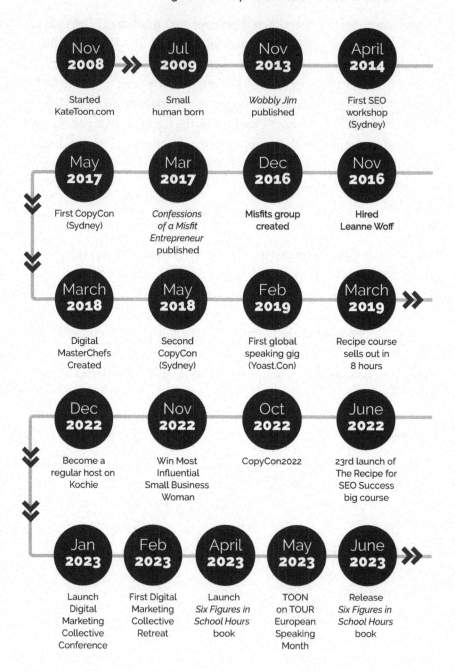

Nov 2008 — Started KateToon.com

Jul 2009 — Small human born

Nov 2013 — *Wobbly Jim* published

April 2014 — First SEO workshop (Sydney)

May 2017 — First CopyCon (Sydney)

Mar 2017 — *Confessions of a Misfit Entrepreneur* published

Dec 2016 — Misfits group created

Nov 2016 — Hired Leanne Woff

March 2018 — Digital MasterChefs Created

May 2018 — Second CopyCon (Sydney)

Feb 2019 — First global speaking gig (Yoast.Con)

March 2019 — Recipe course sells out in 8 hours

Dec 2022 — Become a regular host on Kochie

Nov 2022 — Win Most Influential Small Business Woman

Oct 2022 — CopyCon2022

June 2022 — 23rd launch of The Recipe for SEO Success big course

Jan 2023 — Launch Digital Marketing Collective Conference

Feb 2023 — First Digital Marketing Collective Retreat

April 2023 — Launch *Six Figures in School Hours* book

May 2023 — TOON on TOUR European Speaking Month

June 2023 — Release *Six Figures in School Hours* book

Note: Kochie refers to the David Koch TV Show *Kochie's Business Builders*.

June 2014
The Clever Copywriting School started

Nov 2014
The Recipe for SEO Success started

Jan 2015
First online Recipe course

April 2015
Build #ToonCave

Aug 2016
The Recipe for SEO Success Podcast started

Sep 2015
10 Day Challenge launch

Aug 2015
I Love SEO group founded

June 2015
Speak at ProBlogger

May 2019
Third CopyCon (Melbourne)

Jan 2020
Hot Copy Mastermind

March 2020
Kate Toon COVID Podcast with daily editions

Jan 2021
The StayTooned team grows to 12 members

May 2022
Start Clever Copy Chats podcast

Nov 2021
Released sales page copywriting course

Aug 2021
Paid community membership passes 700 people

July 2021
20th launch of The Recipe for SEO Success big course

Oct 2023
DMC Conference

March 2024
TCCS and DMC merge

June 2024
Launch of The Recipe for SEO Success

July 2024
This book released

Aug 2024
Six Figure Sleepover

What I've learned

This book is a reflection and summary of what I've learned along the way. As I'm not remotely a planner, I can't look back and say, 'Ooh, look, this is when I hit this milestone, and that's why I reached that goal'. It's been a slow evolution, and my confidence and enjoyment have grown with it.

These days, my business is startlingly boring. My days are samey. There are no nasty surprises and no real rushes of excitement. And that's glorious, because I believe that a good business is a boring business. A predictable business. I believe we often mistake stress for excitement and contentment for boredom.

So many business coaches spout the 'DREAM BIG' mantra. 'Imagine if anything was possible!' 'Manifest your success.' 'Reach for the stars.' They encourage their paying customers to aim for something huge, like launching a high-profit course, setting up a billion-download podcast and becoming a global speaker. The bigger, the better.

But the truth is, even with all the encouragement and resources, a huge percentage of people won't reach this massive goal. (The coach then says, 'You didn't want it enough', 'You didn't try hard enough', 'Sign up for another year'. And another, and another…) I know people who have been trying to create things for years and still have nothing to show for it. Why?

Because they set their goals too high – so high they became intimidating, overwhelming and undoable. We may want to be Beyoncé, but perhaps we need to start with a bit of karaoke first. That's why I have a different mantra:

> ***Don't DREAM big. DO small.*** *Start with something small, then build on it.*

Give away a free thing. If 100 people want it, create and offer a low-cost thing. If 100 people want that, make and offer a higher-cost thing, and so on. Iterative development. Testing. Getting things done. Building on our success. Mitigating risk. Because if we're honest, most of us can't afford big risks – risks with our time and/or money. Risking our family. Our mental health.

The truth is, many of those business coaches encouraging us to 'dream big' aren't wearing our shoes *(or slippers)*. They're so far ahead of us that they can't remember what it felt like to be us.

So, start small. Think about what you can achieve today rather than endlessly dreaming about a fictional future. And that's what I'm going to teach you in this book: how to take small, confident steps towards a business you absolutely love that gives you the lifestyle you really want.

PART I:
BEFORE YOU BEGIN

> Inaction breeds doubt and fear. Action breeds confidence and courage. If you want to conquer the fear, do not sit at home, and think about it. Go out and get busy.

Dale Carnegie

Chapter 1

What is passive income?

When I was pitching this book to my publisher, I debated including 'passive income' in the title. Ultimately, I decided against it. Why this debate? Well, let's be clear: the idea of 'passive income' sells. There are so many greasy business coaches selling books, programs and memberships promising that even if you put in no effort, the money will come rolling in if you buy their thing.

It's a beautiful dream, but a dream, nonetheless. **I'm sorry to break it to you, but no income is truly passive.** Or, as George Orwell might have put it if he were an entrepreneur:

> *All incomes are active, but some incomes are more active than others.*

Even with the best idea in the world, there's going to be some work involved – it may be less like work than your current nine-to-five job, but it will be work nevertheless.

Types of passive income

When we talk about building passive income, there are a few different paths you can take.

1. Invest in stocks or bonds

You could invest in stocks or bonds and enjoy the dividends (or reinvest them for more growth). To do this, you obviously need to have the funds to buy these investments in the first place. Also, unless you invest in something simple – such as an exchange-traded fund (ETF) or managed fund – and don't fiddle with it, you could spend hours trying to 'game' the stock market, or even just understand what the hell it all means. Alternatively, you could hire a financial manager to monitor your portfolio, reducing your headaches – but also your profit.

While most finance experts would agree that share portfolios usually increase in value over time, it could take years to see a good return. You're also at the whim of the stock market, and unless you're a high-risk-loving beast, the returns might not be earth-shattering. So, while buying stocks and shares are passive income wealth generators, they are not without their problems.

2. Buy property and rent it out

You could become a landlord, but again, you need the funds upfront to cover that meaty deposit. (Oh, and if you're self-employed, you'll need a great credit history and lots of clean, up-to-date tax returns.) You also need to factor in the time required to find a property and negotiate the sale. After that, there are property reports to be completed, conveyancing fees to pay and a lot of general kerfuffle. Alternatively, you could hire a buyer's agent, reducing your headaches – but also your profit.

And then, even once the purchase is made, you'll have the ongoing labour of dealing with renters and property managers, and you'll lose a chunk for rates, water and repairs. You'll also be at the mercy of the economy when interest rates skyrocket and you're faced with the moral dilemma of whether or not to put rents up for your tenants. Investment properties are generally less passive than shares and often a whole barrel of stress if you don't have a 'forget about it' mindset.

3. Invest in a business or limited partnership

You could invest in a business or limited partnership, but again, those upfront funds need to be there, and you need to have a solid understanding of how the business works and what makes a good investment. You'd ideally want to choose a mostly hands-off investment, otherwise you could end up running the whole damn thing and destroying your passive income dreams.

There are dozens of micro angel investment platforms you can try, where you and others invest small sums collectively in a business, with much less risk. But again, you're not entirely in control, and you might have to kiss a few frogs before finding your business prince.

4. Make an asset you already own available for sale or lease

You could perhaps rent out a room in your house to some random person who paints pentagrams on the walls and plays heavy metal at 2 a.m. Enough said.

5. Develop a product that generates income

This is precisely what we're talking about in this book: you could make a digital product from a service that you can sell with as little effort as possible. The advantages are that you usually don't need upfront cash to get started – just a little time and a little brainpower. You can spin an idea out of your noggin and have it for sale in less than a day. I know because I've done it.

Of course, there are challenges, such as:

· knowing how to get started
· managing time away from your existing business
· dealing with the financial impact of building something new
· coping with the slog of getting your product 'out there'.

But done right – following the advice in this book – developing an online product can be an effective way to create income. It certainly was for me. And once you have that income, you can decide if you want to try out the other passive income strategies I've listed here.

We need a new way to describe this kind of passive income.

I like to call it an 'Automated Digital Passive Income Product' (ADPIP). It's a bit of a mouthful, so let me break it down.

If we accept that passive income is never entirely passive, then perhaps we can think of it as 'automated' instead. That is, you set up a 'system' or 'flow' that generates income. Once it's created, it requires minimal effort from you to keep the income coming in.

The system you set up should be:

- **regular** – your flow should generate income on a weekly or daily basis
- **predictable** – once your flow is optimised, you'll be able to predict revenue each month with confidence
- **scalable** – once the model works, you'll know that the more people who enter your little system or funnel, the more money you'll make.

The benefits of ADPIPs

I don't think you'd be holding this book in your sticky little hands if you didn't understand the benefits of earning money passively rather than by showing up and performing tasks each day. Exchanging your time for money limits you in so many ways. You are hindered by your:

- health
- age
- location
- motivation
- clients
- boss's idiosyncrasies (if you have a boss).

Even if you're a healthy beast and love what you do, there is a definite ceiling to how much you can earn. (I dig into this more in Chapter 2.) On the other hand, systemised passive income from ADPIPs allows you to earn money at virtually any age and in any health condition (within reason). It also gives you more freedom to choose how you spend your time.

TL;DR

Passive income has many forms, but not all passive income is that passive. ADPIPs bypass the need for upfront cash and, with a little time investment, can pay off big time.

OVER TO YOU

I hope this chapter helps you gain an understanding of what passive income really is. No idea – no matter how good – will let you lie in a hammock for all but four hours a week (at least not in the early years).

Now, grab a piece of paper or the *Six Figures While You Sleep* workbook (free from my website) and answer the following questions:

- Do you have a lump sum you could invest in property or shares right now?
- Do you feel confident about buying and trading shares independently, or do you know a reputable financial advisor?
- How long (in years) will you wait for a return on investment?
- Are you a high-risk or low-risk kind of person?
- How much time a week could you spare to work on a passive income project?

Chapter 2

Why trading time for money sucks

I'm going to guess that right now, you're either working for 'the man' and feeling like a wage slave or working for yourself and feeling like a time slave. We live in a world that commodifies time as money. You do the thing, you get the cash. For most people, that means you work hard to earn a decent living and yet never have quite enough money to go around.

Over the years, I've worked with thousands of small business owners, encouraging them to charge a decent rate that covers their expenses, needs and wants. I've also suggested they move towards project rates rather than telling the client the exact number of minutes they spent on each task.

Some have even moved to value-based pricing – setting their prices on the perceived or estimated value of a service (rather than the literal cost of production). But regardless of whether we price hourly, by project or by value, ultimately, when we quote, there's a whisper in our mind of, *I can get that done in X hours.*

Sometimes, we win – the job comes in massively under our quoted time (and then we feel guilty about our initial pricing). Sometimes the client wins – we spend hours longer than anticipated (and gnash our teeth about the injustice of it all). Either way, the whole process of pitching for jobs, pricing jobs, winning jobs and doing jobs feels like jogging on a LEGO®-covered treadmill. It's painful, it's relentless, and it's getting us nowhere.

Working out your hourly rate

Obviously, having an hourly rate is a starting point, so if you haven't calculated yours, you can read the full process of working this out in my previous book, *Six Figures in School Hours*.

Here's a summary:

1. Sit down with a pad and a calculator and work out your monthly living expenses and business expenses. These will give you your minimum viable income – what you could survive on if the poo hit the fan.

2. Calculate your 'nice to have' expenses, debt clearance, savings and investment goals. These are your next goals to hit (in this order).

3. Add them all up. You should now have defined the blob of money you'd need to earn each month.

4. Divide that blob by the hours you have available to work each month. Be realistic. You may think you have eight hours a day, but once you take away staring mindlessly into the fridge and doomscrolling, it's probably reduced to six hours. Then you need to factor in that (in my experience) most people spend only around 60% of their time on billable work – tasks that have an immediate return. Oh, and that you might want to take, say, a month of holidays a year (or more if you're a parent). Consequently, your hours could look like this:

   - **Starting point** – you have, say, 38 hours a week to work over 52 weeks ÷ 12 months = 164-ish hours a month.
   - **This is reduced by faffing/fridge stare time**, which I think is about 10 hours a week = 43 hours a month. Now we have only 121 hours a month.
   - **If we take the reality of billable hours into account, then we can only make money for 60% of this time** – 60% of 121 hours is just 73 hours a month.

I know this maths is hard *(it made my editor cry)* but stick with me.

At 73 billable hours a month, you have 876 hours a year to work. But perhaps you take a month away for holidays – now you have 803 hours.

If your goal is to make six figures per year – say $100K before tax – in those 803 hours, you need to be charging $124-ish an hour.

Easy, right? And $122 an hour is not a huge amount; that's doable. But we haven't factored in those weeks with no clients, the sick days and school holidays. And let's be honest, $100K before tax in this economy isn't exactly going to give you a luxury lifestyle. Now, you can start to see the problem with exchanging your time for money. But let's dig in a little deeper.

Why is exchanging time for money so sucky?

You might be sitting there thinking, 'What's so wrong with charging an hourly rate? At least I have control. And if it's not enough, I can put my hourly rate up (and up)'. *(I used to think that way, too.)* Let me explain some more reasons why exchanging time for money, no matter how much you charge, sucks.

Your hourly rate invites comparison

As soon as you whack a price on your time, you make it easy for customers to compare your rate with other people in the market. And unless you're excellent at explaining value and have reached level 'smug' with your testimonials, you'll have to justify your rate – again and again.

And who are you competing with? Those overseas freelancers? The hobby businesses? Or those just starting out with much lower expectations and expenses? And while you may gnash your teeth over how they can possibly charge such ridiculous rates, there's nothing you can do about it. Someone is always going to be cheaper.

Clients love to compare apples with watermelons, not appreciating the years of experience that led to your pricing. If there was ever a time for a Picasso story, this is it. Pablo Picasso drew a little doodle on a napkin. A lady recognised him and asked how much she would have to pay for the napkin. Picasso said, '$20,000'. The lady was shocked. 'But it only took you two minutes to draw!' Picasso replied, 'No, it took me my whole life'.

I admire Picasso for knowing his worth and sticking to it. But it took years of running my business before I realised that the people who appreciate and are willing to pay for that napkin are few and far between.

Scaling is tough

If you stick with the 'time for money' model, you're going to come up against the undeniable reality that there are only so many hours in the day. Time is a finite resource. If you want to do more work in the same amount of time, you're faced with the vaguely hideous prospect of outsourcing parts of your business or *(shudders)* hiring other people to work for you. And as anyone who has ever had staff will know, hiring good humans who will stay with you and won't disappear on a whim is one of the biggest challenges in business. People are flaky AF, and it's exhausting hiring again and again. Then there's the tax to deal with, KPIs to set and all the HR obligations to meet.

> **TOON TIP** One of the key reasons I went down the digital product route is that I didn't want to manage a team of humans. I never wanted to be responsible for anyone else's mortgage – hell, I don't even want to be responsible for mine. Having been a 'boss' and managed a team, I found that someone was crying at least once a day, and often that someone was me. If you feel an itchy aversion to staff, you're reading the right book.
>
> Ironically, several years into my digital product journey, everything got so big that I did, in fact, need to hire staff to manage it all. Life's funny that way!

Hampered creativity

While we might think there's something romantic about artists starving in garrets *(are garrets still a thing?)*, there's nothing glamorous – or creative – about poverty. Whether you see yourself as a freelancer or not, running a small business is often a hideous rollercoaster of feast and famine – too much work one minute, an empty inbox the next.

And even if you do master your financial management and pay yourself a salary, it's nerve-wracking and exhausting.

From a creative point of view – and by 'creative' I mean inventive, innovative and inspired – it's incredibly hard to be your best self when there's a nagging sense of terror in your belly about where your next dollar is coming from. It's far easier to be creative with a juicy, full bank account and a steady, predictable income source.

The on/in dilemma

The most common complaint I get from my members is that they have zero time to work **on** their business because they spend all their time working **in** it. With a time-for-money mentality, any time spent on anything other than actual client work feels frivolous. Marketing feels like a luxury that only other business owners can enjoy.

So, we lumber on with ugly, outdated websites we never have time to update and sparse social media accounts. Working on new business proposals feels like a Russian roulette of time versus potential gain, and every rejection is gutting as it's time you could have spent on paying clients. Instead, we're stuck with our old, reliable, low-paying clients.

And while networking sounds like a great idea as a way to meet potential new clients, you can't really afford the four hours out of the office. Consequently, you see no one and end up isolated and feeling like a hostage to your business.

No work, no pay

In a time-for-money world, sick days and personal emergencies are a constant source of tight-sphincter terror. I know business owners who have worked on the way to hospital with a burst appendix and others who were answering client emails just hours after pushing out a tiny human.

Holidays are a double whammy. Not only is there the cost of paying for the hotel and airfares, there is also the added financial gut punch of not earning while you're away. So, we work through public holidays and never take our kids anywhere nice – then wonder what it's all for.

People can't work with you

Now, many of you are likely reading this like proud puppies, confident that you're charging your worth and earning a decent living. That's the point I'd gotten to. My quotes were high but fair. I liked to call myself 'reassuringly expensive'. It had even reached the point where fancy clients like Telstra and American Express hesitated slightly before signing off on my proposals.

And all this was glorious, and I could have stopped there – I'd clearly reached the top rate in my industry. But honestly? I'm a greedy little beast – I wanted more. I wanted to pay off my mortgage faster and buy a Mazda 2. I also missed working with smaller clients, start-ups and low-budget businesses, but my prices had become a barrier to entry.

Burnout and blues

I've never been one to burn the midnight oil – in truth, I find it hard to burn the 3 p.m. oil, so conditioned am I by the dreaded school run.

But it's amazing how much you can flog yourself in a regular eight-hour day. The constant search for motivation and energy left me panting with exhaustion. I struggled through a daily dance of triple-shot coffee mornings and too-many-glasses-of-wine nights. As I lay in bed at night, worrying about everything in the world, I sniffed the smoky aroma of burnout.

Now, I'm not suggesting that ADPIPs will allow you to lie in bed all week, but believe me, they make life so much easier.

You're someone's creature

If you started your own business to escape from an oppressive, irritating boss, let me break it to you: you now have the worst boss ever. Yourself. You'll push yourself harder than any previous taskmaster, deny yourself days off, criticise your work and rarely give yourself a bonus. And even if you're relatively kind to yourself, you're at the whim of your clients. Their urgent deadlines become your urgent deadlines. You pick up the phone at the Coles checkout because you're waiting for them to pay that final invoice. You might feel like you're the captain of your own ship, but someone else has a firm hold of your rudder.

Missed opportunities

Most business coaches will tell you to take a 'head down, bum up' approach to business: stick to a plan and don't stray from the path. I believe this is an acutely terrible approach.

You're so busy with client work that you have no time to learn new skills or improve existing skills (allowing you to charge more). You're so focused on quick wins and clearing immediate tasks to get the money that you miss out on bigger opportunities. You're so focused on one-to-one client work that there's no chance to diversify.

🐹 This is where our guinea pig, Ingrid Fernandez, finds herself at the time of writing. Her established customer base and reputation make her a prime candidate to stop trading her time for money. She's done the hard yards to understand that her available hours are 20 per week, and she knows she'd love to expand and create a more diverse income stream that's not 100% reliant on being at her desk 24/7. She's ready to start thinking about changing her business model. Even though it feels a bit scary, she knows it's the logical next step.

I could go on, but rather than lurking in the negatives, let's explore strategies that move beyond the time–money exchange and towards a more sustainable, enjoyable and lucrative business model.

TL;DR

Exchanging time for money is a roundabout to nowhere. Time is a non-renewable resource, and exchanging it for cash limits scalability, creativity, freedom and the chance to take a mini break.

OVER TO YOU

If you stick with the 'time for money' model, you're going to come up against the undeniable reality that there are only so many hours in the day. Time is a finite resource.

Grab a pen and paper or the *Six Figures While You Sleep* workbook and jot down your responses to the following:

· What is your monthly minimum viable income?
· What's your stretch goal that covers all those nice-to-haves and investment goals?
· Be super honest about how many actual work hours you have in a day and calculate your required hourly rate. What is it?
· Do you often feel pressured by client demands?
· Are you worried about where the next dollar is coming from?
· When was the last time you took a two-week holiday from your business?
· Do you feel you spend all your time working **in** your business rather than **on** it?

Chapter 3

The one-to-many model

If we accept that charging by the hour sucks and secretly know that even when we try to charge on a 'value-based' approach, we're still thinking about how few hours we can spend, then we can begin to realise *(at least, I hope you realise)* that the problem is time.

There are only so many hours in the day. So, if we don't want to be working through the night, what's the solution? Ideally, we want to be waking up to a bucket of cash alongside our bowl of cereal.

As I mentioned earlier, one solution is to employ a team, work out your margins for that team and become a manager of people. But that ain't what we're covering in this book. Instead, we're digging into ways to make money on your own with as little stress as possible.

One of these ways is the one-to-many model.

What is the one-to-many model?

The one-to-many model can be applied to several concepts, but in the context of generating 'passive income', it's all about taking those services you currently deliver one-to-one and finding a way to repurpose them and sell them to many people at once.

In my case, I was doing individual SEO audits for clients, which I found time-consuming and monotonous. I could only do so many in any given week, so my income was capped.

After running many in-person SEO workshops, I created an online course that allowed clients to run these audits themselves. Not only did this mean that more people would be able to learn, but they also had more time to understand the process and come away feeling more empowered. I break it down a little further in Table 3.1.

Table 3.1: One-to-one versus one-to-many

	One-to-one model (SEO audits)	One-to-many model (SEO courses)
Time taken to complete one	5 hours (each time)	40 hours (once)
Cost	$1000	$500
Number I can do in a week	2 (around other work)	10 (but infinitely scalable)
Total income per week	$2000	$5000

Now, of course, that looks super attractive. I mean, who wouldn't want to earn $5K instead of $2K? However, this is the highlight reel, the bit where the white-toothed entrepreneurs lure you in with that potentially thigh-shudderingly awesome financial return.

What they don't tell you is how to create the thing, build the audience, market it and keep those customers happy. But don't worry, I explain all of that in this book. Before we dive into that though, let's look at a few more reasons why the one-to-many model works so well:

- **Much higher profits.** Because you are delivering a service once and selling it to many, instead of repeatedly delivering it to just one person at a time, the time involved is hugely reduced, therefore increasing your profits. Of course, this only makes sense if you consider your time an actual expense in your business, which many business owners don't.
- **Broader market reach.** You're no longer tied to working with businesses in your local area or even in the same country. Instead, you can reach a much larger, even global, customer base.

- **Increased scalability.** Once you've made your digital product, you can potentially sell it as often as you like to as many people as you like. This means it's entirely scalable with relatively little effort from you.
- **Time and location.** I've sold digital products while on the loo, shopping in Kmart and quite literally while I'm sleeping. In fact, at one point, I had to turn off my phone notifications as I was being woken by a cacophony of PayPal pings.

Digital products mean you sell your product or service on your terms – when and where you wish – especially if you create evergreen (year-round) products. But, more importantly, it means buyers can buy and access them at their convenience. No sitting on a waitlist until you become free. No waiting for a Zoom appointment. They can enjoy all you have to offer when **they** want it.

> **TOON TIP** Not all products are scalable or evergreen. In fact, some take a heap of maintenance and updates to keep them going. I learned this the hard way. I talk more about the type of product you can create in Part III.

Now, of course, this isn't a passive income, rose-coloured-glasses love story. There are negatives, too, which I reveal throughout the book. Here are the first challenges that come to mind:

- **Time investment.** Creating your digital products will obviously take time away from your existing clients. It's a big commitment and possibly also a financial setback. But it's an investment in your future, and obviously, there will be a lot of fear around that if it's not paying off as quickly as you'd like. I talk more about managing your time and money in Chapter 23.
- **Managing expectations.** The 'build it and they will come' attitude stuffs up so many budding entrepreneurs. They spend months beavering away on their digital product, only to launch it to crickets. But don't worry – I'm going to help you avoid that.
- **Creating mass appeal is hard.** With a one-to-many model, you need one important thing – the 'many'. However, the 'many' brings new challenges, including more customer service issues,

the negatives of building a prominent brand and the need to constantly feed the marketing beast with more content. Getting many people to buy from you can be incredibly difficult without a great marketing strategy, but I cover how to create that in Part IV.

- **It's less touchy-feely.** Many digital products lack that personal experience and direct interaction, and some clients may still clamour to work with you directly. In other words, your digital offering may not resonate with every single one of your customers. Some will still want the one-to-one approach. I talk more about this in Chapter 5.

I've experienced this myself. Having watched a great financial advisor on TikTok, I was super keen to work with him, but the only option was to take his course. Despite the course being more cost-effective, I'd have paid double the price just to talk to him directly. But he didn't have that option available, so I moved on.

Why not ecommerce?

Now, you might be thinking, *Ooh, I know, I'll set up an online store. That's digital. That's a great way to make more money. I can make a thing, resell a thing or dropship some crap from Alibaba at a ridiculous mark-up. Easy peasy, right?*

Sadly, I don't believe starting an ecommerce store is the answer, and I won't be delving into the ecommerce business model in this book. Don't get me wrong, I tried having shops *(mostly as a teenager)*. I made turtle keyrings and sold them to my friends. I sold lavender bags at craft fairs. One day I may even own a store of my own.[1]

Yes, I can totally see the appeal and understand the reasons why you might want to have an ecommerce store. For example, over the years, I've seen dozens of childrenswear brands created, adorably named after the owners' children: 'Poppy and Flange', 'Zippy and Nigel', or whatever.

---

1 Edit: At the time of editing this book I have in fact purchased a bookshop in my home-town. Crazy, right? When I wrote this, I had no idea this would happen. I look back at innocent bookshop-less me with moist eyes – little did I know. And yes, my next book will likely be *Six Figures from Your Shop*, although I haven't told my publisher Lesley that yet.

And a few short months later, I see the same business owners dolefully lamenting the fact that they've spent $20K on Facebook ads and only had one sale (and that was their mum).

On the flip side, I have dozens of highly successful ecommerce storeowners in my Digital Marketing Collective membership, running amazing brands making oodles of sales with delicious profit margins. But they would *(and did when I asked)* all agree with me: **ecommerce stores are extremely hard to make successful**.

Before we cross them off our list, I want to briefly explain why they are such a challenge:

- **Competition.** There are not only gazillions of small stores out there already, but you're also competing with the big boys like Kmart and Amazon, who have marketing budgets and a level of wholesale buying power that would make your eyes water.

- **Inventory.** There's the constant struggle of managing inventory levels and having the right amount of stock to make sales without having all your cash tied up. And don't get me started on storage; it's time to say 'bye bye' to the spare room, loft, garage and possibly the kitchen and lounge room, too.

- **Shipping.** Finding viable and affordable customer delivery options is tough, especially in regional areas where couriers won't pick up. You're stuck relying on the big postal companies, then faced with whether to pass those chunky shipping fees onto your customers or give free shipping and let shipping fees eat away all your profits. And that's before you deal with the delays and the angry customer emails flooding your inbox.

- **Sales.** We live in a world of continuous sales. If it's not Black Friday, it's Cyber Monday. We've got sales for Valentine's Day, sales for summer, sales for winter and sales because the day has a 'Y' in it. Not only do all these sales eat into your margins, but creating the campaigns for them is super time-consuming. And things get even worse if you're a reseller and the bigger brand undercuts your pricing. The big brands can afford to take the hit – but you can't.

- **Supply.** With physical products, you'll often struggle with supply issues due to either your own exhaustion from making them or relying on dodgy suppliers who let you down.

  TOON TIP You could, of course, try dropshipping – you mark up products from sites like Alibaba and have them delivered direct to your customers. But again, we won't be going there in this book. It's not my jam.

And this is why digital products rock – the running costs are so very low. There's no inventory. There's no storage (well, other than on your website hosting and backups). You can 'ship' with the click of an email, and you'll never, ever run out of stock. I cover sales and pricing in Chapter 19, but given you're likely to make your money back on the initial effort quickly, everything after that is profit – so you can dial the pricing up and down and still make money.

My amazing ecommerce members also told me about some of their other challenges:

- the set-up and initial costs
- branding and marketing
- building an audience
- having to wear too many hats and learn everything at once
- knowing when to outsource
- difficult customers with unreasonable expectations.

(But the truth is, these are challenges you'll face with your ADPIP as well.)

If you're reading this and have an ecommerce store that's struggling, don't lose hope. There are plenty of successful ecommerce humans in my community; I'm not saying it's impossible. I'm just saying it's a tad harder than ADPIPs, and that perhaps it's time for you to consider diversifying your income by adding a digital product into the mix.

TL;DR

The one-to-many model allows you to build something once and sell it to people multiple times. It offers higher profitability, more freedom and the potential to make money while you sleep.

OVER TO YOU

Can you think of one service you currently offer that could be a one-to-many offer?

If you're an ecommerce person, can you think of one skill you've learned through your store (or life) that you could teach others?

(Psst: Don't worry if you can't; we'll do some more work on this in Chapter 6.)

$\rightsquigarrow\!\!\!<$ $\rightsquigarrow\!\!\!<$

Chapter 4

Be more shark

There's a quote I love on the interwebs from Kyle Creek, aka The Captain (@sgrstk on Twitter – now 'X'):

> *Do sharks complain about Monday? No. They're up early, biting stuff, chasing shit, being scary – reminding everyone they're a fucking shark.*

For a long time, 'Be more shark' was my personal mantra. I had to tell myself to be brave until I became brave. It was all about facing my fears *(and I have plenty, including a morbid fear of buttons[2])* and 'doing the do' regardless. Hopefully, by this point in the book, you're starting to feel a little bit excited about the road to ADPIPs ahead. But you might also be feeling a little bit fearful. You may already have an idea, a goal, a dream. And when you think about it, you're choked with that familiar feeling of terror.

Perhaps you're the sort of person who:

- talks about your ideas a lot but never quite seems to start making them happen
- does everything you can to avoid a task *(a 'procrastifaffer')*
- finds yourself making excuses for why you're not acting

---

2 Fear of buttons is a real thing; it's called koumpounophobia.

- lives in the shadows of past failures and uses this to justify not moving forward
- sets wildly unachievable goals only to miss them and then feel bad about yourself.

Or maybe you just never quite find the oomph to get started. And the fear of getting started is really about what happens if you **do** start and it all goes wrong. So, you keep yourself in a holding pattern of procrastination, thereby avoiding the possible reality that you're not up to the challenge. While the idea is still just an idea, it can't be ruined by reality.

You could even be scared that your idea will go well and you won't be able to cope – that you won't be able to give it the time it deserves, or you'll let people down. When we fear uncertainty, we create obstacles that take us further and further away from our end goal. Sometimes, we even try to substantiate our fear with a 'reason':

- 'I'd be crazy to start an online business when nine out of ten fail in the first year.' *(Yes, you'll make up your own stats as well.)*
- 'I could create a course, but there are too many out there already.'
- 'I could create a membership, but no one has the money to join these days.'

Or perhaps you'll find (or create) evidence of your own previous failures to shore up your lack of action.

The fear mindset

I know, I know, 'mindset' is such a business coach buzzword. But I must use it to help describe the icky brain burps that pop out when we think about doing something new, something challenging. We know it's fear; but do we really know what fear is? Google tells us that fear is:

An unpleasant emotion caused by the threat of danger, pain, or harm. 'I cowered in fear as bullets whizzed past'.

Put simply, fear is an emotional response induced by a perceived threat. That threat can be a real danger happening right now (a giant, moody hippo is about to eat you), or it can be anticipation of a perceived future threat (like when you are going camping and fear a spider will crawl into your ear and lay baby spider eggs – *shh, it happens*).

Fear messes with our bodies – it literally fiddles with our physiology, changing the way our metabolism and organs function. Our heart beats faster, we experience shortness of breath, our palms sweat and our bum cheeks clench. *(Or maybe that's just me.)* We don't make these things happen consciously; they just kind of happen. The mind controls the physical reactions of the body.

Fear also changes our behaviour. That feeling of wanting to run away when you arrive at a networking event? Fear. The need to hide under the duvet rather than work on your ADPIP? Fear. The mind controls what we say, what we do and, more importantly, what we don't do. For many people, fear can be paralysing. They become tongue-tied in social situations, standing mouth agape, unable to utter a word. And as the herd of angry wildebeests (or customers) hurtles towards them, they become rooted to the spot when they should be running for their lives.

Over 2000 years ago, the *Book of Rites* (a kind of Chinese encyclopaedia) identified six core human feelings or emotions:

1. Joy
2. Sadness
3. **Fear**
4. Love
5. Disliking
6. Liking.

We all have this core set of primitive and base emotions hardwired into our systems. We can't escape them, and we can't eradicate them. They're part of who we are; we're stuck with them. These basic emotions are so woven into our humanity that they each have a corresponding, dedicated neurological circuit that triggers an automatic behavioural response.

That means we don't have to think about how to respond. It just happens.

Thanks to these cave human throwback reflexes, we react to doing a Reel on Instagram pretty much the same way our furry ancestors might have reacted when chased by an angry mammoth *(though hopefully with less grunting)*.

One way psychologists differentiate between basic emotions (such as fear) and more complex emotions (such as embarrassment or wistfulness) is to look at children. Let me give you an example. You won't find many four-year-olds who fear looking foolish, because they're not fearful of being perceived in a negative way. But small children **do**, of course, experience fear. They're frightened of loud noises, of the dark. They're also scared of some super weird stuff that seems anything but threatening. Understanding how kids experience fear can help us adults separate 'real' or justified fear from fear that's self-imagined.

Back in 1954, neuroanatomists started focusing on the limbic cortex as the seat of human emotion. And boy, is it primitive. Some refer to the limbic cortex as the 'lizard brain' because the limbic system is all our poor wiggly friends have for brain function.

The lizard brain not only oversees fight or flight but also lots of other lovely 'f' words, like feeding, fear and fornication *(and most likely faffing, too)*. Now, we might like to think that our business emotions are mediated more by the higher processing part of our brain, but how, then, can we explain the abject terror we feel about sending difficult emails?

Why fear matters

Surely, we can't apply this understanding of fear to our terror of 'putting ourselves out there'? Well, yes, because not all our fears are solely dependent on nature – they're also shaped by our culture, relationships and life experiences. However, both humans and animals can control fear through thought and learning.

We can divide fears into two categories:

1. **Rational (or appropriate) fears** – fear of death, fires or knife-wielding maniacs
2. **Irrational fears (more commonly known as phobias)** – fear of open spaces, birds, buttons or mayonnaise. These aren't as relevant to business, so I won't dig into them more.

So, what do we do? Ignoring our fear isn't going to work. We won't succeed by pretending we're not scared and pushing the fear down deep into our belly.

Put simply, fear has a place in our lives, but we don't have to let it control us.

Here are a few things I've learned through my years of 'doing the do'.

When it comes to business, often the reason we feel fear is that we need other people to love and respect us. We don't want to mess up, look foolish or let people down, because if we do, we might lose people's love and respect.

Deep down, right at the bottom of our emotional ocean, there's a feeling of not being enough. We believe there are things we must be, do, say or have to be enough. So, therefore, if we **do** mess up and risk our ability to acquire these things, our 'enoughness' will be compromised.

Fear is also born out of our need for security. We don't want to risk what we already have by attempting something new – especially if we have a family to provide for.

Understand your fears

One easy way to understand your fears is to write them down on a piece of paper and then challenge them. I want to run through some of the most common business fears here.

Fear 1: This isn't really 'the done thing' in my industry

Guinea pig Ingrid told me that the idea she had for her ADPIP wasn't really 'the done thing' in the legal industry. She was fearful her peers would challenge her or think it was a foolish notion:

> *The legal profession has always done things a certain way and hasn't hugely evolved in the way we provide services to digital businesses, and so doing something techie feels unusual and like it could cause some judgement.*

My retort: Someone has to be the first, someone has to be the brave one, and that might as well be you. So many SEO types were sceptical about me running an SEO course. They said it couldn't be taught. But they were likely just jealous, and many of them now have SEO courses.

Obviously, being the first means you get to make all the mistakes *(fun)*, but this book will help you avoid the pitfalls. It also means that others will follow in your footsteps and have an easier time of it, which is rather annoying but kinda just part of the deal.

Fear 2: This thing has already been done

🦉 Guinea pig Stephanie was worried that her digital products wouldn't sell because there was already so much out there in the industry. And, of course, there are a million YouTube videos, courses and resources.

My retort: When writing this book, I was bombarded with Facebook ads for 'Build a Course in 5 Days' programs. But here are two things about this:

1. **People buy more than one thing from more than one person.** We love choice. Do you have more than one book on your bookshelf? Do you buy more than one brand of clothes? There really is room for everyone.
2. **Just because you know everyone in your industry is doing similar things doesn't mean I know that.** I only know you. If you're my trusted person, I will buy from you. So, your job is not to be dramatically different but simply to be deliciously you, and then shout that from the rooftops. (More on this in Chapter 6.)

Fear 3: Who am I to be 'the expert'?

🦉 Guinea pig Tony felt that, despite years of experience and his desire to coach other WordPress people, he wanted to get the **right** level of person. He didn't want to end up with a group full of 'wise owls' who argued with his advice and heckled every post.

My retort: You're not trying to be **the** expert; you're trying to be **an** expert, part of a collective of people who talk about a topic. You've also done this for a while, right? And while people can argue about facts and stats, no one can argue with your lived experience. This is why it's so important to include this experience in whatever you create. Write down everything you've done and achieved, and then read it.

Guess what? It looks good on paper, right? But you're not just good on paper; you're good in person.

Accept that even if you market to the right level of human, at least one person who buys one of your digital products will inevitably find fault with it. Or question you. You're not expected to be an orb of all knowledge; instead, you're sharing your know-how and experience, and no one can mess with that. Besides, that's what the 'delete' and 'block' functions are for ☺.

Fear 4: What if I fail?

I get it; you're scared that if you launch the thing, no one will buy it, and you'll look foolish, and everyone will think you're a failure.

My retort: I remember seeing a post on LinkedIn congratulating a new 'software as a service' company for their amazing launch. The founder honestly replied that it was, in fact, the brand's 17th launch, but the previous launches had all been flops. If you fail:

- Nobody will probably notice, as they're so self-absorbed. We all think everyone is looking and waiting for us to fail. It's both freeing and humbling to realise that no one really cares.
- You can learn, work out the reasons things didn't work and try again (and again).

Fear 5: What if I succeed?

Another fear is that you'll create this thing and it will take off, and you won't be able to cope. Then you'll feel terrible because you let people down.

 Tony said:

If I don't have systems in place, I worry that I'll have people who are itching for information and I won't get back to them in a timely manner, which will lead them to feel less excited by the group and cause me a lot of stress. My other concern is that I'll spend all day answering questions and not be able to complete other work. I'm worried I'll dawdle too much in the group.

My retort: Of course you'll make mistakes. You'll create digital products that don't scale as well as you'd hoped. You'll make promises you can't keep. You'll set up structures that break when too many people say 'yes'. I had this happen with my SEO course. I said I could take 80 people on the course, and I sold 80 spots – it was terrifying, and I could not service them all well. I worked way too hard. The next round, I took 60 people. And it was fine.

You're not expected to be a soothsayer; you can change what you create. And guess what? If you don't like what you've created, you can also stop. It's important to set aside regular time for your ADPIPs and stick with them, but it's equally important to set boundaries so you don't let your ADPIP humans eat you alive.

Realise everyone is terrified

I don't know anyone who wanders around feeling 100% confident and brave all the time.

You may look at someone and think, *Well, it's okay for her, it's so easy for her.* No, it's not. The person you admire who is 'doing the do' has likely struggled through the fear and come out the other side – or, as in my experience, they are still fearful, but they've found ways to cope.

When I launched my first SEO course, I got absolutely trolled by several blokes in the SEO groups I was in. 'You're not even a techie SEO expert,' they brayed. It put the fear of God into me and made me question myself. But I carried on despite my fear. And look at me now. I find it quite comforting knowing that everyone is scared. When I see other humans just like me who have overcome a fear, it gives me hope that I can too.

Appreciate that fear gets bigger with time

The more you think about a thing that terrifies you and don't act, the bigger the fear will grow. It's like a beast being fed – every time you put it off, avoid it and hide from it, the fear grows a little larger in your mind. For example, each day I sat down to write this book, I felt a mass of fear, but as soon as my fingers touched the keyboard, those feelings disappeared. Poof, it's magic. You can't wait for fear to dissipate – it won't. You won't simply wake up one day and not be fearful. You can't avoid the fear. The sooner you face it, the better.

Handling fear makes you happier

Although that thing scares you right now, when you've faced your fear and dealt with it, you'll feel a huge sense of relief. A gigantic surge of self-confidence will wash over you. In *Six Figures in School Hours*, I talked about neurochemicals and the daily DOSE (dopamine, oxytocin, serotonin and endorphins). After I face a fear and those cortisol levels drop, I feel a massive surge of dopamine and serotonin, and with it, a sense of achievement and calm.

You'll also start to spiral upwards, thinking more positive thoughts like, *If I can handle that, what else can I do?* You'll feel happier and more fulfilled knowing that you're able to push yourself out of your comfort zone and survive.

You might have to employ white-knuckle confidence for a while. But, like walking around in uncomfortable shoes, you'll eventually break in that confidence and feel fabulous.

TL;DR

Fear is innate and serves a valuable purpose, but we can learn to overcome our fears and achieve our goals. In truth, we must accept and acknowledge our fears. The goal isn't to eliminate fear altogether and become some mindless, fearless beast. Instead, we can use our fears to build character, teach us lessons and find the courage within to face difficult situations despite our fears. We need to 'be more shark' and change that fear mindset to a positive, abundant, 'There's room for me, I can do this' mindset.

OVER TO YOU

Now it's time to run through your fears:

1. Draw a table with two columns, and label Column 1 'FEAR' and Column 2 'CHALLENGE'. Write down each thing you're fearful of (in relation to creating an ADPIP) in Column 1, such as, 'I'm scared I won't succeed, and it will be embarrassing'.

2. Challenge those fears in Column 2; for example, 'Everyone has failures, and that's how you learn'.

3. Create a list of mantras on sticky notes to help you when the fear starts to nibble at your earlobes. Here are some examples:

   a. 'Anyone can build an online digital product business – even me.'
   b. 'There are enough customers to go around.'
   c. 'My opinions and experience are as valid as anyone else's.'
   d. 'If it doesn't work (the first time) I can try again. Nothing ventured, nothing gained.'

Chapter 5

Before you go passive

I hope by now you're feeling a little bubble of excitement about trying out this systemised passive income thing, and you've managed to shove any fears down the back of the sofa cushions. But before we grab our little business backpacks and start scaling that six-figure mountain, I need you to do a few things.

The biggest reason most digital product businesses fail is an abject lack of preparation. Some people are so keen to have a taste of the passive income pie that they blunder forward, invest a huge amount of time and money into making a 'thing', excitedly put the 'thing' on the market and then don't sell a damn 'thing'. And they think they're a failure, but they just didn't do the groundwork.

Preparation is everything. I'm not a huge fan of planning, but I am a huge fan of setting yourself up for success and scalability. The following tasks will:

· help you overcome any fears that are still lingering
· buoy your income, giving you more money while you create your new empire
· test your ability to try new ways of selling your services
· trial your product in the market.

I know you just want to jump in, and you can – you can skip these steps if you're super keen. But honestly, setting yourself up for success before you go passive would take less than a month. And what's a month in the grand scheme of things?

Task 1: Make your existing services easier to buy

Productising your services is the process of developing an idea, skill or service to make it more marketable to your customers. It's about creating palatable, straightforward lumps of work that you can confidently price and the client can easily understand.

Price is often the biggest barrier for the customer, and they get nervous when they can't see a price on your site. They dread the 'discovery call' where they feel they're going to be pressured into buying your thing. So, putting your pricing on your site is important.

Proudly displaying your hourly rate is pointless; I have no idea how long it takes you to bake a cake or mow a lawn. But outlining a project with inclusions and parameters makes perfect sense.

The benefits of productising your services include the following:

- **Time efficiency.** You're doing similar projects again and again, so the process is the same and easily repeatable.
- **Process improvement.** You can streamline processes and documents because the project flow is familiar.
- **Outsourcing opportunities.** If your process is streamlined, it's easier to identify areas you could outsource and to explain to subcontractors what needs to be done.
- **Focused marketing.** Instead of trying to be all things to all people, you're selling a few productised services to a core audience, which allows for clearer messaging.
- **No more proposals.** Since the client can see all the inclusions and the price on the site, the proposal or invoice is just a next step, not the deciding factor. This takes the pressure off and makes creating the proposal faster. It also reduces time wasted on proposals that don't get accepted.
- **Fewer phone calls.** If, like me, you're not a natural salesperson and tend to talk your customer out of a sale, you'll be pleased to know that having productised services on your site helps reduce the number of phone conversations you need to have.

- **More money.** As you specialise in a particular service or industry, you'll become known for this service and be a 'go to' supplier.

How to productise your services

Start by reviewing your services to find the most likely candidates for productising. I base my decision on the following criteria (see Figure 5.1):

- **Customer demand.** Do enough people want this thing? If you think your plans to start a membership for toad lovers may not be successful, it might be best to broaden it to all amphibians.
- **Ability.** Do you have the skills to do this thing? You might want to start a cooking course, but if you can't boil an egg, it ain't going to fly.
- **Speed.** Can you do this thing quickly? Some things come to us easily and quickly; the faster you can do it, the more likely it will be profitable.
- **Enjoyment.** Will you enjoy doing this thing? This might seem frivolous – we're not here to enjoy ourselves, right? But there must be a modicum of pleasure, or you'll get fed up and won't be able to persist.

You might wonder why 'Makes the most money' isn't there. Well, that's because I find if people want the thing, you're good at it, you're fast at it and you enjoy it, you'll be able to charge a premium and the money will roll in.

Figure 5.1: Criteria for productising a service

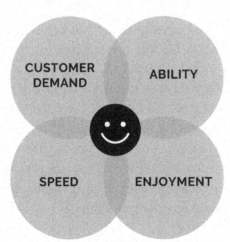

Also, answer these questions:

1. What proven experience do you have?
2. What insider knowledge do you have?
3. What are your interests?
4. Which customers do you most like working with?
5. Who would be your dream client?
6. Which types of work do you have the most testimonials for?
7. Which are your most established networks?

Once you have decided on a service to productise, decide on your model:

- **One-time** – a project-by-project offer with a set price, such as a logo design for a fixed fee. This is easier to sell – you start with $0 every month.
- **Recurring** – a regular payment for work, such as a website maintenance package. This creates consistent income, but of course, there will still be clients coming and going, so it's not entirely predictable (see Task 2).
- **Unlimited** – you could offer an unlimited package, which isn't truly unlimited and generally includes some limitation mechanism, such as one amendment every 24 hours. While an unlimited package is relatively easy to sell and works if your processes are tip-top, they can feel overwhelming. Unlimited packages work well for, say, web developers who are building a site and want to give their clients lots of room for changes.

Once you have decided on your model, outline what you're going to include in your packages. Be clear and concise – for example, how much discussion time is included, what's the actual output, and how many rounds of amendments do they get? Try to throw in some value-adds that are low-cost to you but useful to the client. For example, I used to give away a free copywriting formatting guideline with every website copy job. It was a generic document but was helpful to the client. Also, work out what you'll do if the client goes over the prescribed inclusions. What if they want more frequent conversations or ask for more amendments? How will you charge for this?

Next, decide on your pricing. I like to use the 'power of three' pricing, aka the 'three bears' approach:

i. **Baby Bear** – a low-cost, basic package.
ii. **Daddy Bear** – a mid-price package. (This is the one you want to sell.)
iii. **Mummy Bear** – a top-of-the-range package. (This is just there to make the mid-price one look reasonable! *And yes, Mummy is the head of the family, because f*ck the patriarchy.*)

Then, you can build a simple sales page (see Chapter 19). Ideally, integrate 'buy from the site' methods such as Stripe and PayPal.

> **TOON TIP** You don't need fancy software to achieve this. You can easily get set up with basic WordPress, Shopify, Wix or Squarespace sites. If you need help doing this, head to my Facebook group, The Misfit Entrepreneurs, and I can recommend someone from the group to help.

Finally, make sure you cover your bottom. Ensure that you've clearly explained all your boundaries on your site and in any email correspondence. Also, get some proper terms and conditions for your services; you might want to contact guinea pig Ingrid Fernandez for this.

Ingrid Fernandez is planning to have four core offerings:
1. **DIY** – digital downloads in her shop.
2. **Done with you** – consultation calls and an audit for a set price. This is prime for productisation, as she can create custom packages based on the length and depth of the audit.
3. **Done for you** – customised services with 'from' pricing. This is a bespoke proposal based on discussion with the client.
4. **ADPIP** – which I'm not going to reveal just yet.

Ingrid told me:

I feel there would be such a lightness with this offering, because I know I can help people without it taking over my entire day. I love the boundaries productisation offers. It allows me to help more people and still have balance in my life, which the 'done for you' offering just doesn't let me do right now.

Task 2: Turn your one-night stands into serious relationships

The biggest complaint I get from the people I mentor in the Digital Marketing Collective community is that they hate to sell – not just in terms of cold-calling randoms *(shudder)* but the whole laborious process of talking to clients, drafting proposals and the bum-clenching horror of waiting to see if you've won the job.

And I get it – all that dancing about to win clients is relentless and time-consuming. It's like continually going on a first date when all you crave is someone who will click with you immediately and for the date to turn into a long-term relationship. Don't get me wrong – one-night-stand clients are fun to begin with as you learn the ropes, but they get old rather quickly.

It's lovely to get to the stage where you can stop 'wearing that uncomfortable, posh underwear' and 'plucking your business eyebrows', and instead let it all hang out and just 'be'. It's about reaching a level of understanding and respect with your clients that means 'selling' is moot. The answer to this is **retainers**, which involve:

- agreeing on a set amount of work or hours with your client
- offering a small, sweet incentive (either a discount or priority service)
- the client paying you upfront[3]
- agreeing on a set number of hours (a maximum that will roll over each month).

It's hard to sell a retainer to a client from the get-go. Generally, they're a great thing to offer after you've finished the first job. But if your client is more experienced with using a supplier like you, they may be happy to work this way immediately.

Retainers work well because they help create a steady, regular income and predictability, reassuring you that you've got your essentials

---

3 You can agree to get paid afterwards, especially if you think there will be a variance in hours, but that upfront payment is great for cash flow, so go with that if you can. Also, be aware that many corporates won't be willing to pay you upfront; you may have to work on 30 days or more.

covered. If you're able to get your retainer to cover your minimum viable income, then everything above and beyond your retainer is 'cream', or extra money you can use for nice-to-haves and investments.

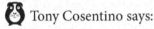 Don't take on too many retainers and leave no space for random jobs and time to work on your own business. Be sure to have a clause in your retainer agreement to review every three months so you don't get stuck on a rate that doesn't match your experience or inflation.

Here's how to set up a retainer:

1. Download the 'Retainer Agreement' from Katetoon.com.
2. Review it and adapt it to your business.
3. Propose a chat with your client.
4. Let them know they'll get priority service and/or a reduced rate, allowing them to budget better, and that you'll roll over a maximum set number of unused hours.
5. If possible, set up some kind of direct debit system, such as Navro.
6. Set up regular times to review the retainer to ensure it's working for both parties.

Tony Cosentino says:

Retainers provide stability, so I don't have a feast-or-famine lifestyle every month. They give me a baseline of money to build on, which means I don't have to cold-sell as much to find new clients every month. The extra benefit is that retainer clients also lead to more project work as they know and trust me. They also recommend me to other potential clients.

Task 3: Go 'done with you' before you go 'DIY'

The next and final task for you to complete before you go passive is to set up some kind of coaching or training offer. Why? Because there will always be people who want to DIY but also want their hand held. 'Done with you' is the bridge between service-based and ADPIP (see Figure 5.2).

Figure 5.2: Done with you – the bridge between
service-based and automated

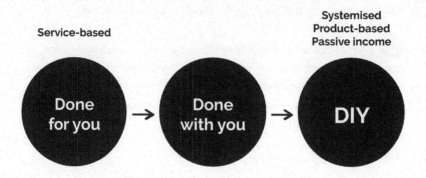

The benefits of offering coaching and training are as follows:

- **More money.** You can charge at least three times your going rate to train people, making each hour you work far more profitable. Why three times? Look, it's an arbitrary number that works for me, but my reasoning is that I can give away a lot more when I'm talking than when I'm doing.
- **Zero set-up.** All you need is a decent mic and video conferencing software such as Zoom.
- **Simple offering.** While you can outline what your coaching includes, I find it's generally best to keep it freeform and talk about the benefits rather than the inclusions – for example, 'By the end of this session, you'll feel more confident about your SEO. You'll leave with a clear action plan of next steps to boost your ranking'.

Of course, training can be draining. I often need an hour to recover after a session and can't do more than three in a day, so that reduces the profitability considerably. Also, if you're introverted, you might find this option too challenging; it's important to be able to think quickly on the spot and be confident.

Be aware that if you're a people-pleaser, you may find yourself running over time, but firm boundaries on this will help (or a free Zoom account that cuts you off after 40 minutes). In my experience, all of this gets easier with time.

The final reason why offering coaching or training is a great pre-step to passive income is that it acts as a pricing positioning tool for your future DIY and passive income options. People will compare working with you to getting coaching with you and doing your DIY option (which will likely be the most affordable). For example:

> *You could pay $10,000 for me to write your sales page copy for you or $1497 for an hour of coaching with me. Or you could join my sales page copywriting course for $1497 and get access to me for an entire year.*

Which would you choose?

To set up a coaching or training session:

1. work out three times your hourly rate
2. create a simple sales page (see Chapter 19)
3. consider offering both 30-minute and 1-hour sessions (and later down the track, you could offer coaching packages, but I'd start small)
4. set up payment mechanisms, such as Stripe and PayPal
5. consider setting up an automatic booking system, such as Calendly.

 It's a good idea to record each session (using Zoom or similar) so that your client can focus during the session and watch it back afterwards.

Be clear on what you're offering in the session. Is it just the literal hour, or are you planning to provide pre-discussion and post-session notes? If the latter, factor this into your pricing, or you'll immediately eat up that lovely profit.

Tony Cosentino says:

> *As the hourly rate is higher, I feel I'm beating the game a little because I'm bringing in more dollars per hour than when I'm doing regular work. The other positive is that I get paid upfront, which helps cash flow, and the time management is pretty easy: just a calendar invite, which is great for my ADD*

brain. Also, it's been especially lucrative for larger clients, as they come back to me regularly when new team members need to be trained.

TOON TIP I don't use an automatic calendar system, as I like to think about when I want to do coaching. My diary, though organised, often has 'air gaps' that I want to keep clear. Instead, I just chat with the customer to determine a good time for both of us. It's a good warm-up to the session.

Bonus idea: Your first taste of passive income

Now, while the ideas in this chapter set you up for ADPIP, they're not really ADPIP. And I know you're keen to have that 'money for nothing' feeling right now! So, here's another tactic you can try. Let's say you have a steady stream of work and occasionally find yourself turning work away because:

- you don't have enough time
- the client can't afford your rates
- it's not quite the right fit.

In this case, try setting up a referral network. A referral network is a collection of other business owners who do the same as you and to whom you could pass on work. Now, you might think you should just pass the work on out of the goodness of your heart, and you absolutely can. But after a while, you might find that while you're giving work out, you're not getting any back, and your referees start to feel a bit guilty.

Instead, you can set up a referral agreement (there's a template on the katetoon.com shop) where you agree on a small fee for passing clients on. It stipulates that the fee is a one-off, and is only paid if the referee completes and is paid for the job.

A referral agreement keeps everything businesslike and above board. The client gets a recommendation to someone good who you trust, the referee gets a client without having to do any of the marketing legwork, and you get a nice trickle of passive income for connecting good people with good people. The standard referral fee across most industries is 10%.

This is a trust exercise – I'm not talking about setting up an affiliate program – so, of course, you have to have an existing relationship with the people you choose. After a while, you could expand your network to include adjacent industries. For example, if you're a designer, you could recommend a good printer or accountant. The referral world is your lobster!

TOON TIP I earned $18K in referral fees in my first year of business, which represented about 20% of my income that year. It was life-changing!

TL;DR

Before you dive into launching your first ADPIP, it's important to squeeze as much juice as you can out of your existing offering and repackage your services into a range of higher-priced offerings. This will also help you to start flexing your sales page and tech muscles, so they're ready for when you have your 'thing' to launch.

OVER TO YOU

So, now it's time to decide which of the three tasks outlined in this chapter you'll tackle. Ideally, you'll do all three, but if you can only do one, I'd go with productising your services. Ask yourself these questions:

1. Which of your services is ripe for productisation?
2. What will your 'three bears' pricing be?
3. What will you include in each package?

(Psst: If you want to work through this with me, remember to check out the Six Figures While You Sleep Program on my website.)

PART II:
START WHERE YOU ARE

"

Start where you are. Use what you have.
Do what you can.

Arthur Ashe

"

Chapter 6

Getting to know yourself

I was never one of those children with a shelf full of trophies and a pinboard full of medals. I am in no way a child prodigy and in fact consider myself remarkably untalented. This is not me being humble, it's the plain truth. I never mastered any instruments *(except the recorder, which I can play with my nose, and a bit of one-finger piano)*. I have zero sporting prowess. I cannot solve the Rubik's Cube or do cryptic crosswords.

Throughout my life I've felt both relief and anger that my parents didn't force me to continue with ballet as a child or even get me started learning Mandarin. I'm okay at a lot of things. Not great, not amazing, but okay. And for a long time, it didn't feel like enough. Until I realised that being an all-rounder is pretty darn useful. Because here's the thing:

You do not need a superpower to be successful.

We've been led to believe that to rise to the top you must have some innate superpower; you must excel in one area; you must be a low-level genius. But it's just not true. We all know the quote 'A jack of all trades is master of none' – what you might not know is that it continues with 'but oftentimes better than a master of one'.

Being 'goodish' at a collection of things can work out just fine. But we must learn to appreciate our skills – however mediocre we feel they are. My own skills have evolved over the years. When I started out, I would have listed my skills in a CV kind of way:

- I am good at project management.
- I can write reasonably well.
- I am good at managing my time.
- I can type 94 words per minute.
- I can use the 'sum' feature on Excel.

However, recently a peer told me that my superpower was that I'm 'super high on fluid intelligence and creativity – the ability to throw yourself at something new, and come up with a totally unique (and valuable) take on it'.

Not only did this make my ego gland bulge and glisten, but it also helped me see that sometimes it's not about possessing a particular career skill – it's more about having the soft skills. I'm hoping by the end of this chapter you'll have fully examined your navel and will have a clear idea of who you are and, more importantly, who you want to be in the business world.

Why soft skills matter

When we're about to embark on something new, the temptation is to gather evidence of why it will fail, and one big document in the evidence folder will be lack of experience. Sure, you might be a fabulous lawyer, a gifted architect or a talented nail tech, but what if you have no experience in digital marketing?

Now, of course, you weren't born out of an egg yesterday. I'm guessing you have used the internet once or twice in your life. And if you were able to learn a skill or a craft so well you can make money out of offering it as a service, you'll be more than capable of learning the soft skills you need to master becoming an ADPIP legend.

But what are these soft skills? I'd say the skills required to thrive in this arena are:

- **curiosity** – the desire to learn about your customers and their problems
- **persistence** – the ability to push through, even when things aren't going well

- **warmth** – you need to genuinely like your customer community (you can fake it, but sooner or later people will work out that you don't care)
- **willingness to learn** – a keenness to take on new things and learn new ideas
- **humour** – the ability not to take things too seriously.

Something else that has helped me is the ability to see the big picture as well as the details. You need to be able to hover over your business in a helicopter, taking a long-term view – such as 'I'd like to build a membership' – but also dive into the details, such as 'Today I need to register a domain name'. You need to be able to complete tasks one by one without the bigger picture distracting you.

These are not a definitive list of needed skills but rather what helped me. I'd also say it helps to have **creativity** (to enjoy creating and writing) and to have a degree of **technical nous**, but if you don't, these things can be outsourced.

Think about what your soft skills are and what you like about yourself. You're going to be spending a lot of time with yourself on this ADPIP journey – so it's important that you and yourself get on.

🐧 Stephanie Holdsworth decided that these are her soft skills:

- **She's a good communicator.** She's able to understand people and learn what she needs to from them quickly.
- **She's not a delicate snowflake** *(her words)*. She is open to, and takes, feedback easily without getting upset.
- **She's relatable.** Unlike lots of people in the allergies industry who wear a white coat, she's a mum with lived experience and know-how.
- **She has a sense of humour.** She's able to make light of a situation and turn dull topics into warm, enjoyable content.
- **She's like a dog with a bone.** She won't give up; give her the green light and she will do it.

This is a great list of skills for someone who wants to be an ADPIPer – it's going to take hard work, a strong sense of self and a great sense of humour.

Embracing personal branding

Okay, so, now that we're starting to like ourselves, we must decide which bits of ourselves we want to put 'out there'. It's a well-known fact in marketing that people buy from people (as opposed to brands), and that people want to buy from those whose values align with their own. No one wants to invest in a course from some grinning entrepreneur on Instagram only to find out they're a rampant racist *(unless they are a rampant racist themselves)*.

But for people to trust you, they first have to like you. I know, I know, business shouldn't be a popularity contest – but it is. You don't need everyone to like you, but you do need enough people to like you to make your thing viable. You don't need to be Insta-famous, but you do need to become well known for what you do. To attract the right people, you're going to have to develop some kind of personal brand. And most importantly, **you** need to like you. Tough, eh?

Why is branding important?

Jeff Bezos said, 'Your brand is what other people say about you when you're not in the room'.

What would someone say about you, your business and the services you offer – or would they have nothing to say at all?

Since we're throwing quotes about, we can add this one from Oscar Wilde: 'There is only one thing in the world worse than being talked about, and that is not being talked about'. The truth is, if we want to have a successful business, we have to have people talking about us – and in positive ways.

Now, of course, I know you probably buy from Kmart and don't know the name of the CEO *(I'm betting it's John)*, but that's Kmart, a huge global monster brand. You are not a huge global monster brand, so you need the marketplace to be talking about you and your business positively from the get-go.

Earlier I covered the fear of putting ourselves out there. But we can't worry about some little troll living in his mum's garage writing snarky remarks on our posts. We can't let the 1% of negative people hold us back.

TOON TIP I resisted building a personal brand for a long time. I was worried that I didn't have enough credibility, that I wasn't likeable, that I didn't have big enough boobs or neat enough hair. I hid behind my brands. That was a mistake!

I know the idea of a personal brand might give you the heebie-jeebies, and I'm not saying it's not possible to build ADPIP with a faceless brand, but it's just so much harder. Remember, you don't immediately have to start dancing naked on Reels – you can start small with a few Instagram Stories.

The Madonna Factor

The great thing about investing in a personal brand is that it's timeless, and it travels with you. You can move seamlessly from idea to idea and people will follow you without question because they're following **you**, the person, not the brand. In my business lifetime I've been a copywriter, an SEO expert, a speaker, an author, and now a business mentor and digital marketing coach.

I've reinvented myself numerous times. Just like Madonna, from conical-bra me to Britney-kiss me to senior stage-dance beast. The business ideas may change, but I stay the same (*if a little older and wiser*).

Let's start with values

Okay, it's time to dig deep and decide what your personal (and therefore business) values are going to be. These will form your brand values, which dictate how your brand behaves and how it comes across in the world. A good way to start is by asking what you stand for – and what you won't stand for.

I believe my values are:

- **generosity** – I share my knowledge and advice; I don't hoard it
- **honesty** – I don't pull any punches and I give you the absolute truth
- **humour** – I add gentle humour to soften my approach and make dry topics more enjoyable
- **transparency** – I'm open, I share my ups and downs; this makes me more approachable and friendly.

But how do I know these are true? Well, for example, I give away a lot of free content, and of course it gets ripped off, repurposed and resold, and at times this has made me question whether being generous works as a brand value for my business. However, after some soul-searching, I've realised it absolutely does. It brings me leads, it's who I am and it's what stand I for.

Figure 6.1 shows a little cloud of words you could use for your values. Take a moment to circle three or four that seem right, or add more of your own.

Figure 6.1: A word cloud of values

Once you've settled on your values, write them on a Post-it note and stick it to your computer, and whatever you do in business, go back and check the action against your values. Remember, your values should be genuine – don't try to create values that don't quite fit but look good to others, because you won't be able to sustain the pretence.

Find a personality

If values are what you stand for, then personality is how you come across. How do people describe you? If you're a one-person band, then this will be your brand personality, whether you like it or not. If you're the leader of a company, it's inevitable that your personality will become part of your company's culture.

I like to think of myself as friendly, smart, funny and a little bit odd. That's how I'd like the world to see my brands, and conveniently, that's who I feel I am.

It may seem weird to 'create' a personality, but we're really 'curating' a personality. We're deciding which aspects of ourselves to show. Now, I'm guessing you're not a perfect person. Perhaps you can be a little impatient, you're fanatical about typos, or people avoid talking to you before your morning coffee.

Embrace your less-than-admirable qualities, because no matter how you try, they will come out. For example, I'm a massive control freak and deeply sarcastic. I talk about this in my socials – it's who I am, and my customers are going to find out sooner or later.

It's often hard to describe ourselves, so I find asking someone else is a good idea. Try popping this onto your Facebook page:

Hi Facebook friends,

I'm working on my branding. Can you help me?

Please give me four words you'd use to describe me. Don't hold back. I can take it.

Other ways to think about your brand personality and test your brand values are to ask yourself:

- If your brand were a movie star, who would play it?
- If your brand were a person, what type of person would they be?

Or finish these sentences:

- 'People describe me as…'
- 'I am definitely not…'

TOON TIP If you've been in business a while, you can look through old testimonials to find common adjectives that people use to describe you.

Once you have some options, write these on a different Post-it note and ask yourself, is the content and messaging you're creating in line with your personality?

Decide on your unique selling proposition

Your unique selling proposition (USP) is the reason that your product or service is different from, and better than, the competition's. I find that people struggle hugely to write their USP, but let's be honest – if you want to sell your product to someone else, you must sell yourself on it first.

Your USP is the major advantage your product has over the competition. It must be different from your competitors **and** strong enough to attract new customers.

Here are three different formulas you can use to write your USP:

1. [Name of brand] is the only product/service that [does something awesome] for [your audience] by [what makes you different].
2. [Name of brand] helps [type of customer] do [thing you do], and we do this by [how you do it].
3. [Name of brand] is a [category] company that provides [target audience] with [end benefit] by [points of difference].

Here's an example for my biggest seller, The Recipe for SEO Success:

The Recipe for SEO Success is the only course that effectively explains the foundations of SEO to small business owners in an easy, fun and digestible way. The Recipe for SEO Success helps small business owners master SEO with fun, easy to understand and affordable SEO courses and resources.

If you're struggling with the formula, just try asking yourself these questions:

· What do you do?
· Who do you do it for?
· Why do you do it better than anyone else?

Now, of course, at this stage you might not yet have found your Big Little Idea (see Chapter 8), and you may be working this through just for your existing business. But whatever your ADPIP is going to be, the USP will likely fit – with a bit of a nip and tuck.

🐹 I worked with Tony Cosentino to decide on his USP for his business, and then we looked at how that would change to be a USP for his ADPIP.

Here's his current service-based USP:

I'm an experienced WordPress specialist who helps ensure your website integrates seamlessly with your existing processes and platforms. My calm, friendly, jargon-free approach to website support and training gives you the competitive edge in the business battle. And my focus on client relationships means I've got your back and I'm here for the long term.

We'll talk about his Big Little Idea in the next chapter, but generally, he wants to position himself as a coach for starter WordPress developers, helping them learn from his mistakes, providing guidance and support, and improving their overall business approach.

So, he might tweak his USP like this:

Tony Cosentino is an experienced WordPress specialist, speaker and coach who helps newish WordPress developers create a business that truly supports their lifestyle goals. He provides help with business structure, sales tactics, support plan creation and project management, and gives advice on the best tools to invest in. His calm, easygoing approach to training makes everything seem more achievable, and his willingness to honestly share his highs and lows is refreshing in the WordPress world.

Decide on your mission

Yes this sounds a bit woo-woo. Your mission may be simply to earn a bit of money with as little stress as possible and have time to watch some Netflix at the end of the day. But trying to think of a small 'why' for your business and the products you want to put out into the world can really help you 'stress test' your idea and keep going when things get tough.

Figure 6.2 shows my little mission statements.

Figure 6.2: My mission statements

 Stephanie Holdsworth told me this story:

When I was a new mum with a 21-day-old fussy baby sleeping beside me who started crying, I picked her up and put her on the bed to change her, and she threw up – blood. Even though I was a paediatric nurse, I had no idea what was happening. My husband and I raced to the hospital at 3 a.m. and I remember being terrified. My daughter was transferred to Sydney Children's Hospital and had all the tests and scans, to be told, 'It's just bad allergies'. But it's not as simple as that. I was up all night googling, and felt stressed, tired and like I had no support. I want to change that for other parents out there.

Stephanie defined these as her mission statements:

- 'Help someone when they're at their worst, googling at 3 a.m. to get the right information.'
- 'Remove fear and stigma around allergies and eczema.'
- 'Provide support and education in everyday language that's jargon-free and relatable.'

Share your quirks

We all have strange little habits and secret passions. Maybe you're a huge Barry Manilow fan; maybe you collect cheese. Don't hide these fabulous quirks – share them with the audience.

For example, I'm obsessed with the British crisp brand called Frazzles, and I'm a mad-good hula hooper. These things have nothing to do with my business, but I share them freely because they show I'm *(gasp)* human!

In this time of AI and chatbots, we need to show our humanity, and that often means we need to share a little non-professional stuff.

Again, we don't need to share all our sad or bad stories. If you have a secret S&M den in your garden shed, that isn't necessarily something you'd put on LinkedIn *(although it would make great OnlyFans content)*. You don't need to share your daily breakfast or your kids' school pictures. Start gently with the odd picture of your dog, or some personal stories about what you did on the weekend. Even if it's just one post out of every ten, I think you'll be surprised how much that content resonates with your audience.

When I spoke to Ingrid Fernandez about sharing her quirks, she told me that the thought of sharing makes her feel like not doing it:

> I have huge fear around being visible, and although I know logically I don't have to share everything, it still feels so vulnerable to be public in this way. As a lawyer, we spend so much time doing invisible work – hidden behind contracts and other lawyers – so this is extra uncomfortable.

We discussed this, and Ingrid felt one thing she could start sharing is her love of house plants. Sounds odd, but bear with us.

'I love plants, but I'm not always great at looking after them', she told me. 'Some are taking over my house, and some I just can't keep alive, a bit like business. Sometimes you think it's all good and then you find your plant is dead.'

I love this idea – plants are related and relatable, which is exactly what we're after. Like Ingrid, you can start by sharing personal things in this analogous way, and before you know it, you'll be sharing naked pictures of yourself in the bath *(jokes)*.

Share your failures

Nothing is more humanising than lovely fat failure. Sharing your struggles will help people to identify with you – and build a personal connection to you and your brand.

Sharing flops doesn't undermine your ability, your professionalism or your brand. Now, of course, I'm not talking about terrible mistakes, legal issues or hideous faux pas, but rather mistakes that help you learn, flaws that make you human – the spilled coffee on your top before an important meeting, or the launch that didn't fly. Save the dark stuff for your diary.

 Stephanie Holdsworth told me one of her failures:

> *When I first started dealing with eczema allergies, I was focused on the price and how expensive everything was. So, I started Allerchic in saviour mode. I wanted to help everyone, so I set my prices low. Of course, it was successful, but it wasn't profitable or sustainable. Now I've learned to charge my worth, both for my products and for my educational content.*

Understand your EEAT

You might not know it, but Google knows everything about you. Yep, it knows every weird thing you've typed into the search engine at 3 a.m.; it probably knows what colour underwear you're wearing right now.

We all have a digital footprint (much like our environmental one), and Google uses this to understand who we are. To Google we are all 'entities' – little data blobs that connect to other data blobs.

So, say you're putting yourself out there as an authority on SEO, or dogs, or cake. How does Google know if it's true? It establishes this using a process called EEAT:

- **Experience** – what is our proven experience in this area?
- **Expertise** – what expertise have we shown?
- **Authority** – where have we been quoted as a source?
- **Trust** – where is there proof that we know what we're talking about?

This is why your experience to date in business counts – and why, to some, degree when it comes to ADPIP you should stay in your lane. If you're a well-known psychologist who suddenly decides to bring out an accountancy course, it's going to be an uphill battle. Your audience and Google will be looking for previously established EEAT.

Examples of EEAT that you could share on your website and on your socials include:

- qualifications you've earned
- brands and companies you've worked with
- press you've been featured in
- podcasts you've appeared on
- testimonials you've been given.

Don't worry if you don't have much EEAT yet – it's also something you can build along the way. I cover this when I talk about your slippery funnel (Part IV).

Have a brain blurt

If all this seems a bit challenging, just try having a brain blurt – think about your business (and possibly rope in a friend or partner) and just have a good old brainstorm. Write down words, phrases and sentences that come to mind when you think about your business. Then, perhaps, print them out and pop them on your office wall as a little reminder of who you are and why you do what you do. Figure 6.3 shows my brain blurt.

Figure 6.3: My brain blurt

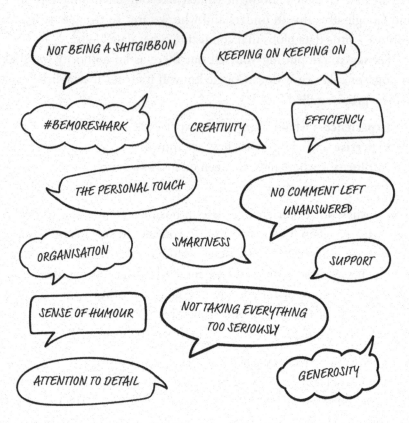

TL;DR

Knowing who you are – your superpowers, values, personality, quirks, flaws and what you offer to the world – is vital. You're not just going to be selling a product, you're going to be selling yourself, and you have to know and like yourself for it all to work.

OVER TO YOU

Grab a pen and paper or the *Six Figures While You Sleep* workbook and get to know your:

- brand values
- brand personality
- USP
- mission
- quirks
- failures
- EEAT.

And if all else fails, grab a big piece of paper and blurt out any words that come to mind. You can always polish them up later.

Chapter 7

Understanding your customers

Once we've gazed deeply into our navels long enough to discover who we are, we can move into gazing into our customers' navels (*figuratively that is*). Because, of course, we're trying to make a thing that will appeal to other people, and we're working towards a one-to-many model, so it needs to appeal to **many** people. I've said it already, but business is a bit of a popularity contest. For our ADPIP to work, we need a mass audience – and that means appealing to as many people as possible.

Now, we can't be all things to all people. We established our personality and brand values in the previous chapter; we can't abandon these just to make people like us. But we can be some things to the right people. If we can really gain insight into our ideal customers' problems, we will appeal to them and offer solutions they will buy. It's shockingly simple.

So, now it's time to get to know our customers – what they like and don't like. It's time to firm up our customer profile.

Step 1: Describe your ideal customer

Let's cover the basics of your ideal customer (I'm afraid it has to be a little bit more nuanced than 'anyone with a pulse and a credit card'):

- Gender
- Age
- Location

- Profession
- Income
- Marital status
- Interests
- Second-favourite flavour of jam.

You can go further than this and create a full avatar of your client, giving them a name, a cat and a passion for Taylor Swift. The more fully rounded your vision is, the easier it will be to 'talk' to them.

You may have more than one avatar, and that's fine too, but if you start to develop a *Downton Abbey* cast of customer creations then maybe you've gone too far. It's hard to market to everyone – you really need to market as if you're talking to just one person.

TOON TIP If you struggle with this, I think it helps to imagine an actual customer, perhaps one you've met in real life. In my head I'm always marketing to Sue McGary from French Affair. Sue has a wonderful tablecloth business; she was on my email list for years before becoming a member of the Digital Marketing Collective. She's lovely, and I always think, *If Sue will like this, then it's probably a good thing.* You need to find your 'Sue'.

Step 2: Identify your customer's BDF

The next thing you can do is look at your ideal customer's BDF:

- **Beliefs** – what are their attitudes to your product and your industry?
- **Desires** – what do they want? What are their goals?
- **Feelings** – how do they want to feel after working with you or buying your things?

I like to use a divorce lawyer as my example of BDF. If you're going to hire a divorce lawyer to handle your separation, what would your BDF be? Perhaps:

- **Beliefs** – expensive, talks jargon, boring
- **Desires** – to resolve it as quickly as possible and spend as little as possible
- **Feelings** – stress-free and relieved.

Ingrid Fernandez has asked herself these tough questions. So far, she knows her target audience is small business owners:

- Their pre-conceived **belief** is that legals are too hard, scary and expensive.
- Their **desire** is to run a legally compliant business and be able to sleep at night without worrying whether their legal bum is covered.
- Their **fear** is that they're doing the wrong thing without knowing and missing something that may get them into legal trouble, but also that they can't afford to pay a lawyer to fix it all for them.

Step 3: Find their Clive Google Factor

Most of us stick to demographic land, listing out the shoe size and number of nostril hairs our customers have, when really this doesn't help us sell them things at all. So instead, I like to use the Clive Google Factor (CGF).

I like to think about my customer – let's call him Clive. He's 66, he's married to Maureen, he drives a Volvo and has a sausage dog called Barbara.

It's 3 a.m. and Clive has woken up from a restless night, Maureen slumbering beside him. He reaches for his phone and starts to google. What is Clive googling?

Now, of course, there is a myriad of things he could be searching for, some probably not fit for printing in this book, but imagine he is worrying about a strange itchy feeling. For a few days now he's had itchy armpits and he's ignored it. Life is busy – there's golf to play and the lawn to fertilise. But tonight, they're so damn itchy. So, he googles 'why is my armpit itchy', and there you are, the first result – a well-written blog titled '10 reasons your armpit is itchy and what to do about it'.

Clive reads, feels comforted, makes a note to buy some itchy armpit cream in the morning and falls back into a deep, restful sleep. The next day, he's back on your site with his credit card in hand, ready to buy.

If we can be there for people in their hour of need, they will remember us when they need to purchase. We need to move beyond shoe size and into pain points. So, ask yourself, what is your ideal customer googling at 3 a.m.?

🐧 Ingrid has worked out that her ideal customer's Clive Google Factor is, 'What happens if someone asks for a refund a year after they've purchased my product?', or, 'How do I handle someone breaking my terms and conditions but having a heart-felt reason for doing so, such as illness or death?'

She needs to ensure her ADPIP delivers to this audience and helps them sleep better.

Step 4: Identify their problems and pain points

Now, let's try to articulate your customers' pain points. Another way to think about this is, what problem are you trying to solve?

🐧 Here are the pain points for Ingrid's customers:

- 'I'd love to get legal documents for my website, but I can't afford it.'
- 'I'm worried I'm going to get stuck working with a client that I don't like and won't be able to get out of it.'
- 'If I call it a "deposit", do I have to give it back?'

Step 5: Find the right solution

Now that you have customer pain points and a clearer insight into what problem you are trying to solve, you're getting closer to identifying the right solution and being able to dig into some more practical considerations, namely:

- budget
- time
- level
- connection.

🐧 What are the pain points for Tony Cosentino's target audience –newish WordPress developers?

- Overwhelmed by the sea of too-general WordPress business advice

- Fearful of wasting money on the wrong tools
- Struggling to find clients and keep them for the long term
- Unsure and lacking confidence about pricing and productising their services
- Unable to effectively project-manage and stay productive
- Looking for a safe space to get advice without being judged by their peers.

🦉 Steph Holdsworth thinks the gap for her customers is people who are:

- waiting an age to see the right specialist with no idea what to do (it can be up to a two-year wait to see an immunologist)
- overwhelmed by the incomprehensible medical information online
- struggling to find the right solutions and feeling helpless
- feeling unsupported, exhausted and like there's no one to turn to
- looking for a safe space to get advice without being judged by other parents or medical professionals.

It's time for another Venn diagram, people! (See Figure 7.1.)

Figure 7.1: Practical considerations to help you find the right solution

What is your customer's budget for this?

Budget is often defined by potential return.

Say you've identified your ideal customer as someone who crochets. They want easy demonstrations on how to make new projects. Their budget is low – it's a hobby, just a fun thing, not something they're going to invest big bucks in. This doesn't mean they're not a good ideal customer, it just means you'll need to manage your income expectations or get a lot of people to join if you want to make big money.

On the other hand, if you've identified your ideal customer as a real estate agent looking for advice on how to improve their sales and bring in more leads, their budget might be high. If they make good home sales based on your tips, it could mean huge financial gain for them, which makes the solution you can offer them a great candidate to turn into an ADPIP.

How much time does your customer have to solve their problem?

Our crochet lover might have lots of time – perhaps they're no longer working and are looking to be absorbed in something new. Our real estate agent, by contrast, has little time – they want fast results and to get in and get out quickly.

What is your customer's existing level of understanding?

Is your audience at a beginner, intermediate or advanced level? Each will take you down a different path:

- There are more people at the **beginner** level, but they will be less willing to invest heavily.
- There are fewer people at the **intermediate** level, but they will be more likely to have bigger budgets.
- There is a much smaller pool of humans at the **advanced** level, but they will be willing to pay a premium for the right solution.

What kind of connection does your customer want?

This ties back to 'time' in some ways, but it's slightly different. How much 'touch' does your customer need?

A beginner crochet person might want a lot of support, the ability to ask questions, ongoing assistance and other crocheters to talk to. This isn't a bad thing, but you'll need to factor it into your time planning and budget.

The busy real estate agent may not want to be rubbing shoulders with other real estate agents in his local area. They may be looking for more of a VIP offering, with one-on-one support where they can talk in private.

And Ingrid's legal-seeking humans from earlier? They might just want to buy a quick template and be done.

Understanding the level of support needed is going to dictate the kind of ADPIP product you develop. This, my friends, is the most important part of the book – stop now, take a sip of coffee and read this carefully:

Most potential ADPIP people do not do this important work to understand their customers. They build the product they want to build, not the product their customer wants – and then wonder why it doesn't sell.

Put simply, there's no point making a six-month course for someone who hasn't got the time to take it, the money to pay for it and the need for that kind of learning.

> **TOON TIP** It's so tempting to go out on social media and say, 'Hey I'm planning on building this thing, who wants it?' and then lap up all the comments that affirm your decision. But remember, people will often say 'yes' just to be nice – the true test is when you ask them to pay for said thing. Then, suddenly, they're hiding in the bushes.

TL;DR

While I know you want to dash out and start making the thing, you're at risk of making a thing that doesn't appeal to the right people. It's important to do the work to distinguish between what your customers think they want and what they need.

OVER TO YOU

Grab a pen and jot down ideas about your potential customers:

- Their demographics and shoe size
- Their beliefs, desires and fears
- Their Clive Google Factor
- Their pain points
- Their budget, time, level and connection needs.

Chapter 8

Coming up with your Big Little Idea

At a certain point in life, you realise you're never going to be a rockstar. You pack away your shimmering dreams of being an A-list celebrity, along with the fanciful notion of becoming 'the next big thing'. Perhaps you thought you were going to invent something amazing and impress the investors on *Shark Tank* or *Dragons' Den* with those new self-cleaning knickers or that revolutionary blend of kumquat soup.

But now, you grunt when you get up off the sofa, and you have pairs of socks older than most of the entrepreneurs online, and you're thinking, 'My chance has slipped away'. But has it? The truth is that it's often the pressure to come up with a big idea that stops us in our tracks. We're racking our brains trying to think of something so new, innovative and revolutionary that it causes our brain to fog over, and we achieve nothing.

In my experience, the big superstars, the ingenious inventors and the big idea stories are few and far between. The true genius is in the little idea – taking something small that already kind of works and making it better. Looking at something you already offer and finding a new way to deliver it.

In this chapter, I want to give you permission to stop looking for your big idea and instead find your Big Little Idea.

Here's how.

Step 1: Find your selfish reason

It's all very well and good to want to help other people, but of course, we must rummage around to find our own oxygen mask first. What's in it for you?

When I ask people why they want to start an ADPIP idea, they usually have one of five reasons:

1. To make more money
2. To spend less time working
3. To avoid burning out emotionally and physically
4. Not to rely so much on a single income source
5. To avoid the tedium of doing the same thing again and again.

What's your reason?

🦉 Stephanie Holdsworth, who runs a successful online store, was relying on one supplier who suddenly decided to shut up shop in Australia. This caused her a lot of stress as she scrambled to replace them. It would have been nice if she'd had some ADPIP income to cover her during this period.

Step 2: Find your altruistic reason

Right now, you might not have an altruistic reason, and that's fine to start with, but long term you're going to need something more than cold, hard cash to keep you going. Remember your mission back in Chapter 6? How does this tie into your ADPIP?

Perhaps you want to:

- help more people than you can currently
- help people when they need it rather than making them wait
- lower the price barrier to work with you.

Step 3: Find the frustration

Think about what frustrates you about how you work. Perhaps it's being asked the same questions again and again, or how long it takes your clients to give you the information you need. Perhaps it's the time you spend onboarding new people, or how difficult it is to justify your prices.

There are gems in those frustrations. For example, if you're frustrated by lots of questions, then the solution could be a community or FAQ bank where all those questions are covered. If you're frustrated by onboarding struggles, then you could use a checklist of assets that need to be gathered and a tutorial on how to do it faster.

You can also think about what frustrates you about your industry. This was my route into ADPIP. The SEO industry is kinda full of cowboys and those pretending that it's some dark art or genius-level process that only gurus can master. This frustrated me, and I saw the need for an honest, plain-English SEO course that normal humans could master.

Step 4: Find the gap

Now, there may be absolutely nobody offering what you're planning on offering. When I started my SEO course there was, I think, only one other in Australia, and only a few worldwide. There were also no courses at that time offered by a female SEO expert, and none that made SEO fun *(and, at times, funny).*

> *If you're a true pioneer, the land before you is empty to travel as you wish – but you're going to have to tread your own path. However, if similar products already exist, it doesn't mean all is lost. Look at what's out there already and see how you could make it better. Perhaps there's already a course teaching people how to use a certain software, but it's general and not specific to your industry. Maybe there's a beginner-level offering, but you could offer advanced (or vice versa).*

There's also potential for finding ADPIPs offered in one market that aren't tailored to your market. For example, you've seen there's a subcontracting agreement for copywriters, but you can produce one that's perfect for graphic designers.

A few of my students have taken what they learned in my SEO course and created similar Spanish- and German-language versions – obviously not out-and-out copying me but adding their own ideas and flavour.

Tony Cosentino told me:

I feel there's a gap in the market for a support system and community for newish WordPress developers. Existing products are focused on one theme, or one niche set of tools. Or they come in too high a level for the newbies, making them feel afraid to comment or share. I'd also say that many existing WordPress communities are male dominated and heavily focus on tech, rather than sales and customer relationships, and they can be a little chest-beaty.

I want to create a diverse and inclusive space where everyone feels they can comment and share (and no theme-shaming – that's a WordPress developer joke).

Step 5: Paint the future for your potential customers

Okay, so far, we've been super practical, but now I'm going to let you dream a little. Imagine you're one year down the track and your ADPIP is working – what does this look like?

Take your customer avatar and describe what you've helped them do, how they feel and what improvements your products have brought to their life. You can even take it a step further and write out your dream customer testimonial. I know it's a bit woo-woo, but it's a nice exercise to give you the good feels. Even better, soon you'll be able to compare that made-up testimonial to the real thing.

 Here's Tony's dream testimonial:

Since joining Tony's community I feel so much more confident about my skills and my business. I have one spot to learn every-thing and am no longer falling down research rabbit holes as I can jump into the group for a quick answer from Tony and the other members. I've made great connections in the community, and it's led to some wonderful referrals. I now have a good flow of clients, am better at managing my time and feel I can hold my own in the WordPress world.

A. Customer. WordPress Developer, Wagga Wagga, Australia.

🐹 At this point, let's be clear on what our three guinea pigs have decided is their Big Little Idea:

- Tony Cosentino wants to set up a membership for junior WordPress developers where they can learn about tech, sales, customer service and project management.
- Stephanie Holdsworth wants to create a series of small workshops, and potentially a course, aimed at parents about allergies and how to manage them.
- Ingrid Fernandez wants to create a membership, and potentially a mastermind, for small business owners needing legal support.

TL;DR

This preparation work may seem like overkill, but any time you invest now in planning your ideas will save you months (and possibly years) of effort and disappointment down the track. It will enable you to create something that flies off the virtual shelves and that you enjoy delivering.

OVER TO YOU

Work through the following questions to identify your Big Little Idea:

- What is your selfish reason?
- What is your altruistic reason?
- What makes you frustrated?
- Where is the gap?
- What does the future look like?
- What does your dream testimonial look like?

Chapter 9

Stress testing your idea

In Part III I'm going to walk you through the pros and cons of what I see as the four core delivery methods for your ADPIP idea: digital downloads, courses, memberships and masterminds. For now, though, I'm going to assume you're already thinking about one of these, and I know you're desperate to get started, but I just want to stress test your idea and give you a realistic slap in the face about the necessary time, money and other impacts of your idea.

Unless you are extremely productive, this isn't going to get built quickly, and unless you're unusually lucky, this is not going to take off overnight. You don't want to destroy what you already have by reaching for something completely new. Instead, you need to weave your new idea into your service-based work with as little impact as possible.

Test 1: Why, why, why?

I know, enough already with the 'why's – you've established you're going to be good at this, customers want it, there's a gap, and you have both selfish and altruistic reasons to do it. So, what now, Kate?

My question here is, do you really want to do this, or do you just like the idea of having done this? We all know that the people who run marathons, while of course they enjoy crossing the finish line, also have to enjoy getting up at 5 a.m. on soggy mornings and running 20 kilometres with no audience and no applause.

Can you enjoy the journey as much as the destination? Can you enjoy the struggle?

I see a lot of people announcing when they're going to do a thing. 'I'm going to launch a course'; 'I'm going to set up a membership'. Everyone gathers in the comments to pat their bottoms and wish them well. And the proud business owner gets a rush of dopamine, the neurochemical reward. It's lovely, it's exciting – but it's not deserved. They just haven't earned it yet, baby. *(Cue The Smiths.)* If you're in this for the dopamine, the truth is it's a long, long way off; instead, you have to enjoy the slow serotonin of developing something quietly.

The other advantage of not announcing and working behind the scenes is that no one can poo on your bonfire (or copy you). Believe me, as soon as you announce you are straying from the well-trodden path of 'time for money' exchange, someone, somewhere, will pooh-pooh it. Mostly, I find, it's because they are envious. Don't take advice from people who are not in the arena fighting the same lions as you. Find your other ADPIP gladiators.

Test 2: Time-check

As I've mentioned before, nothing is ever really passive income – there's always work involved. And with ADPIPs, a lot of that investment is at the start, which makes it even more terrifying as you have to invest the time hoping it will work. But how much time?

In Part III, I'm going to provide you with a breakdown of the tasks involved for each type of product, but for right now we can use ballpark figures. Want to make a template? How long do you think it will take? Got a number in your head? Okay, double it. Then add 10% ☺.

The average template in my shop takes around eight hours to produce:

1. Writing – 3 hours
2. Proofreading (not me) – 30 minutes
3. Design (not me) – 2 hours
4. Amendments and fiddling – 2 hours
5. Coding into the site – 30 minutes.

And of course, that doesn't include the time to create the site to host it on, installing the software to deliver it, integrating the payment methods, the marketing and the support for people who have any issues purchasing, downloading or using it.

And where do those eight hours come from? If your reason for moving into passive income was wanting more money and spending less time, then this is the exact opposite.

Here's the thing: you're going to have to take a step back to find a way forward. The time is not going to appear in the middle of your day, and you're not going to be able to fire all your clients while you work this out. So, you're going to have to do that thing, working harder than other people are willing to in the short term so you can have the life you want in the long term.

This might mean 5 a.m. wake-ups. It might mean late nights. It might mean weekend working. And if that isn't possible right now, that's okay – you can plan for it. Remember, in reality, no one is waiting for this thing you're making. You have time. You might worry that someone else will do it first, and they might, but that's no reason to drive yourself into the dirt to get it done faster. There's enough room for everyone; you won't lose 'the race'.

Test 3: Shag, marry, kill

For many of you, there simply won't be any extra time available to you. You're up until 3 a.m. with a small child, so 5 a.m. wake-ups aren't going to happen. You spend your weekends ferrying your teen to sporting events, so they're out too. But something's got to give. You're going to have to look at your list of weekly tasks, the work that you're currently doing, and take a 'shag, marry, kill' approach:

- **Shag** – what's the work you really love that's super high-income? Do more of this.
- **Marry** – what's the work that you kind of enjoy and has solid income? Keep on doing this.
- **Kill** – what are the low-income (possibly admin) tasks that take a lot of time and make no money at all? You gotta kill those, or at least outsource them.

I would not have been able to build my ADPIP empire if I'd continued to reconcile my Xero for an hour each morning (I hired a bookkeeper) or kept fiddling around trying to design things in Canva (I hired a designer).

I had to dig out some weeds to create fertile ground to plant my new ideas. And if you're thinking, 'I don't have the money to pay for someone else to do this', I'm sorry to say you've got to get real. This is an investment. Your ADPIP isn't going to appear out of thin air. You're going to pay with either time or money – but believe me, it will all be worth it.

 This is Stephanie Holdsworth's shag, marry, kill:

- **Shag** – maintaining the website, choosing new products and fulfilling orders
- **Marry** – marketing and promoting the shop, doing finances, general admin
- **Kill** – customer service and going to the post office.

For her kill, she could hope to hit an order threshold which means Australia Post would pick them up, or she could hire a local teenager (with a driver's licence) to take products to the shop for her. For customer service, she could easily outsource this to a virtual assistant, or create some more comprehensive FAQs and perhaps even a chatbot.

Test 4: Parkinson's law

I'm obsessed with time, that finite resource that slips by so quickly. How we invest it is everything. Your passive income project will eat as much time as you give it. Why? Because you want it to be perfect. Because of all those fears we talked about in Chapter 4. If you keep fiddling and fixing, you'll never get to launch the thing and see if it actually works.

You must be brutal and apply Parkinson's law – the idea that a task takes as long as you give it.

If I tell you it should take you six to eight hours to create your first template, that's all you're going to spend, because I know otherwise you'd still be working on it when you're old and grey. It won't be perfect. You'll sell a copy and then notice a typo; you can fix it. Your course videos will make you cringe; you can re-record them. Your membership will flop on the first launch; you can launch again.

The price of progress is giving up on things being fabulous the first time around. I could write 'Done is better than perfect' here, but I won't, because it's a cliché.

TOON TIP I have an admission to make. I made a video for my Recipe for SEO Success course and loaded it onto my site. A year later *(a YEAR, people)* my friend Anu, who was doing the course, sent me a message: 'Hey I don't mean to sound odd, but you know that video in module one? Do you burp at about minute six?' I listened back. I burped. And I hadn't edited the burp out. It wasn't a little polite burp; it was a major toad burp. About 200 people had passed through the course in that year. And all heard the burp. While it was mortifying, I survived. And now, #BURPGATE makes me smile *(sometimes)*. So, don't worry if you fail to edit out a burp in a video you make and then leave it available for a year.

Test 5: Work out the money, honey

In my previous book, *Six Figures in School Hours* (and briefly in this one), I talk about the importance of setting an hourly rate for yourself. Whether your business is service-based or ecommerce, it's vital to give your time a value and then use that when you're deciding on your priorities. If your hourly rate is $100, that template I mentioned earlier is going to cost you $800. You might decide to outsource the proofreading and design, which brings your hours down, but the total cost will likely be the same. Now, say you sell that template for $40. You need to sell 20 copies to break even. But you need to sell many, many more to cover the future marketing time.

A course might take you 100 hours to create and require you to hire a myriad of helpers. Perhaps you'll spend a cool $20K before you're done. Selling it at $2K a pop means you'll have to make ten sales to break even.

Test 6: Identify the first step

Obviously, this book is a way to work through the whole process of creating ADPIPs (and if you need more support, you can join the Six Figures While You Sleep Program). But right now, let's think about your first step. After you've done the exercises covered in this chapter, what's the first thing you're doing to do to make this real? *(Hint, it's not announcing it on Facebook.)*

Perhaps it's:

·   time-blocking your calendar
·   hiring a proofreader
·   writing some copy for your future sales page (more on that in Chapter 19)
·   firing a low-income client to make space for your ADPIP.

Stop now and identify the first step – one that gives you no glory or dopamine and is possibly the thing you least want to do.

Test 7: Make the commitment

I'm guessing if you're reading this book, you've been thinking about passive income for a little while. You may have spent years mulling over an idea but haven't ever managed to make it happen. It's time to make a commitment. I prefer to write mine down, but you can say it out loud if you want.

Something like this:

I commit to building my [THING] by [DATE]. I understand that it will cost me [MONEY] and take up [TIME]. But I'm willing to make the sacrifice now to build a better future for myself and my family.

Test 8: Paint your future

In the previous chapter we painted the future for our customers. Now it's time to use the paintbrushes for ourselves. What would life look like if all this worked out? (Sorry, **when** all this works out.)

Think about what your new average day will look like. Right now, maybe you're commuting to a job you hate, or you're a slave to your clients' demands. Your day involves doing the same work again and again, and you dread heading to your desk on a Monday. You're beholden to a few clients that you don't really like working with, and you're in a constant state of financial feast and famine. Future you will still be working (how much will depend on your model and success), but your day could look much different.

Back when I started all this in 2015, I was an exhausted mum with a five-year-old. I had a huge mortgage, was the main income earner and was working all the hours I could to earn a crust as a copywriter. We didn't travel, I spent 90% of my time in pyjamas, and I did zero self-care.

Now, and not to sound like a smug cow, I work around 20 to 25 hours a week in my home office. I have no mortgage and two investment properties and am building generational wealth for my son. I take regular trips both for work and pleasure. I race to my desk each Monday. I still spend 90% of my time in pyjamas but invest more effort into self-care.

Life isn't without its challenges, don't get me wrong, but they are more enjoyable challenges with bigger, scalable rewards.

🐧 So, earlier, Tony Cosentino painted an imagined future for his members and wrote his dream testimonial. But what does **his** future look like when his membership is up and running, and successful? I asked him to imagine how it would feel to have 127 happy members:

> I love the fact that I can focus on the group and go down as many rabbit holes as I want daily to solve issues for my members.
>
> I love hearing about their successes, and I love being able to give back. I am spending more time doing what I truly enjoy – being able to fix problems and help these people and make money while I do it. My membership has become part of my daily routine and I'm as happy as a clam.

TL;DR

You need to turn your passive income pipe dream into a plausible reality. This is going to require some cold, hard figuring out of your time and money commitment, and the sacrifices you're going to make. You may have to do it tough in the short term to live well in the long term.

OVER TO YOU

Now it's time to test your idea:

- What is your why?
- How much time do you think you can allow?
- What can you 'shag, marry or kill'?
- Apply your hourly rate to your time allowance above – what's the end cost?
- What is the first step you can take towards your passive income goal?
- Write out your commitment.
- Write out your 'paint the future' statement.

PART III:
CHOOSING YOUR ADPIP

Nothing is more difficult, and therefore more precious, than to be able to decide.

Napoleon Bonaparte

★☆ ★☆

Chapter 10

Creating digital downloads

As I've mentioned, the biggest mistake I see people making with ADPIPs is not taking a long enough view. Most budding ADPIPers dash out there and start building the 'thing' in its entirety and then try to sell it. They start by creating a huge 12-week course when they haven't even been able to get someone to download their freebie. They spend hours recording video content for their membership when they only have four followers on Facebook.

You must **start with the end in mind**. When I created my first digital download, I had no idea that I would later have a big fat SEO course and two memberships stuffed with humans. But things evolve over time. Your Big Little Idea can be sold in several different formats, and you need to start somewhere, or you'll never start at all.

It's a good idea to understand the pros and cons of each ADPIP option and weigh up which is the best fit for you and your customers right now. So, let's start with the easiest option – digital downloads.

What is a digital download?

Digital downloads come in many different forms, such as ebooks, worksheets, checklists and templates. Essentially, they all serve the same purpose: to solve a customer's problem and help them do something quickly.

For example, my first digital download was a copy deck template, something I'd developed over many years in the advertising industry. This solved several problems for other copywriters:

- It gave them a way to present their copy professionally.
- It made them look more experienced and like experts, even if they were just starting out.
- It provided ideas to improve and enhance their copy.
- The 'fill in the blanks' format sped up the copywriting process for them.

Why choose digital downloads?

As discussed in previous chapters, digital downloads are probably the quickest of all the ADPIPs to create. Also, after the initial set-up, they are relatively easy to maintain and need little support and customer service. This makes them higher-profit assets.

Digital downloads are also a great way to test the market; you may even choose to give your first digital download away for free to gauge the level of interest (see Chapter 19).

TOON TIP Remember, if someone isn't willing to give you their email address to download your freebie, it's unlikely they'll ever give you their credit card details to pay for your main product.

It's also fine to just do digital downloads and nothing else. If a course or membership feels like too big a commitment, creating templates is a great way to get a nice little burst of extra income every now and again with minimal effort.

Who suits digital downloads?

Digital downloads are relatively low effort and don't require a huge, ongoing commitment. So, they're an easy way to dip your toe into the ADPIP pond, test the water and see if you enjoy the process. You'll likely need to make more digital downloads for your courses, memberships and masterminds, so if you struggle to create these, it's possibly an indicator that you'll struggle to create a whole course. But remember, you can always outsource and get help.

Remember also that your first digital download is likely to be a freebie, which you'll use for lead generation (see Chapter 17). But it still needs to be as good as a paid download to show the quality of your overall product. You want people to think, *Wow, if this is what she's giving away for free, imagine what her paid stuff is like.*

Creating your first digital download

If you've never made a template before, I'm guessing the idea of creating your first public digital download and selling it might be kinda scary. So, Figure 10.1 breaks down of the steps I take to create mine.

Figure 10.1: The steps to create a digital download

1 PLANNING   2 TYPE   3 NAMING   4 WRITING

8 SUPPORT   7 LEGALS   6 SELLING   5 DESIGN

Step 1: Planning

Hopefully, Chapters 8 and 9 motivated you to start developing your Big Little Idea. It's important to ensure the idea:

- solves a problem and empowers the user to act
- provides more value than a free downloadable
- positions you as an expert and authority
- encourages the user to buy more templates or your 'bigger thing'.

TOON TIP A great way to distinguish between a free digital download and a paid one is that the freebie often just covers the 'what' and the 'why'. The paid version also covers the 'how'.

For example, my aim with this book is to give you direction and as much of the 'how' as I can squeeze into 77,000 words. Obviously, there's going to be a whole lot more 'how', support and accountability in my paid program (the Six Figures While You Sleep Program). And that's okay. Your products must be helpful, but they don't need to give everything away.

Step 2: Decide on your digital download type

Are you going to create a template, a checklist, a spreadsheet, or something else? Remember, the idea is to help the user and speed up something that would normally take them ages.

TOON TIP I don't think ebooks make great digital downloads. For me, they just create a problem for users – a big old chunk of text they have to read. While I do sell my books as ebooks, I don't consider them ADPIPs – not least because a book like this one takes months to create, is hugely costly and has a terribly low profit margin.

Step 3: Give your digital download a compelling name

You need a relevant, compelling and memorable name for your digital download that clearly conveys its benefits to the user. You can use AI tools like ChatGPT and Magai to help you with this. Remember to consider SEO and findability too (more of this in Chapter 16). As with any branding exercise, you need to create something relevant and memorable – and possibly also unusual so it will be easier to find when people search for it online.

If using an AI tool, use a prompt like this:

Please suggest a compelling and engaging name for a digital download checklist that helps business owners understand the first steps with SEO.

For example, here's one of mine: 'The Ultimate SEO Checklist: How to grapple Google and get more sales'.

Step 4: Writing

Okay, now you need to write your digital download, and this can feel daunting. That's why I love to start with checklists. They help you get comfortable with the writing process, and pretty much anyone can compile a list:

1. Imagine you're writing a list for a business buddy on how to do 'the thing' that you do.
2. Write out the names of the steps (and try to keep to around ten).
3. Flesh out each step by explaining why it's important.
4. Add some detail on how to do the step.
5. Give an example of a result.
6. Repeat.
7. Top and tail the checklist with an intro from you and an outro outlining the next steps.

Again, you can use AI to help you here with a prompt like this:

Please write me ten checklist points that a small business owner needs to think about when starting out with SEO.

Obviously, the key here is to embellish the content with your experience (remember EEAT?), so add some little comments, tool recommendations and tips here and there.

(Psst: If you want to see an example of a free digital download, head to my website at katetoon.com and download my Personal Branding Workbook.)

Step 5: Layout and design

Now it's time to make your download sexy; a basic Word document might not be enough to get customers excited. If you're not a great designer, I recommend outsourcing design so your downloadables look super professional and polished.

Remember to:

- use consistent colours, formatting, fonts and image styles across all your downloads
- include your logo
- ensure YOU are featured on the digital design; perhaps even include a photo of you so everyone knows you are the creator.

If you don't want to include your face, consider using an illustration. You can hire an illustrator to create something for you or use one of the gazillion AI generators out there. But remember, a real face is always more powerful.

Canva is a great tool to help you create sexy digital downloads, but just be wary. If you read the small print on Canva, it says:

> *Generally speaking, if you're the creator of an original design, you're also its copyright holder. But if you used third-party content (e.g. stock Content from the Canva library) in your design, your ownership is subject to those third-party rights. Canva gives you non-exclusive licenses to use stock Content in your designs.*

Canva allows you to sell some templates yourself, but if you use pro elements you might need to sell via the Canva shop. It's not a biggy; just be careful about which bits and bobs you use, and possibly avoid pro elements for now. Don't forget to add page numbers and your branding to every page, as well as your URL and a clear call to action at the end of the download.

(Psst: Don't worry, we're going to cover the file types, uploading and tech in just a minute.)

Step 6: Create a sales landing page

You may want to create a sales landing page for your digital download, but the time you invest here needs to be measured against the return on the template. Most of my templates I simply sell via my 'shop' with a short product description. I talk more about sales pages in Chapter 19.

Step 7: Legal bits

Ensure you're clear in your product description about how the product can be used, how many times it can be downloaded (I set the limit at three) and whether the user can resell it to others.

Oh, and pop a copyright statement at the bottom of all your templates. Something like this: '© Kate Toon 2025. All Rights Reserved.'

TOON TIP Remember, you must have a valid privacy policy and terms and conditions on your website. As you begin to reach a wider audience, there's more chance of encountering litigious humans, so please cover your bottom and speak to a lawyer (maybe guinea pig Ingrid Fernandez).

Step 8: Consider customer service

As I mentioned, customer service is light with templates, but there will be some people who can't download them, miss an email, and so on. So, you'll have to make time to respond to these people promptly and factor this customer service into your costs.

Understanding the tech

Thankfully, adding digital downloads to your website is easy. Let's break it down.

Step 1: Decide on the file format

Choose the most suitable file format (such as PDF, Word doc, ePub, XLS or Google Doc). Here's some more information about some popular formats:

- **Editable Word docs** are great for action plans, templates and digital downloads that allow people to use the document in their business, and for ideas that aren't overly reliant on images. I've used these for copy templates, tone-of-voice documents, branding documents and more. (Google Docs works well for this too. I'm just old-school and prefer Word.)

- **Editable spreadsheets** are great if you want formatting and formulas. And they're not just for money-related digital downloads. For example, I have a snazzy keyword research Excel spreadsheet that auto-calculates the length of your copy snippets and colour-codes them. *(I know, how cool!)*
- **Editable PDFs** I love, mainly because you can make them look so snazzy. I use editable PDFs for most of my templates and include fields and check boxes to make them super interactive. I work with a designer to create these – thanks Sue! She uses InDesign to make them and exports them as PDFs.

TOON TIP Consider how your downloadables will print. Although you might like to complete documents on screen, many folk love to print things out. Try to keep the colours simple and minimal so your documents don't look bad or chew up all the yellow ink.

Step 2: Optimise for speedy downloads

Keeping file sizes small is especially important if using PDF format. There are lots of PDF compression tools out there. Just google 'Free PDF compression tool'.

Step 3: Create the download mechanism

Now, of course, you could upload your template to Etsy, but the fees and level of competition are off-putting. I suggest adding it to your own site. How you do this will depend on the platform you're on. Shopify, Squarespace and WordPress all have digital download functions and plugin options.

I use WordPress for my website, and there are a few options to select from. Here are two of my favourites:

- **Easy Digital Downloads** is a simple plugin that allows customers to browse products, add to cart and check out. It includes various payment methods and detailed customer records. This option also works with most themes.
- **WooCommerce** has the flexibility to sell memberships and subscriptions as well as products. I chose to install it because I planned to sell more than just digital downloads.

TOON TIP No one expects you to become a WordPress developer overnight. Setting up your site is a relatively straightforward process for a developer and won't cost a fortune. If you need a recommendation for a good developer (for whatever platform you're on), head to my Misfit Entrepreneurs group on Facebook and ask.

Step 4: Hook up your payment methods

When it comes to payment methods, at the very least, you'll need PayPal and Stripe. I'd say about 30% of my customers pay for my ADPIPs via PayPal and the rest via Stripe. Yes, you'll pay fees, but your bottom is also covered if things go wrong. (Oh, and don't worry – you don't have anyone's credit card info; that's all in the payment software and not your responsibility.)

Hooking up payment systems is surprisingly easy on all website platforms. Just be prepared for a slightly painful verification process when you sign up to the payment tools.

Step 5: Connect your email platform

Most digital download plugins and apps come with a simple set of emails that send the template out to the person with a link to download (or view, if using Google Docs). You'll need to connect your email platform so you can gather their email addresses and sell them more down the track. (More on this in Chapter 17.)

Depending on which email platform you use, you might need to get a little tech support here.

My tech stack

Here's an exact list of what I use for digital downloads:

- **Website** – WordPress, hosted on SiteGround with Divi theme.
- **Download mechanism** – I use the free WooCommerce plugin. My online shop has different categories and individual product pages.
- **Format** – I write my digital downloads in Word and use a graphic designer to turn them into editable PDFs.
- **Payment** – I've integrated PayPal and Stripe for payments.

- **Emails** – WooCommerce comes with ready-to-use set-up emails to send your digital products out, but I also use ActiveCampaign for ongoing emails.

Selling your digital download

Now comes the tough part – selling your digital downloads. It's not the *Field of Dreams* – just because you build it, they won't necessarily come. You have to start by building awareness and creating demand (see Chapter 16).

It's natural to get excited when you test your download and discover it all works wonderfully. You announce your new template on Instagram and then… tumbleweeds. No one cares about it, let alone buys it, except perhaps your mum.

Remember, there is no 'correct' price. You can do a Google search to see what templates are out there and try to price-match, but really, you are pulling a figure out of your bottom.

The challenges

It can be just as hard to sell a $7 template as a $7000 mastermind. Remember, nothing is 100% passive. You can't just plop a download on your site and expect the sales to come flooding in. As I said, it's critical to create awareness, explain the problem you're solving to build desire and offer proof to show how effective it is.

Now, I'm sure the fear pig is snorting in the back of your mind, and you might be thinking, *Why would anyone grab my digital download when they could just use AI to make something themselves?*

Here's the thing: just because I can use AI doesn't mean I want to. You may feel semi-confident using AI tools, but most people don't. And even if they do, they can't be bothered or have better things to do. I can attest that sales of my templates have not dropped at all since AI came out.

We'll run through how to market and sell your digital downloads in Part IV.

You might be thinking, *What's to stop someone from downloading my digital product and giving it to other people – or worse, selling it themselves?* The answer is absolutely nothing. I could write a whole book about copycats, but it would be bitchy and boring. So instead, I choose to ignore the content stealers and keep on keeping on.

The possibilities

By this point, you might be feeling enthusiastic about creating your digital download, but perhaps also a little overwhelmed. Remember, if you want more support to create your digital download you can:

- grab your free *Six Figures While You Sleep* workbook
- sign up to Six Figures While You Sleep: The Program
- join my membership, the Digital Marketing Collective.

Digital downloads are a slow-burn ADPIP – they're a gentle trickle, not a tsunami of income. I still get pleasure every time I hear a little PayPal ping from something being bought in my store because I made most of these templates years ago. Also, once you've created a digital download, making the next will be much easier.

Let's use Ingrid Fernandez as our guinea pig for a hypothetical digital download.

Ingrid wants to create a community of business owners who need legal support but can't necessarily afford to hire a lawyer. Ultimately, she'd like to have some kind of membership where they can gather, and she can serve them on a one-to-many basis. To start with, she's going to trial a checklist template in the form of a digital download.

Now, she could call it 'Website Law 101: A Compliance Checklist for Entrepreneurs', but that's boring. So, she decides to use an AI tool to come up with something sexier.

She begins the checklist with a professional headshot and a personally written intro to explain the template.

Next, she lists the four core documents that website owners need to consider and includes a checklist of key points that each document must cover, explaining why each is important and the legal ramifications of not ticking it off.

She also provides some examples of how each issue can be addressed – for example, explaining to users that the copyright statement on their website footer should be formatted like this:

© Copyright <name of business> <Year>

She also adds links to tools and other useful resources.

Finally, she closes with an outro, summarising the content and including a call to action to encourage the customer to take the next step, which might be to:

· book a 'done with you' call and audit (the coaching option outlined in Chapter 5)
· book her premium 'done for you' service
· grab more digital downloads
· join her membership.

After she's done, she hires a developer (guinea pig Tony) to add the WooCommerce plugin to her site and connects it to Stripe and PayPal. She then gets training on how to upload the template so she can do it herself in future. Now, she's ready to market and sell her digital download.

TL;DR

Digital downloads are a relatively quick, low-cost way to start your ADPIP journey. It's important to ensure they solve a customer problem and move them down your funnel to bigger and better things. That said, many ADPIPers stick with digital downloads – I had a happy year of just selling templates before I dived into ALL THE THINGS. It was simple and easy.

OVER TO YOU

Grab a pen and paper or the *Six Figures While You Sleep* workbook and plan out your first digital download:

- What type of download are you going to create – template, checklist, spreadsheet?
- What file format are you going to use?
- What will the name of your digital download be? (Use AI tools to help.)
- What tech will you use?

Chapter 11

Creating online courses

A course is possibly the most obvious ADPIP. When I was planning this book, I admit I felt a little wobble of imposter syndrome, as there are SO MANY resources out there teaching you how to make and sell courses. But most of them are rubbish.

Here's the thing: it's not necessarily making the course that's the hard bit; it's selling the course.

I've seen people slave for months trying to create some fancy 82-module course, spending a fortune on sexy in-studio videos, debating for weeks about which course platform to use, mapping out content and downloads, planning an elaborate launch and then – you guessed it – not selling a single spot.

In this chapter, I want to give you some clear direction about creating an online course, and possibly a mini course, before you head off and start on the behemoth. **I could write an entire book on this topic alone, but I'm not, so I'll keep to the core points.**

I also share the good and not-so-good realities. I've sold thousands of my smaller courses, and at the time of writing, I just ran the 27th round of my Recipe for SEO Success course (with 1505 students so far). So, I've seen my fair share of ups and downs when it comes to creating, launching and running courses.

What is an online course?

Online courses come in many shapes and sizes. They can be a simple two-video tutorial or a comprehensive beast. They can come with or without live sessions or a Facebook group and can be launched at set times or run all year round (evergreen). The price point varies hugely as well.

For example:

- My smaller course, the 10 Day SEO Challenge, costs AU$247 at the time of writing. It has 10 learning sections, 10 videos that run for around 7 to 12 minutes, and 4 or 5 templates. It's unsupported, evergreen and includes one year's access.
- My larger course, The Recipe for SEO Success, costs AU$2997 at the time of writing. It has seven modules each with 10 to 12 sections, 104 videos that run for around 7 to 12 minutes, and 41 templates. It comes with 12 weeks of support and 12 coaching calls, and it's launched three times a year.

The goal of a course is generally to provide a 'DIY' or 'done with you' experience at potentially (but not necessarily) a lower cost than when someone engages you to do the work for them (the 'done for you' experience).

Why offer an online course?

Online courses can, if done well, provide a genuinely huge revenue stream at very high profit margin. The main issue with courses is the time to produce and manage them. **A good course lives or dies by the support.**

People often ask me, 'Why would I pay for a course when I could just watch YouTube videos?' And often, the only argument in support of your course is that **you** are there to help. I can leave a comment on a YouTube video asking for an explanation, but I'm unlikely to get a response.

Obviously, the level of support impacts the price, which, in turn, guides people's expectations of support. People are happy to pay a couple of hundred dollars for my unsupported 10 Day SEO Challenge, but I doubt they'd pay almost $3K to wander through my larger course alone.

The other core reason is that a lot of 'content' out there is fluffy, waffles on and is not specific to the audience's problems. The idea of a course is that **you** have distilled exactly what the user needs to know into the shortest possible format.

Who suits online courses?

Now, obviously, creating an online course requires you to have proven experience and results that you can share with your students. They don't want to learn from someone who just learned the thing yesterday; they want a tried-and-tested expert. Also, given that great courses come with great support, I think you have to enjoy teaching people, and have a nice bedside manner and a huge amount of patience.

Not everyone will learn at the same speed, and you'll find yourself repeating the same explanations again and again. If you don't genuinely enjoy helping people reach their 'aha moment', I think you'll struggle.

> **TOON TIP** There's a relatively new hideous phenomenon called 'Master Resell Rights', which allows you to buy a course, rebrand it and sell it as your own. I feel this is a somewhat dangerous model because students could potentially be taught by someone with no experience who may have only purchased the course a week before. Also, the model predicates the idea that you'll make money just by having a course, which isn't true – you have to be great at selling that course too.
>
> I don't offer Master Resell Rights on my courses.

Creating your first online course

I want to keep this process as simple as possible, so I'm limiting it to 13 points. You've already taken the time to choose your niche and identify your audience. You've also identified that you have the skills to be the 'teacher' on this course and banished that ugly imposter voice from your brain. Now comes the deeper work.

Step 1: Define the learning objective of the course

What do you want the user to be able to do by the end of the course?

For example, for my sales page copywriting course, I want them to be able to write a professional, high-conversion sales page and plan out the design. For my free SEO Nibbles course, I want people to understand what Google is looking for in a website to rank it well.

Step 2: Name your course

Naming a course well is even more important than naming a digital product. You need to pick something:

- **relevant** – ideally, it describes the audience or the outcome
- **available** – you need to check the landscape to ensure it is clear of competitors
- **memorable** – ensure it's something snappy that sticks in the brain and makes your course easy to recommend.

Again, you can use AI to help you come up with a list of good ideas. The main thing is to Google them first. Your ideal name may already be a podcast, a book or someone else's program.

Once you've chosen the name, I recommend buying the domain name. A great way to check out your name before you buy it is to look it up on namecheckr.com.

> **TOON TIP** I googled over 200 different titles for this book before I landed on this one.

Step 3: Create an outline for the course modules

Break down the big objective into steps and put them in a logical order – this will become the roadmap for your course. Then, decide on section titles and write a brief paragraph about what you'll cover in each section. So, for my sales page copywriting course, I broke the big objective down into four phases:

1. **Learning** – what are sales pages and how do they work?
2. **Planning** – gather everything you need to write the sales page.
3. **Creating** – this is the actual writing part.
4. **Reviewing** – evaluate the sales page after you've written it to ensure it has all the necessary bits.

Step 4: Plan your content

People like to learn in different ways – some like to watch videos, others like to read; some like to listen, others prefer to visualise; some learn best through doing, others through discussion.

In all my courses, I include:

- **videos** – usually no longer than ten minutes and featuring me on-screen presenting over slides
- **text** – bullet-point summaries of the videos
- **demos** – me doing the thing I just taught you
- **templates and digital downloads** – to help you do the thing I just taught you.

Step 5: Break the course content into smaller modules

Once I have the big chunks worked out, I can then break them down further into smaller, digestible lumps. For example, under 'Learning' in my sales page copywriting course, I have smaller sections:

- What is a sales page?
- How long does it take to write a sales page?
- How long should a sales page be?
- Understanding copywriting formulas
- Conversion copy confidence
- Simple copy tips.

Step 6: Write your content and create your slides

Once I've completed my outline and decided on my smaller modules, I shoot out the bullet points I want to make in a Word doc. Typically, I know I can deliver ten or so core points in a single video.

Once I have these bullet points, I turn them into slide decks, thinking of interesting examples, images, photos and text formats I can use to make them engaging. I use a designer to make my slides, but you can use Canva or PowerPoint to make them yourself.

Again, this can be a great time to use AI. You can use it to help you with your outline and then flesh out each point into meatier bullets. But you have to know your stuff, as AI can be a bit of a people-pleaser, in that it will generate a completely gobbledegook wrong answer just to give you something back. This means you need to be the judge of whether the content is correct.

Step 7: Record your videos

Next, I sit and record the videos. I use software called Camtasia. I load up my slides and then record myself speaking over the top of them. This creates a picture within a picture look, with a little me in the corner explaining the slides on the screen (see Figure 11.1). I don't write a script for myself. Instead, I have the bullet points I've drafted from the content and run through those. I do, however, try to elaborate a little – a few ad libs, some jokes, some examples. Hearing someone dully read out bullets from a slide is not a fun way to learn.

Figure 11.1: An example still from one of my videos

TOON TIP I don't use a teleprompter, so occasionally I have to look at my notes, but I'm fine with that. You don't have to fix the audience with a permanent stare to be a good teacher. But if you want to use autocue software, there are heaps out there.

You could head to a studio and record professional videos for your course, with nice backgrounds and an artfully placed succulent. I don't do this because:

- it's expensive
- it would take a huge amount of prep to be ready to record all the videos in one day
- It would be exhausting to record them all in one day – I have to batch mine out
- I like to be able to swap out videos as and when I need to – recording them at home makes the swaps less obvious (other than my ever-changing hair).

Step 8: Upload onto your site

Now, you'll need to upload your videos. (I put mine on a private Vimeo account and then embed them into my WordPress site.) We'll talk more about the different platforms in a moment. You'll also need to create a password-protected area on your website that requires a login. I then add my bullet points underneath each video.

> **TOON TIP** You can use rev.com or otter.ai to create transcripts if you wish. Also, Vimeo will automatically add captions to your videos, which is great for people who have hearing issues, prefer to read or – in my case – can't understand my northern English accent.

Step 9: Create digital downloads

Think about any digital downloads you might want to create to support your course. Examples include templates, worksheets and spreadsheets that help make completing your course easier.

Step 10: Create completion elements

It's nice to offer your students some kind of reward on completion of your course. This can be a badge or stamp they can download and use on their site or socials, or a completion certificate. I use a straightforward, editable PDF for my courses, but there are more sophisticated options out there.

There's more you can do later down the track if you want to, such as adding quizzes, leaderboards, incentives and rewards, but my advice would be to create something basic first and see if you can sell it before you invest in all the fancy bells and whistles.

Step 11: Create a sales landing page

You'll need an amazing sales landing page for your course, which will grow with more testimonials and proof points each time you launch. More on this in Chapter 19.

Step 12: Legal bits

Courses raise different challenges. Can people use your content to teach others? What happens if they don't like it after a month; do you offer refunds? You'll need to work out all your business rules and turn them into a terms of use policy before you start selling.

> **TOON TIP** I offer a 100% money-back guarantee, but it must be taken within the first two weeks of the course. This offers prospective buyers reassurance but means I don't give away too much before the deadline. So far, I've only refunded three times in the last six years, all due to illness.
>
> I believe I've achieved this through extremely thorough marketing. I don't hide my pricing; I list all inclusions and have detailed FAQs and easy-to-read terms and conditions. I don't use FOMO or tricky tactics to get people on my course. This means no one ends up on my course 'by accident', wondering how on earth they got there. And no one has buyer's regret the day after buying the course.

Step 13: Consider customer service

If you're launching on a particular day, ensure you have people around you to help you onboard your new students – more on this in Chapter 20. And consider ongoing support – covered later in this chapter.

Understanding the tech

The problem with tech for courses is not that it's complex but that there are so many options. Let me break it down for you as best I can.

Hosted course platforms

There are lots of pre-made course platforms you can use to build your course. These make creating your course somewhat easier and help with all the elements, like having a sales page and logins.

I have always avoided this method because I do not want to build my empire on someone else's land and get stuck with a platform that's difficult to leave. Instead, I chose to build my course on WordPress. But if you're daunted by the prospect of WordPress (don't be, I can recommend guinea pig Tony as a great WP human), then here are a few hosted platforms you might want to consider:

- Kajabi
- Thinkific
- Coursera
- Udemy
- Skillshare
- Podia.

Just ensure you read the terms and conditions, and are clear on who 'owns' the course and what happens if you want to move your course to another platform later.

A note on Kajabi (as it's the most frequently mentioned course platform, I thought I'd give my thoughts): It's a super popular option among entrepreneur types, generally because they're affiliates and earn a fat ongoing payout for everyone they sign up. I can see the appeal of this platform, because for a relatively low fee (around $200 a month at time of writing) you can do the lot – funnels, sales pages, courses, memberships and even podcasts. But be aware of a few things here:

- It's a new platform to learn, which might slow you down. See what you can do on your existing platform first to 'prove your concept'.
- The fees might be low now, but they will increase over time and as you scale.
- Once you're in, it will be hard to get out later down the track. It's a big commitment.
- If you already have a website on another platform, you'll now have two spaces to maintain.

WordPress course options

There are themes and plugins for WordPress specifically made for courses – often referred to as 'learning management systems' (LMS). Again, these make it easier to create sequential content and allow you to plug your content into an existing framework. However, I didn't choose this option either as I don't like their linear approach to courses. I want to allow people to jump ahead, revisit and so on. I also wasn't particularly keen on most of their user interfaces.

These days there are some learning systems that allow people to jump around a little. Basically, there are a lot of options out there, so do your research, but don't get lost in it.

My tech stack

Here's an exact list of what I use to make my courses:

- **Website** – WordPress, hosted on SiteGround with Divi theme.
- **Selling mechanism** – WooCommerce memberships and subscriptions allow me to sell my course, restrict content, have password-protected zones on my site, drip feed content and have content expiry dates.
- **Course back end** – Standard WordPress pages (password-protected by Woo), which allows me to set my own design style and format for the pages.
- **Videos** – hosted on Vimeo pro and embedded into the site (uploading videos direct to your site can really slow it down, which is bad for SEO and usability).
- **Digital downloads** – uploaded to my media files in the member area of the website.
- **An online form** where people can submit questions before the live Zoom session – Gravity Forms plugin.
- **Coaching calls** – I run my coaching calls via Zoom.
- **Community** – I use Facebook groups for my discussion forums. (I've tried other platforms, such as Circle, but my students are already on Facebook, so it just makes life easier.)

Over the years, I've added a few more bits and bobs: a glossary of terms, an FAQ library, quizzes and more. But I regard them as nice-to-haves – I don't think you have to have these to make your course.

I want to stress here that although the tech seems like a barrier, it's not the thing that's going to make or break your course's success. There is no perfect tech set-up, and everyone does it slightly differently. Again, it can be a good idea to outsource the set-up of your course so you can focus on the content, support and sales.

Other big online course considerations

Once you have created your course, there are some other things you'll have to think about.

1. The degree of support you want to give

I have some supported courses and some unsupported courses – support comes with a much higher price.

Support for my big course involves:

- a Facebook group for course members
- weekly one-hour Zoom calls, which are uploaded and added to the course
- expert guests joining some of the Zooms.

After the course support period is over, I encourage course members to join my membership for ongoing help (see Chapter 12). Live support really helps students engage and leads to higher course completion rates and more reviews.

2. Ongoing updates and upgrades

Depending on the topic you've picked, the course may require regular updates. You might also want to improve the course, add new bonuses and keep the course fresh.

TOON TIP Be super careful about mentioning dates and adding dates to your file names. Some of my content is evergreen, but if I revealed the year the file was first saved (2021), some people would think it was out of date.

Also be careful about including software demos in your courses, as they can date quickly. A button only needs to move a few pixels to the left and people won't be able to follow your tutorial. If you decide to do demos, ensure you make a list and set reminders, as these will likely need to be updated every three to six months.

3. Access period

Decide how long people get access to your course – I recommend at least one year.

TOON TIP Don't offer 'lifetime' or 'unlimited' access. I used to do this, and despite the meaning of 'lifetime' being clearly articulated in my terms and conditions, some felt that my version of lifetime (the lifetime of the course) was unfair. 'You should deliver the course from the grave', they cried. I jest, but remember, most won't read the legal bits and bobs, and it's best to set clear expectations.

4. Evergreen or launched?

While evergreen might seem easier, the problem is that it's harder to sell. Without firm opening and closing dates, the customer has no incentive to join; it's always there and always available, so what's the urgency? A launch creates urgency – but I talk more about that in Chapter 22.

Evergreen courses are usually unsupported, which is fine if they're simple but not if they're complex. For this reason, I keep my smaller, unsupported courses evergreen. This means that people can join and start any time. In contrast, my bigger, supported courses are always launched.

An approach you could take is to offer an evergreen unsupported version of your course year-round **and** a launched version, with the option for evergreen humans to upgrade.

Selling your online course

When I created my first online course, I built the sales page first, sold 20 spots and then built the course – week by week, often by the skin of my teeth. Those were the days before NBN in Australia, and my internet was so slow that I had to make videos, transfer them onto a USB stick, pop that an envelope and post it to my virtual assistant so she could upload them using her faster connection. While this was stressful, it meant that I didn't invest the time and effort into making a thing before I knew if I could sell it.

Back then, I didn't really understand funnels and iterative development. I also didn't understand the acquisition model.

Based on my experience today, an acquisition model goes something like this:

- One hundred people download your freebie.
- Ten people purchase your low-price thing (a digital download or small course).
- One person buys your big thing.

I got lucky with my first course – I sold those first 20 spots to previous clients. As time went on, that would have gotten harder if I hadn't built my list. More on this in Part IV.

In terms of price, remember, you can always go up, but you can't come down – if you do, you risk annoying those who paid the higher price. You also need to leave room to offer early-bird discounts and other sale offers.

Again, there is no right price for your course; you can choose to price it low and try to get lots of people, or price it high and get fewer people. Do you want 100 people paying $47, or 10 people paying $4700? Again, considering the level of support you're willing to give is critical here.

Here's how my pricing changed over the years:

- 2016 launch 1: $497
- 2016 launch 2: $657
- 2016 launches 3 to 5: $1097
- 2017 launch 6: $1195
- 2017 launch 7: $1426
- 2017 launch 8: $1526
- 2017–8 launches 9 to 12: $1695
- 2018 launches 13 to 14: $1735
- 2019–20 launches 15 to 20: $1899
- 2021–22 launches 21 to 23: $1997
- 2023 launches 24 to 26: $2197
- 2024 launch 27: $2697

The challenges

The biggest problem people talk about with courses is getting students to complete them. Now, you might think, *Who cares? I've got their money.* But if people don't finish your course, they won't give you testimonials and become advocates for your products (see Chapter 21).

Here are some meethods to improve this:

- Offer constant reassurance to prevent people from falling behind.
- Give them permission to take tiny steps – 'Just watch one video'.
- Don't use leaderboards or reward high achievers – it makes those achieving less feel like poo.
- Give them little milestone rewards *(I love an end-of-module quiz)*.
- Don't link your coaching calls to your modules – allow the calls to meet people where they are. Otherwise, if someone hasn't completed Module 3, they won't turn up for call number three, and you'll lose them.
- Offer them a next step when support for the course finishes, such as an ongoing membership (see Chapter 12).
- Reframe the word 'completion'. While a course has a start and an end, it's also a learning resource that can be used again and again.

I use all these methods, and they have helped me improve completion rates hugely.

My biggest challenge has been keeping my courses up to date. For my big course, I chose a highly changeable topic (SEO) – staying up to date and creating new content every year is a big time-suck.

On average, it takes me and my team about one full week to create a single module of content. Breaking it down, this includes:

- planning out the module (usually 10 lessons) – 2 hours
- writing and researching the course content – 5 hours
- planning the slides and briefing the designer – 3 hours
- design work to create slides (outsourced) – 3 hours
- proofreading (outsourced) – 3 hours
- recording and editing videos – 10 hours (my videos are usually less than 10 minutes in duration, as I've found that's the average attention span, but each of these videos takes around an hour to

record due to fluff-ups, edits and barking dogs next door; I usually have around 10 videos per module)

- uploading content to my website (outsourced) – 6 hours
- checking content for errors – 2 hours.

That's **34 hours in total**, usually spread across several weeks.

Remember, this is just the time to create one module. And there are seven modules in my big course. Obviously, I don't need to update everything every year, but it's a big job each January to refresh the course.

> **TOON TIP** I am **much** faster now than when I started. Back in the early days, one ten-minute video could take an entire day to produce. Be kind to yourself. As you become more confident and experienced, you will speed up.

On a positive note, my successful sales page copywriting course takes minimal updates. So, while I sell fewer, it's far more profitable. Consider this when choosing your course topic.

The possibilities

Although my ADPIP journey started with a single copy deck template, it took off with my course. My Recipe for SEO Success suite of products (the big course and smaller courses) have earned me literally millions at an average profit margin of around 78%. It is the cash cow of my business – it's allowed me to pay off my mortgage, buy investment properties and shares and create generational wealth. It was my ultimate Big Little Idea. While there were existing SEO courses on the market, I made my course fun, found a niche and solved a real pain point. In return, it changed my life.

It may not be the sexiest of topics, and occasionally, I wish I'd chosen a different niche. But The Recipe for SEO Success is largely responsible for my success, and I'm thankful for it. This is why I haven't included a guinea pig example in this module, because I am the guinea pig for this topic.

Now, obviously, this has been a high-level overview of course creation, giving you a general direction and starting point. My main point is to start small. One of my most popular courses started as a collection of ten blog posts before it turned into videos and glued together. Don't try to create a James Cameron epic – start with a home movie.

Remember, people care more about great content and quality support than they do about high video production values and sexy features.

If you want more support to create your course, you can grab my *Six Figures While You Sleep* workbook or join my membership or program.

TL;DR

Courses can be bigger than Ben Hur, but it's better to start with something small. Consider support and maintenance from the get-go, and don't let the tech overwhelm you. My SEO course is my most lucrative and one of my highest-profit products, but it's not without its headaches – especially the need for constant updates.

OVER TO YOU

Let's roughly map out your first course:

- What problem is your course going to solve?
- Are you going with supported or unsupported content?
- List the titles of your core modules.
- Plan out some topics for your first module.
- Consider your tech set-up and pick the options you find easiest to grasp – what are you going to use?
- Create a dot-point summary of your content.

After this, you'll move onto selling your course – I cover how to do that in Chapter 19.

Chapter 12

Creating online memberships

While templates and courses may offer high profit margins, for me, nothing beats a membership. I've been a fan of online communities since my early days as a copywriter. Back then, I set up a Google+ Group and invited about 40 copywriters to join. Several told me to sod off, but 20 or so joined, and for the next few years that community was everything to me.

We shared ideas, resources, tips and tactics. We celebrated each other's wins and commiserated with each other when we had PITA (pain in the arse) clients. That little community offered me support when I needed it most; it was a light in dark places, and I'm still in contact with many of those OG copywriters today.

After running that community for a while, I wondered if other copywriters would like something like this, too. And so, my first membership, the Clever Copywriting Community, was born.

What is an online membership?

An online membership is an ADPIP that provides exclusive access to learning content, community, accountability and support (see Figure 12.1).

Again, memberships come in many shapes and sizes and with different inclusions and options, but essentially, the model is as follows:

- signing up to the membership for a given period (usually a year)
- paying a recurring fee (a subscription)
- gaining access to some kind of resource library
- getting ongoing support from the membership owner
- being part of an online community.

Content within the membership can take various forms and is often a mix of digital downloads, short courses, masterclass videos, tools and templates.

Figure 12.1: Online memberships

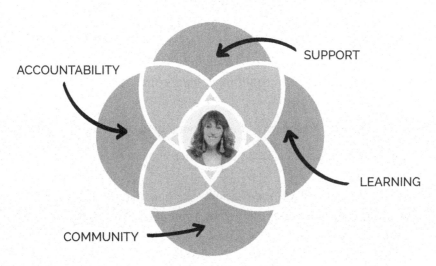

Why choose online memberships?

I love online memberships for four main reasons:

1. **I am not a fan of one-on-one coaching.** I find it a little intense and draining, and I don't have enough hours in the day to fit it in. Memberships allow me to coach many people at the same time (a one-to-many model). It's a lighter touch, and that suits me better.
2. **They provide consistent revenue.** I love having the recurring and predictable revenue that memberships offer. There are peaks and troughs throughout the year (around launches), but the regular income is my 'bread and butter' and gives me security.

3. **I genuinely love my community.** It's more than a resource to learn and get accountability – it's a gang! Social media is packed with little groups of what appear to be 'cool kids'. I used to find it hard to watch and felt like an outsider. But here's the thing: nearly everyone I speak to feels this way, even when from the outside it looks like they are part of the 'in' crowd. It's all about finding your people, and the Digital Marketing Collective crew are my people.

4. **We all learn from each other.** Although people join the membership to learn from me, I learn just as much from them. I have 18 or so subject matter experts in my membership who provide regular updates on their topics. This means I have one spot where I can learn 'all the things' and stay up to date. We all draw from each other and learn as a collective. Honestly, this also reduces the need for me to have all the answers and do all the work. Yes, I educate on some areas, but in other areas I simply facilitate the discussion.

From an altruistic perspective, the membership allows me to provide:

- **ongoing support** – helping people when they need it on a long-term basis
- **unstructured and ad-hoc support** – helping people with an answer to an urgent question or an immediate block that they can't receive in a course due to its linear, restrictive nature
- **a safe space** – enabling members to ask questions they might not feel comfortable asking in a wider forum.

Oddly, I believe people come because they think they want account-ability, content and to learn from some fancy coach, but what they need – and what they stay for – is the community. Owning a business can be lonely, and having a gang is so helpful.

Who suits online memberships?

To run a membership, you must accept that it's a long-term commitment. You can't sell it to 40 people and then not turn up. Memberships require you to set aside regular time each day to help people. I don't think you can fob off this work to underlings or community managers. While I have group experts, as the leader, I need to be present. So, it's important to establish boundaries.

In the early days, I would be online to respond to comments on weekends and holidays. These days, I'm firm with myself on this. I also give myself December off in my membership, with no real interaction or new content.

I think you also have to love people and enjoy interacting with them to run an online membership. You need confidence in yourself that you have what it takes to provide valid help to your customers. (Of course, this is true for all ADPIPs, but it's especially true for memberships as you're so visible.)

Creating your first online membership

I could write a whole book on memberships – in fact, maybe I will. But for now, I want to give you some direction and know-how to get started with your membership, as they're not as complicated as they sound.

1. Define the theme of your membership

The world is your lobster here. You can create memberships around pretty much anything: crochet, mini pigs, digital marketing, aged care, education, bangles – you name it.

Your aim is to gather people together with a common interest or problem.

> **TOON TIP** I think free communities should throw the net wide, and paid communities should be more specific. For example, your free community might be about crafting in general, and your paid community might be about selling crafts on Etsy. You don't need a free community to start a paid community, but it helps build awareness. I discuss free communities a little more in Chapter 20.

2. Name your membership

When it comes to naming your membership, the same rules apply as with online courses (see Chapter 11). But you may want to append the word 'membership', 'club' or 'community' at the end of whatever brand you create.

3. Decide on your monthly content

I don't map out my membership content for the next 12 months. Rather, I try to respond to what my members want – and I discover this by asking them ☺. You might prefer to have a roadmap of ideas for the first few months of your new membership, but be prepared to be flexible.

> **TOON TIP** The idea is to start with minimum viable content (MVC). You don't need to have months of videos lined up. Instead, you can make content on demand and add it to your resource library.

I do, however, have a set structure for content each month:

- **2 × Ask Me Anything sessions** – Q&As with me and other experts in the group
- **2 × masterclasses** – training with me or experts on relevant topics
- **4 × Toon in the House sessions** – weekly one-hour drop-in chats to chat through members' issues, copy, strategies, email funnels, product descriptions… you name it.

All the content is recorded and uploaded to the back end of the membership so people can watch it back later (see 'My tech stack' later in this chapter).

As the membership has gotten bigger, I've found the one-on-one hot seat sessions too hard to maintain, with only four spots available to members per month, so I now do weekly live sessions in the group for an hour each week.

4. Decide on your levels

Some memberships have different levels, such as Basic, Premium and VIP, with various perks for each level. My membership is flat – everyone is treated equally.

However, I do offer incentives for those paying annually, such as member gifts and a listing in our member directory.

> **TOON TIP** I suggest you start with only one level; you can always add a premium level further down the track.

5. Consider support and boundaries

Especially in the early days, the membership will essentially be you banging your drum and shouting into the abyss. It can be hard to build user engagement at the start – and so you'll need to push hard during the first 30 to 90 days. That said, you also need to have boundaries, as mentioned earlier. I could be in the group all day, every day. I could respond to every comment (and I mostly do), but I have to balance that with the return on investment.

It can be daunting to think of doing something all year round, but the model is flexible enough to allow for holidays and illness. As I mentioned, I take the month of December off every year with no calls or new content. If you're explicit about what you're offering, there's no reason for people to complain.

6. Establish community rules and guidelines

A membership is essentially a community, and every community has a 'vibe', which you are responsible for setting. You'll also have to be a leader in the group and establish clear rules and guidelines for behaviour. More importantly, you will have to enforce these rules, which may be awkward. You can head to any of my free or paid groups on Facebook to check out my group rules. (I think you'll especially like rules 1 to 3.)

Facebook comes with its own group rules, which you can add to your group. I've included a list of my rules in the *Six Figures While You Sleep* workbook, which you can download for free from my website.

> **TOON TIP** Facebook has a feature that allows you to approve every comment before it goes into the group. I believe it's fine to use these for free groups, but in your paid membership I think you should allow people to comment whenever and whatever they like.
>
> I find that after a while, the group culture becomes self-policing. People see other people behaving in a certain way, and they follow. In addition, if someone is out of line, another member will often put them in line, so I don't have to. But all that said, I have to be 'the bad guy' sometimes – it's tough, but you can't have one rotten egg spoil the egg sandwich. Take it from me, though – it gets easier.

7. Attract advocates and experts

As your membership grows, you won't be able to do everything yourself, and you may decide to outsource community management or bring experts into your group to help you. I have a team of around 18 subject matter experts in my Digital Marketing Collective membership. In return for their support and expertise, I give them free membership and lots of promotion on the sales page, in socials and via email.

My group experts need to:

- be present at least one day a week to answer questions
- run at least one masterclass a year.

My membership is also a happy hunting ground for potential clients for them, so it all works out.

> **TOON TIP** I don't think you need extra experts in the group when you start; you really need to establish your own credibility and dominance for the first few months. Also, choose your experts carefully. You don't want someone who comes in and does more than you, or has an agenda to create their own membership and nick your members.
>
> Select non-competing people first. As time passes and your confidence builds, you might want to consider letting competitors in – but keep an eye on them!

8. Manage churn and retention

Naturally, members will come and go. Some people join a membership for a reason, others for a season and some even for a lifetime. (I have members in The Clever Copywriting School who have been with me for nine years!)

I could do a whole chapter on retention strategies, but in short, I think it's important to:

- **have a great onboarding process** – make new people feel special
- **be consistent, show up and do the thing** – don't disappear after people join
- **set reasonable expectations for content** – don't set the bar so high that you can't maintain it over the long term

- **create advocates in the community** – they start conversations and support others
- **respond to your members' needs** – offer content and support.

Don't be disheartened if people leave; there will always be new members coming along to bring new ideas and life to your community.

9. Create a sales landing page

Establishing a sales landing page is critical. You want to emphasise that it's not a course but more of a community. I dig into this in Chapter 19.

10. Sort out the legals

Be sure to define your membership terms upfront and whether you offer cancellation and refunds *(I don't)*. Also, be clear on permissions regarding data and intellectual property ownership of the content you share.

Remember, even though the group is private and you'll encourage people not to share content outside the group, they shouldn't add anything they wouldn't want to let the world see anyway – things will inevitably leak from the group. I highly recommend having a super watertight set of membership terms and conditions. (Consult a lawyer – maybe our guinea pig Ingrid Fernandez?)

Understanding the tech

With memberships, there are a few tech options and platforms to consider – Memberful and Mighty Networks are two that come to mind. But I like to keep things simple, so I built my membership with WooCommerce on WordPress. This allowed me to create a sales page and set up products that give access to other memberships. I also use WooCommerce subscriptions to manage regular payments.

Compared to other ADPIPs, memberships are super low-tech, especially if you use an existing platform to manage your group, such as Facebook. Sure, it's risky, as Facebook often makes changes, but whatever happens, you'll have enough notice to move off Facebook if they suddenly make running groups difficult.

My tech stack

Here's an exact list of what I use to create and run my memberships. You'll notice it's the same as my course set-up; that's the very reason I chose WordPress, as it's so versatile.

- **Website** – WordPress, hosted on SiteGround with Divi theme.
- **Selling mechanism** – WooCommerce memberships and subscriptions allow me to sell my course, restrict content, have password-protected zones on my site, drip feed content and have content expiry dates.
- **Membership back end** – Standard WordPress pages (password-protected by Woo), which allows me to set my own design style and format for the pages.
- **Videos** – hosted on Vimeo pro and embedded into the site (uploading videos directly to your site can really slow it down, which is bad for SEO and usability).
- **Digital downloads** – uploaded to my media files in the member area of the website.
- **Calls** – I run my coaching calls via Zoom.
- **Community** – I use Facebook groups for my discussion forums. (I've tried other platforms, such as Circle, but my members are already on Facebook, so it makes life easier.)

Over the years, I've added a few sexy bits and bobs, such as a job board and a directory (I use the Sabai Directory plugin for this). But essentially, the back end of the membership is a collection of password-protected content, while the community is a simple Facebook group.

You will likely need help setting this up, but it's a one-off thing, so it's worth investing in a good WordPress developer, such as guinea pig Tony Cosentino.

Pricing your online membership

With memberships – as with digital downloads and courses – there is no right price. You can look at your competitors and test the market, but ultimately, you'll have to slap a price on it and see how it goes. Remember, you can always put the price up, but you cannot put it down (without pissing off your existing members).

The general rules of pricing a membership are as follows:

- **The price members join up for is their forever price** unless they leave and try to come back. Some don't offer this, but for me, it's a no-brainer because it rewards loyalty and creates a desire to stay to avoid the higher price.
- **Members are charged a set fee** for a monthly subscription and incentivised to sign up for an annual subscription – the annual fee is usually ten times the monthly fee (or two months free).

Often, the higher price for paying upfront is seen as a 'poor tax' decision, where those who can least afford it are charged more. But the reality is that monthly payments often fail (lost cards, and so on), meaning they require a lot more admin than annual payments. I have some members who I have to chase every single month.

Now, you might think that because your membership is likely to be offered at a lower monthly price point than a high-ticket course, it's going to be an easier sell (more on pricing in Chapter 19). **But the problem with memberships is the commitment.**

If you go with a 'cancel any time' model, then you risk someone joining for a month, grabbing all your content and leaving. Also, the admin of onboarding and offboarding members will likely eat up that entire monthly fee.

There's also the comparison trap with other monthly payments. How much are they paying for their accounting software, website hosting or virtual assistant? And how does your membership measure up against those?

So, most memberships require an annual commitment. You may have monthly, six-monthly and annual payment options, but make it clear that they're paying for a year.

For a simple blanket rule on pricing, I suggest starting with $47 a month for founding members, including GST – which means $470 a year. And I recommend increasing it by $10 every relaunch.

Working out the profit

I know this revenue doesn't seem like a lot. But you need to understand that there's a tipping point with memberships.

For the first ten members, it's not going to feel that profitable. You're earning $470 a month and likely putting in about ten hours of work a month, so that equals $47 an hour.

But then you hit 20 members, and now your hourly rate increases to $94.

And then you hit 30, and your hourly rate is $141.

When you hit 100, your hourly rate will be $470, which ain't bad.

The time invested doesn't really change; the profitability does.

TOON TIP A note for Australians: I recommend putting your prices in Australian dollars if your primary audience is there. Don't use US pricing just to look all global and fancy.

I also recommend including the GST in your pricing so there are no nasty surprises for your customer at the checkout.

The challenges

People often ask what comes first: the membership or the course? I don't think it matters. I created the course first, but I could have easily created the membership first.

These days, I'd say about 30% of my members joined after completing my big SEO course (even though the membership is not specifically about SEO), and the other 70% joined via other channels.

Selling a membership requires you to have built a reputation. Even if you just see yourself as 'holding a safe space' for people to get together and talk about the chosen topic, it's still **your** safe space. And its popularity will largely depend on whether people trust, like and respect you.

The challenges of trust and reputation can be overcome with the right funnel and sales page (see Part IV).

The possibilities

While my big course injects large sums of money into my business three times a year, my memberships provide a regular, predictable, recurring income every month. I can predict my income from the memberships over the year and calculate the retention rate.

Obviously, some people will leave over time, but new people join (I launch three times a year), and they join at the new higher rate.

Memberships are hugely scalable because regardless of how many people join, they can all enjoy the same content. This is not the case if you include one-on-one elements, though, so try to avoid this, or move them into a higher-cost tier.

Let's see how this model could work for Tony. He's already established his audience as newish WordPress businesses. How best can he support them with content?

He thinks he could offer the following each month:

- **1 × 60-minute Business Masterclass** with him on topics including sales, money, systems and processes, and client acquisition.
- **1 × 60-minute Tech Masterclass** showing members a new tool, a way of coding something, the latest plugin or a challenge they can overcome.
- **1 × Q&A session**, an open forum for chats.
- **1 × Hot Seats session** containing 4 × 15-minute member chats (which he realises might be slow at the start as people might not want to volunteer).

He's also going to share other advice and tips around best plugins and themes, and offers from his fave hosting platforms. This is more than enough for him to get started. If he begins with this framework, he can add to it later depending on what the group needs, calling in other experts and creating content as required.

So, this equates to around six hours of work per month – four hours of live hosting and two hours of content prep. Earlier, we established that Tony might have about ten hours a month to work on his ADPIP, so this leaves around four hours for commenting, or around 15 minutes a day.

As you can see, that's not a lot of time, and he might need to double that in the early days to build momentum. This reduces his profit but creates an attractive library of content for new members in the future.

TL;DR

Memberships are a glorious way to offer your customers ongoing support and create a recurring revenue stream for yourself. Although they might seem like a big commitment for both you and your customers, this can be managed with solid rules and clear boundaries.

OVER TO YOU

Plan your membership:

1. What problem will your membership solve?
2. What kinds of content will you offer in the group?
3. Map your content ideas for the first few months.
4. Make a list of a few 'friends' who could be bums on seats in the early days.
5. Make a list of a few experts who would be happy to be in the group and help in exchange for membership.
6. Decide on your tech set-up and select the options you find easiest to grasp.
7. Decide on your pricing model.

After this, you'll move onto selling your membership – that's coming up in Part IV.

Chapter 13

Creating online masterminds

Masterminds are often seen as the pinnacle of passive income and online coaching, possibly because people often charge a stupid amount of money for them. But in truth, my courses and memberships generate far greater profit and are much more passive. Why? Because often people join your mastermind to get close to you, to get a 'piece' of you, and there are only so many pieces to go around.

Unless you're dead inside, after you've taken $10K from a business owner for your six-month mastermind (even if you believe they can afford it), you're going to seriously want to help them. You're going to desperately want them to get results. And you might go overboard trying to achieve that. *(I did.)* Masterminds are not for the faint-hearted. Turning up and chatting with the same people month after month can be challenging. You'll get to know them on an intimate level, and I personally found I got way too emotionally invested in everyone. *(I'm too much of an empath.)*

The key with masterminds is to understand that even with the best guidance in the world, some people won't achieve everything they set out to. And often, that won't be your fault as the mastermind host.

What is an online mastermind?

An online mastermind is a private group or training program where a group of humans come together to help achieve their individual goals.

Generally, the idea is that members inspire and learn from each other, providing accountability and support. There is, of course, a leader (you) who guides these discussions and creates a safe space.

The idea is that each member presents the challenges they're facing and gets constructive feedback from other experienced business owners and, of course, you. Possibly, these are issues they can't talk about with their partners or peers, so the value is in the multiple perspectives that expand their thinking and help them push through their pain points.

This all sounds very rah-rah and aspirational, but an easier way to define it is a small group of like-minded souls with similar goals, sharing their highs and woes and finding a way forward. For example, Wendy might suffer from imposter syndrome, and Elise might have found a way to deal with that. However, Elise might not be great at selling, while that's Wendy's favourite thing.

Depending on the focus of your mastermind, you could also end up attracting people from different industries, which can be both helpful and difficult to manage.

Some masterminds are just group chats with a host. Others *(like mine)* could be considered 'programs' and include online learning components, digital downloads, invited experts and get-togethers.

Everyone uses the 'mastermind' term differently, so it's important to clearly define what's included in yours.

While it's not entirely passive, as you're showing up on a regular basis to 'do the do', it is a high-revenue, often high-profit, one-to-many offering. You're charging your highest rate to people who want to get as close to you as possible and suck all the goodness from your brain.

Why choose online masterminds?

The idea of masterminds is to have a 'high-ticket' offering. Unlike a membership, they're usually a 'price them high, stack them low' offering. They're as close to one-on-one coaching as you can get without offering one-on-one coaching.

Who suits online masterminds?

I feel there is an ethical imperative to be at the top of your game before you run a mastermind, or at least substantially ahead of those you are masterminding. Many would argue that's not the case – that as a coach, you're there to help your customers come to their own realisations, and you don't need to be a guru to do that. But if I'm paying a big wodge of cash to a mastermind leader, I kind of want them to have most, if not all, of the answers.

Creating your first online mastermind

Here are some things to think about if you're starting an online mastermind.

1. Define the theme of your mastermind

Usually, a mastermind is far more niche than a membership. Either it's drilling down into a particular topic or industry, or it's the same topic but at a deeper or higher level.

Start by defining the outcome or goal your mastermind offers. For example, Six Figures While You Sleep: The Program has the goal of helping you create and launch your first digital product (and possibly more) in a six-month timeframe.

Once you have decided on the theme and niche for your mastermind, it's important to stick to it. It can be tempting to let anyone in (as you want the money), but I generally recommend not doing this.

TOON TIP My last mastermind was focused on helping service-based businesses increase profit, improve processes, get more sales and be more confident in raising their profile.

We did, however, have one ecommerce person. While this kind of threw off the sessions, the ecommerce human was just an amazing being *(Hi Deb!)* and brought so much warmth, experience and perspective to the mastermind that it was great to have her there.

2. Name your mastermind

Often, masterminds are extensions of an existing membership and can therefore be named the same thing but with a term like 'VIP', 'Inner Circle' or 'Elevate' attached to them.

I'm not a fan of this as it implies that my membership members are somehow lesser, and I don't like elitism, so perhaps I'd just simply add the word 'mastermind' instead. Again, as with courses and memberships, be sure to google it first.

3. Decide on the duration of your mastermind

Masterminds can last anywhere from six weeks to 12 months, but around six months seems to be the norm.

Both masterminds I've run were six months long (one with a month-long break in the middle to allow people to play catch-up). Six months may not sound like a long time, but to me it felt like a marathon!

By the end of the mastermind, we were so bonded that I considered buying us a house so we could all move in together.

Have a good hard think about whether you want to get in and get out (more suited to short coaching sessions) or if you have what it takes to turn up week after week and talk to the same people. Running a mastermind is a serious commitment.

4. Decide on your role

The degree to which you need to be a leader in the space is up to you, and this is where I struggle. I can't help butting in and giving my opinion, offering advice, offering help and even doing the damn thing for my members. By month two of my last mastermind, I found myself up late at night rewriting people's sales pages!

When I run my next mastermind, I'll be much clearer beforehand on what I'm providing (and what I'm not).

In my next mastermind, the Six Figures While You Sleep Program, I will:

- provide educational content each month, which people can watch in their own time
- provide my members with easy-to-use templates

- offer weekly coaching calls with all the mastermind members
- provide a private Facebook group for members
- offer an upgrade with one-on-one coaching, as not everyone loves one-on-one.

5. Choose between group and one-on-one

While most masterminds are just group sessions, some masterminders also offer one-on-one sessions – usually one at the start, one in the middle and one at the end. This is totally optional, but it will improve the perceived value of the mastermind, as many people really want one-on-one attention.

> TOON TIP Think hard about this. While giving one person three hours of your time might seem doable, what happens when you sell ten spots? Coaching can be super draining, and the admin around people cancelling and rescheduling is a pain in the bum.

6. Decide on your content

Given that the main features of the mastermind are discussion and idea-sharing, you might not think you need content. But I find having some resources and videos can help.

For example, with my new mastermind program, I'd like to have a video for each stage of the journey – partly to help with comprehension and partly so I don't have to explain it again and again.

I also think creating some templates along the way can be helpful. But I'd argue that a mastermind is less content-heavy than a course or membership. It's really about peer-to-peer and mentor-to-mentor advice, permission and encouragement.

7. Work out your meeting schedule

Work out the frequency and duration of all the meetings and include that information in any sales materials. There's no point in someone signing up if they can't make most calls.

Try to keep to regular times so people can lock their mastermind time into their diaries.

8. Decide whether or not it will all be online

Most of my masterminds have been online, with regular Zoom sessions and an online support forum. But there's something rather lovely about bringing your group together in person. Whether you decide to include a lavish tropical retreat or just a meet-up in a local city, there's something special about meeting these people you've talked to for months in a more personal setting.

9. Sort out the legals

Establish some rules and agreements about confidentiality. You may even want to have a screening process to ensure there's minimal competition. However, if you've niched it down, you could end up with a mastermind of similar people. Make it clear that if you share an idea, someone else on the mastermind could adopt that and use it themselves.

10. Consider post-program alumni

After your masterminders have finished the program, you could allow them to stay and pay month by month. Of course, they've already consumed most of your educational content by this point, but they might want to stay for the accountability and coaching.

Understanding the tech

Masterminds can often use most of the tech you've set up for your courses and memberships.

My tech stack

Here's an exact list of the tech I use for my masterminds.

- **Website** – WordPress, hosted on SiteGround with Divi theme.
- **Mastermind platform** – WooCommerce allows me to create an area for my masterminders to download resources.
- **Mastermind back end** – Standard WordPress pages (password-protected by Woo), which allows me to set my own design style and format for the pages.

- **Videos** – I use Google Drive to upload videos for one-on-one and group sessions, making it easier for members to download and keep the videos for future reference on completion of the mastermind.
- **Digital downloads** – uploaded to my media files.
- **Coaching calls** – Zoom is my choice.
- **Discussion forum** – I use Slack (but I will use Facebook next time as I didn't love Slack).

Some masterminds also offer unlimited email support. But I think this is a little ambitious (*I can't think of anything worse, actually*) and likely to lead to a lot of stress, so I like to keep all discussion in the discussion group.

Pricing your online mastermind

As with previous ADPIPs, there's no right price. In general, though, the price will be substantially higher than your membership. The members are paying for:

- a smaller group
- more attention from you
- more time
- more advanced tactics
- more tailored advice.

Some would argue that masterminds suit those who have been in business for longer (generally because of the investment), but I see no reason why you couldn't have a start-up mastermind if the price is right.

When working out your pricing, I suggest you start by reviewing your coaching rate, which I discussed in Chapter 5.

Let's say you're charging $400 an hour for one-on-one coaching, and you have eight people in your mastermind. In that case, you could argue that they should pay $50 each per session. So, if you're offering four sessions a month over six months, that equates to $1200. Then, perhaps you could offer one more session at the start and another at the end, bringing the cost to $2000.

Additional fees could be considered if there's a group, a Slack channel or email support, and more if you also offer templates and training. And more again if there's a retreat included.

At the time of writing, I'm seeing folk similar to me offering year-long masterminds with some one-on-one coaching and a retreat costing anywhere from $5K to $20K.

As always, what you charge depends on the perceived value and your level of confidence.

The challenges

While it would be nice to think you could leap straight from being a service provider to launching a $1000-a-month mastermind, I think you might struggle. For people to pay this much to be guided by you and be in your intimate business circle, you need a high level of knowledge and trust. I believe you need to be known and respected in your industry and by your peers before starting a mastermind.

The majority of my masterminders are already in my membership and have had years to see me 'do the do'. They're paying to get a bit more attention and some direct advice.

How to deal with dropouts

Since masterminds are high-commitment, high-cost offerings, you may possibly have people wanting to drop out. Thankfully, this hasn't happened to me, but on the flip side, I know many people who signed up for high-ticket offers and ended up stuck in them and feeling resentful.

You need to make the commitment clear on your sales page and in your legals, including penalties for leaving. However, when push comes to shove, and someone asks to leave halfway through due to illness or some family crisis, you're really going to have to think hard about how you enforce your rules and still sleep at night.

TOON TIP Personally, while I get that when you pay, you understand the commitment, I also think that as business owners we need to be human and have empathy. I sleep better with my ethics intact than I do holding onto someone's money when it puts them in financial distress.

The possibilities

Masterminds allow you to earn a large sum of money each month from fewer people. Some people much prefer working with a smaller one-to-many group than a larger group. They also offer the opportunity to help transform people's lives. Unlike courses and memberships, where you might get brief contact with each member, masterminds foster deep connections over long periods of time.

I genuinely enjoy seeing how people grow and helping them reach their version of success.

TL;DR

Masterminds are a great way to regularly earn large sums of cash while working with fewer people for significant results. They are not entirely passive income as they will involve a lot of your time, but that can be mitigated, meaning a solid ROI. Just have a think about whether you can commit to helping people in this way over a long period.

OVER TO YOU

Grab a pen and plan out your mastermind:

- What problem will your mastermind solve?
- Who is your ideal mastermind member? (You should be able to imagine a few people you already know.)
- What kind of content (if any) will you provide?
- What will be the duration of your mastermind?
- Will there be an in-person element? If yes, what will that look like?

$\succ\hspace\prec$ $\succ\hspace\prec$

Chapter 14

Additional ideas

I wanted to include these ideas as although they're not exactly ADPIPs, they are ADPIP-friendly and work great if you have a one-to-many model. They could be something to add later down the track, or you could include them from the get-go so you're ready to scale.

Affiliate marketing

Affiliate marketing is a performance-based marketing strategy where a business rewards affiliates for each customer they deliver. When you become an affiliate of a business's product or service, you're given a unique code which you can then promote via your own website, emails and social media. If a customer clicks on your link and makes a purchase, you earn a commission – usually a fixed percentage of the sale price.

This works great for ADPIPers because we're often making recommendations for lots of tools in our digital downloads, courses, memberships and masterminds. The companies offer you a convenient selection of banners and graphics to use, and you can plop them wherever you please. Often the affiliate fee is recurring, paying out every month or year, so it becomes a nice little passive income earner.

Easy money, right?

Well, yes and no. Here are a few affiliate marketing tips:

- **Declare that you're using affiliate links.** I think it's important not to hide it. Some people get funny about paid recommendations, so it's best to be upfront.
- **Be selective.** I am only an affiliate to a handful of software applications, all of which I've used and would recommend even if I weren't an affiliate.
- **Don't be greedy.** Recommending something that's not very good just because you're getting a wad of cash undermines your trust and authority. It just isn't worth it.
- **Be realistic.** Unless you put some serious energy into it, you're not going to make heaps of cash from affiliate marketing. And if you do spend energy here, you could be taking time away from marketing your own products.

Most software companies have a link to their affiliate program in their footer – just click on it and follow the steps to sign up. They'll ask you a few questions about your site and your following to see if you're a good fit. If you can't see a link, then email customer service.

Becoming an affiliate is a smashing way to get another income stream into your business. I don't put a huge amount of effort into prompting the platforms I'm an affiliate for – just a few socials posts here and there, links in emails and the occasional demo. Affiliate marketing probably represents about 2% of my overall income, but it's always a nice surprise when I see the payments come through.

The other reason it's great to sign up to affiliate programs is that it can help you understand how they work, so that further down the track, when you're looking to create advocacy for your own ADPIPs (see Chapter 21), you can create your own program.

Directories

An online directory is a website (or part of a website) where businesses can list their products and services into logical categories. They usually include images, a description, contact details, products and services. They're a great potential touchpoint for new customers to discover your business, and a great listing can be a powerful way to drive leads (and the backlinks help SEO).

A directory could be an ADPIP in its own right, but this raises some challenges:

- There are a lot of free directories to compete with.
- To make your directory attractive, you're going to have to show the volume of traffic you receive each day (which is hard when you're starting out).
- To drive a lot of traffic, you're going to have to really know your SEO and have the time and energy to promote your directory.
- The perceived value of your directory could be low (unless it's extremely specialised and has amazing traffic stats), which means you can't charge much for a listing.
- The admin around directories can be tricky. While most systems make creating a listing easy, I've found the level of 'user error' is incredibly high, which means you'll need customer service on hand.

So, rather than creating directories as standalone ADPIPs, I've used them as additional bonus incentives in my courses and memberships. Initially, I created a directory of my Recipe for SEO Success graduates, but later I replaced that with a directory for my Digital Marketing Collective membership. Members are incentivised with a free listing in this directory for the duration of their membership if they pay annually rather than monthly. I used the Sabai Directory plugin on WordPress to create my directory.

Job boards

If your ADPIPs are business-related, obviously a huge incentive is to provide customers with job opportunities. For my copywriting membership, the job board we created was a huge driver for membership and retention. External businesses can post on the job board for free, and the board itself is a simple display of opportunities that members can then click through to see the full job description.

Again, this could be a standalone ADPIP, but if you make it a paid product you will have to set expectations around how many jobs will be posted each week. And then you'll have to go out there and actively find jobs to put on your job board.

I'm lucky – as a high-ranking copywriter on Google (even though I haven't actually written copy in five years or more), I get a lot of enquiries, which I shoot through to my job boards. I've also built a reputation as a 'connector' of people, and that word-of-mouth recommendation helps my job boards stay full.

But I'm not a recruiter and don't want to be, so I use my job board as another incentive for membership rather than as a standalone ADPIP. I manage expectations around the number of jobs we're going to post, and while members enjoy these opportunities, they don't join my memberships solely because of them.

Advertising and sponsorship

As you move into the one-to-many model and build an audience (see Chapter 16) you're creating valuable and sellable business assets:

· That podcast you created has an audience that other businesses would like access to.
· Your free Facebook community could be the perfect spot for businesses to advertise in.
· Having a large group of relevant people in your audience is certainly not something to be sniffed at.

You could now consider selling advertising.

I'm not talking Google ads placed on your site, but rather advertising packages that give businesses access to your audience – you offer them X in return for a fee.

Obviously, this has challenges too:

· You don't want to be seen as a 'human for hire' who will share anything if they are making a buck.
· You need to be careful that the things you advertise don't conflict with, or drown out, your own offerings.
· The admin and time to negotiate the deal can lead to a poor return on investment and take focus away from your real money-making ADPIPs.

However, it can also associate your brand with other great brands. In my time I've had my podcast sponsored by Ahrefs, Yoast and Supermetrics. Xero, Hnry and Rounded have sponsored my podcasts and conferences. I've also done some Reels here and there for members of my community – mostly just for fun.

Again, when these deals come along, they're a nice little bonus, but I try not to invest too much time here.

ADPIP overwhelm

It's easy to get distracted by all the possibilities of the ADPIP world. Don't get me wrong, I love a little business diversity, but it's important to focus on your core product (which we covered in Chapter 5, but see Figure 14.1 for a refresher).

Figure 14.1: The ingredients of a great ADPIP

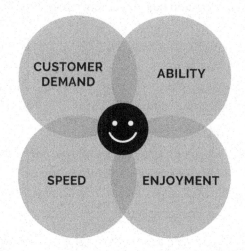

Yes, there might be a bit of a customer demand for sponsorship, and I might enjoy it, but I'm not a sponsorships manager, and I think my time is better spent elsewhere.

Yes, my members love the directory, but they're not going to be willing to pay the fee to make the admin worthwhile, and I don't enjoy fiddling around with people's listings.

Everything is a balance.

Say I charge $300 for an annual listing in my directory and get 30 people. That equates to $9K a year. Is that enough for me to invest time myself (or in a third party) to build the traffic and handle the customer service? For the same amount of revenue, I could sell just three spots on my big course. Something to consider.

TL;DR

There are many other potential ADPIP revenue streams, most of which won't really be possible until you have a strong customer base. But just because you can, doesn't mean you should. Try not to get distracted by shiny objects, especially when you haven't sold many of your main ADPIPs yet. If you're going to pick one of the ideas in this chapter, I'd start with affiliate marketing.

OVER TO YOU

Focus on affiliate marketing:

- Make a list of all the software you regularly use and recommend in your business. Then, find the affiliate link and join up. Make a note of your affiliate link so you can add it to your website, and later your email funnel, social media, lead magnet and ADPIPs.

PART IV:
SLIPPERY LITTLE FUNNELS

> **"**
> A good teacher, like a good entertainer
> first must hold his audience's attention,
> then he can teach his lesson.
>
> John Henrik Clarke
> **"**

Chapter 15

Understanding funnels

I've said it already, but it bears repeating: to make the one-to-many model work, you need the **many**. And the number-one reason why most people fail at ADPIPs is because they invest all their time in building the product and zero time building an audience.

I talked about understanding our customers in Chapter 7. We know their beliefs, their fears and their desires. We know their pain points. We've created our Big Little Idea to suit them *(and ourselves)* perfectly. Now, how do we get them to know about it? And more importantly, how do we get them to trust us enough to buy it?

We use sales funnels.

What is a sales funnel?

A sales funnel is a traditional marketing concept that shows the steps customers take from awareness to purchase (and beyond). The idea is that it's like an ever-narrowing tube, with a lot of people entering at the top and fewer people making it to the bottom.

There are few different ways to describe a sales funnel, and I've included four different ways of approaching it, but if you're time-poor or easily overwhelmed, just jump to number four.

1. The TOFU, MOFU, BOFU model

An easy way to understand the sales funnel is to think of it in three stages (see Figure 15.1):

1. **Top of funnel (TOFU).** Customers are becoming aware of you and their interest is growing. They are following and interacting with you on socials, or listening to your podcast. You need to start a conversation without pushing product. These people are **problem aware**.
2. **Middle of funnel (MOFU).** Customers are considering getting involved with you and have engaged with your brand in a more meaningful way. They are signing up for your lead magnet or offer, or buying something small. (See Chapter 17 for more on lead magnets.) They're not clueless, but they're not ready to buy yet. These people are **solution and product aware**.
3. **Bottom of funnel (BOFU).** Customers know who you are and what you offer, and now they want your pitch. They are at the buying stage. These people are **brand aware**.

Figure 15.1: The TOFU, MOFU, BOFU model

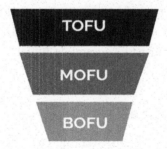

TOON TIP You could also add FU (f*ck you) – people who are totally unaware and don't need what you're selling – but you'd be making your job a lot harder. Trying to attract people who don't have a problem that you could solve and trying to convince them they do is tough. It's even tougher to sell to them, so don't try.

2. THE AIDA model

The AIDA model consists of four steps (see Figure 15.2):

1. **Awareness.** A customer becomes aware of your brand and discovers a problem they might not have really known they had.
2. **Interest.** The customer actively wants a solution to their problem and researches your brand and its offerings.
3. **Desire.** The customer is ready to decide and starts comparing your brand to others.
4. **Action.** The customer slides out their credit card and spends their sweet, sweet moolah on your ADPIP.

Figure 15.2: The AIDA model

Now, ideally, we want this funnel to be as slippery as possible without being greasy. What I mean by this is that we want to people to slide towards buying your product with as little friction as possible, but equally, we don't want to use greasy sales tactics to get them there.

3. The awareness model

The awareness model looks at your customers' awareness of their problem and how that influences what they need at each stage of your funnel:

1. **Unaware.** They want peace, so leave them the hell alone (the FUs).
2. **Problem aware.** They are seeking a solution.

3. **Solution aware.** They want proof that you have the solution.
4. **Product aware.** They want a push to buy your product rather than someone else's.
5. **Brand aware.** Often at this stage it's about price, perceived value and some kind of urgency to buy.

4. The customer journey model

The customer journey is my favourite model as it offers the most comprehensive view of the entire customer experience, from first sniff to final snog. It encompasses the phases of the TOFU, MOFU, BOFU and AIDA models but also includes what happens after a customer makes a purchase. The customer journey model considers all of the customer's interactions with your brand and all the little touchpoints, such as signing up to email lists, engaging on social media and buying your thing.

There are six core stages in the customer's journey (see Figure 15.3):

1. **Awareness.** Your customer becomes aware of your brand, product or service.
2. **Interest** – your customer starts to research and consider your offerings.
3. **Desire.** Your customer really wants what you have to offer.
4. **Action.** Your customer makes a purchase.
5. **Retention.** Your customer continues to engage with your brand and becomes a repeat customer.
6. **Advocacy.** Your customer becomes a mini brand ambassador and tells their friends, family and pets about your amazing stuff.

This all sounds rather wonderful, but of course it's not this simple in practice. Some customers might leap straight to Action and then completely disappear. Others may stay in Desire mode for ages until they have the need, time or funds to do your thing.

> **TOON TIP** Patience is so important with ADPIPs. the aforementioned Sue McGary from French Affair spent nearly seven years in my funnel before she reached the Action stage, but it was worth the wait. She's now a huge advocate of my brand (as I am of hers).

Figure 15.3: The customer journey model

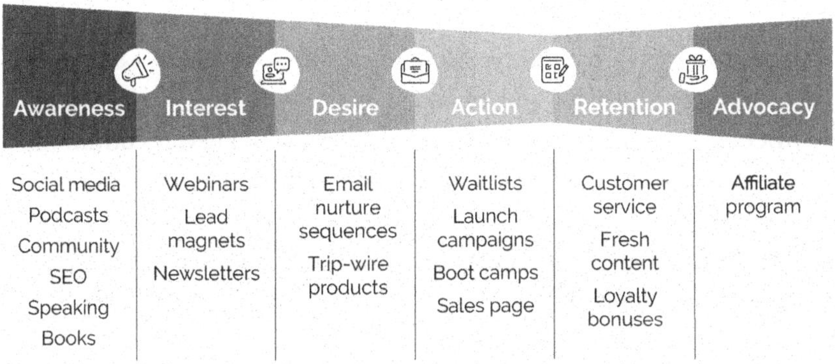

Awareness	Interest	Desire	Action	Retention	Advocacy
Social media	Webinars	Email nurture sequences	Waitlists	Customer service	Affiliate program
Podcasts	Lead magnets		Launch campaigns	Fresh content	
Community	Newsletters	Trip-wire products	Boot camps	Loyalty bonuses	
SEO			Sales page		
Speaking					
Books					

Creating your customer journey

Now that we have our big idea and our chosen destination, let's map out our customer journey and understand what we need to do at each stage. (We'll use the customer journey as our model as it's the most comprehensive.) If you haven't already, you can grab the *Six Figures While You Sleep* workbook for free from katetoon.com to see a template for your customer journey, which you can use throughout the following chapters.

But before we work through it, let's go through two examples – my funnel for The Recipe for SEO Success and a potential funnel for one of our guinea pigs.

As you know, one of my Big Little Ideas was to create an SEO course for normal, non-technical small business owners and ecommerce businesses. To get paying customers, I have to move them from vague interest to handing over several thousand dollars for a course. Here is how I do this.

1. Awareness

Here's how I build awareness of me and my offering:

· **Social media** – I share a combination of tips, advice, case studies, tools and funny videos about SEO across Facebook, Instagram and LinkedIn.

- **Podcast** – I have a regular podcast where I share short tip episodes and interviews with well-known SEO experts. I'm also a regular guest on other people's podcasts.
- **Community** – I have a free group on Facebook called I Love SEO where people get tips and advice.
- **SEO** – I use blog posts on my site and others to answer commonly googled questions about traffic and the best way to make more website sales.
- **Speaking** – I speak at regular events around Australia (and occasionally globally).
- **Books** – I write books (like this one).

2. Interest

I use the following methods to turn that awareness into genuine interest:

- I run regular free **webinars** that cover the basics of SEO and show how doable it is for normal people.
- I have not one but two different **lead magnets** – a comprehensive SEO checklist and a free mini course called SEO Nibbles *(not 'Nipples', as I say throughout the course)*.
- I send a monthly **newsletter** with tips, advice and news about SEO.

I also promote all of these on social media.

3. Desire

After they sign up for my various freebies, I nurture my customers, creating desire and showing them what they can achieve. I do this by:

- **creating an email nurture sequence** – a short series of emails that address customer pain points and helps with advice and offers
- **creating a trip-wire product** – a low-cost product that paves the way for the customer to buy a more expensive product later. (More on this in Chapter 19.) Mine is called the 10 Day SEO Challenge and it's available all year round (evergreen).

  TOON TIP Trip-wire products should have solid value in their own right. My small SEO course is an appetiser for the main course but also serves those who could never afford the big course.

Don't think of your trip-wires as a way of tricking people into a large purchase, but rather as teasers for what's to come.

4. Action

Now for the real action – it's time for the customer to sign up to the big SEO course. To facilitate this, I:

- create a **waitlist** where customers can sign up to be the first to know when the course opens (and I send a series of emails pre-launch to overcome any final objections)
- run **launches** at three set times a year to create some excitement and urgency
- run a **social media campaign** of launch content
- run **boot camps** to get people excited about what can be achieved, give them some quick wins and encourage them to sign up to the big course
- create a super sexy **sales page** to convert users.

5. Retention

Since the course is a one-off thing, there's no real retention model there, but students can sign up for additional years of access. On top of that, after the course finishes, I try to migrate them to my more generalised digital marketing and business membership, the Digital Marketing Collective, which is where I focus my retention efforts.

I do this by promoting the Digital Marketing Collective at the end of the course and offering a small ongoing loyalty discount. Once members join, they are fixed at their initial price, which means there's an incentive to stay – if they leave and come back, they'll have to pay more.

On top of this, members are given fresh content every month and access to a growing library of content, resources and tools. They're also listed in my directory and have access to a job board offering them ongoing opportunities. I recognise and reward members, giving gifts, offering them promotion opportunities and inviting them onto my podcast.

6. Advocacy

Students are offered various proof elements when the course finishes, including certificates of completion and graduate stamps. I encourage them to provide video and written testimonials for the course, which I can then use in my social media and emails for the next round to build trust. I also offer an affiliate program solely to Recipe students, which allows them to be rewarded for recommending the course.

*

I like to refer to my Recipe funnel as a 'tube of joy', because I'm a strange human. Figure 15.4 shows what it looks like.

Figure 15.4: My Recipe tube of joy

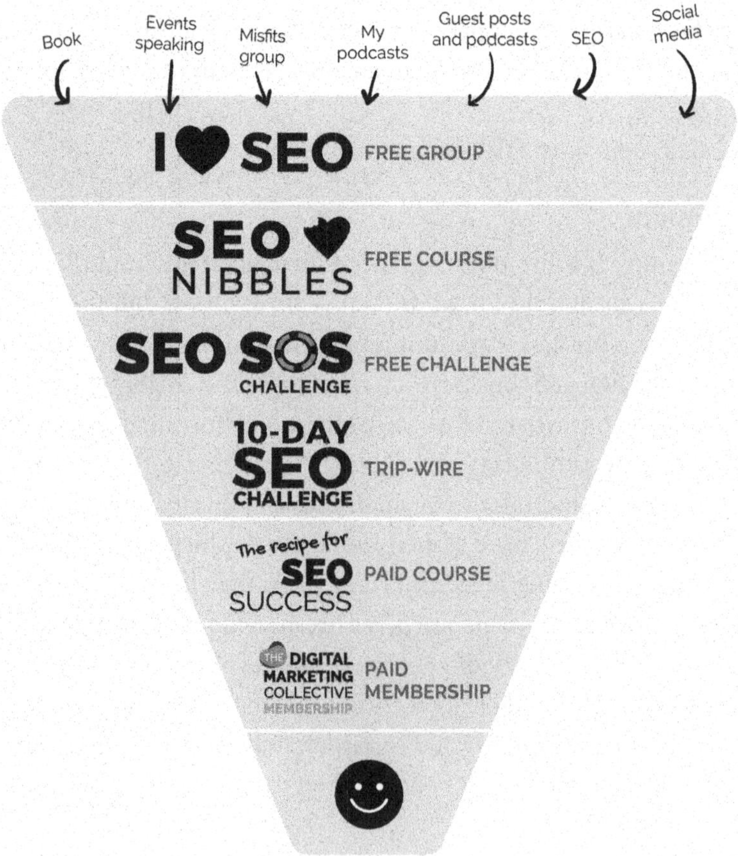

While this funnel all looks very sexy now, it wasn't always this way.

When I started out, the 10 Day SEO Challenge – now a paid trip-wire – was free, the Facebook community was deserted, and I had no podcast listeners and no lead magnets. It took several years for it all to come together and for me to fill the gaps – partially because I'm a working mum and had minimal time.

Be patient with yourself. I cover more about managing your money as you build your ADPIP in Chapter 23.

Here's how a simpler version could work for one of our guinea pigs Tony Cosentino. Remember, his Big Little idea is to set up a membership for junior WordPress developers where they can learn about tech, sales, customer service and project management.

1. **Awareness.** While Tony is known as a developer, he's not known as a coach, so I'd suggest he create a social media schedule that focuses on providing tips and advice around his four core membership content pillars: tech, sales, customer service and project management. He could share a mix of content including tool recommendations, demonstrations, advice, encouragement and real-life case studies. He could also use short form video content through such platforms as Instagram Reels, YouTube Shorts and TikTok to connect his face and voice to his brand. If he has time, he could even resurrect his podcast and produce short, snappy episodes providing tips for junior WordPress developers (to position him as a subject matter expert) and interviews with successful WordPress developers (to increase awareness of the podcast). All of these brand awareness efforts could have the same call to action – to sign up to his lead magnet.

2. **Interest.** Now that Tony has warmed up this audience, he needs to offer them a next step. The simplest way to do this is to create an email sign-up with a sexy lead magnet – something that helps junior WordPress developers feel more confident. I'd recommend he has one solid lead magnet before he creates any more.

3. **Desire.** Now that Tony's audience is keen and educated, he's ready for the next step. To keep things simple, I'd suggest short, paid, live online workshops that help take his leads through what he thinks are the five most important steps for building a successful WordPress business. This would be his trip-wire product. He could also set up a short email series (his nurture sequence) to nurture his leads.

4. **Action.** In previous chapters, I talked about how memberships are often a harder sell, not because of price but because of commitment. Tony could set up an ongoing membership at a low price to get some bums on seats, gradually increasing the price as he becomes more well known. He'll need a sales page, sales emails and social media launch content to do this.

5. **Retention.** I wouldn't worry overly about the retention stage upfront. It's more important to get people in. But I would recommend that Tony roughly maps out at least three months of content and lines up some great guests to come into the group. He can create minimal content, and instead schedule time and **commit to showing up** for his members. Remember, people want coaching, not content. (The difficult part here is that it often takes as much effort to serve three members as 30 or even 300, so the early stages can feel like a real slog and slightly thankless! It will get better.)

6. **Advocacy.** Again, no point stressing too much about advocacy when you're in the early stages. But some ideas might include elevating long-term members as experts in the group, offering them the chance to be on the podcast and creating a simple affiliate program.

So, Tony's funnel shopping list (in order of priority) is:

1. a social media plan with short videos
2. a lead magnet
3. a nurture sequence
4. a workshop outline

5. a sales page
6. three months of roughly planned content.

Now, if all that sounds a little overwhelming, don't worry – in the coming chapters I break down each of these stages in detail, why they matter and what you need to do.

Understanding the numbers

I talked about pricing a little in Part III, and I'll talk about it more as we go on. Price is one dial you can twiddle to drive up revenue, but the other dial is the number of people you lure into your funnel.

Just recently, one of my Digital Marketing Collective members announced that he was launching a new membership and was planning for 30 people in the first launch, which was only a week away. While I never want to poo on someone's bonfire, I did have to give him a reality check.

Table 15.1 shows how the numbers could work for your funnel, using both a generous 10% conversion rate and a less generous 5% conversion rate.

Table 15.1: Two examples of how the numbers could work
for your funnel

Conversion rate	10%	5%
Number of humans who see your messages in a given period	10,000	10,000
Number of humans who sign up for your freebie and join your email list	1000	500
Number of humans who pay for your trip-wire	100	25
Number of humans who buy your big thing	10	1.25

As you can see, even with the more generous 10% model, my Digital Marketing Collective member would have needed at least 30,000 people on their email list to get 30 people for their first launch.

These conversion rates may seem low – and obviously, the more targeted your marketing efforts are, the better these rates will be – but that's why it's important to manage expectations. Getting 20 people into your membership in the first week might be ambitious, but getting 200 over a few years is entirely possible. ADPIPs require patience – your numbers will improve as you build trust and awareness..

It's important not to set your expectations too high at the start, or you'll set yourself up for failure. It's the first few years that will be the hardest. For perspective, Table 15.2 shows my numbers for The Recipe for SEO Success course over the first few years.

Table 15.2: The Recipe for SEO Success course
attendance numbers over the years

Course number	Date	People
1	February 2015	20
2	July 2015	30
3	August 2015	53
4	October 2015	30
5	May 2016	44
6	January 2017	22
7	February 2017	42
8	July 2017	64
9	October 2017	72
10	June 2018	69
11	February 2018	64
12	October 2018	74
13	June 2019	82
14	March 2019	83
15	October 2019	80

The Kevin Bacon Factor

One thing to be aware of is what I like to call the Kevin Bacon Factor (also more boringly known as the 'six degrees of separation'). When you first start your thing, you'll be marketing it to your warmest audience – friends, family, old colleagues and previous clients. These are easy fish to hook. My first 20 students on Recipe were all already known to me in one way or another. This can give you a false numbers boost – I was patting my own bottom thinking my membership was going to skyrocket. Then after a few launches (when I'd used up those early people), it got harder – look at my dip in 2016 above. I thought I'd lost my touch. I hadn't; it just gets harder. Be aware that you can't sustain a business selling only to your mum and your long-lost school friends.

As time goes on, you'll need to work hard to draw more people into your Kevin Bacon circle and use those advocates to do the Bacon creation work. We'll cover this in Chapter 21.

TL;DR

The biggest mistake people make when launching an ADPIP is not building an audience before (or at least while) they create their thing. If you don't want to be selling to crickets, then you need to start building awareness, sparking interest and creating desire from the get-go. And if you're wondering when to start, the answer is **today**.

OVER TO YOU

Grab a pen and paper or the *Six Figures While You Sleep* workbook and map out your customer journey, thinking about what content, vibe and products you need to offer at each stage. These can be top-level thoughts at this stage; we'll flesh them out in the coming chapters.

Chapter 16
Brand awareness

Awareness | Interest | Desire | Action | Retention | Advocacy

Right now, you're probably thinking, *No one knows who the heck I am; how on earth am I going to build this big audience?* You're at the bottom of a big, snowy mountain ready to start scaling, and someone has stolen your backpack. Well, it starts by understanding the brand awareness stage. I know it sounds like a fancy marketing term, but put simply, it means how familiar your target audience is with your brand.

Why is brand awareness important?

The more people who know about you, the better, right? But they must be the right people. In this awareness stage (or TOFU) we want to:

- **build recognition** – customers become aware of your brand's existence through your marketing efforts, and they can recognise your name and logo
- **improve comprehension** – customers start to understand what you offer and what problems you solve

- **improve recall** – customers can remember your brand when they need something you offer; your brand is top of mind
- **foster trust** – customers feel comfortable with your business (remember, people want to buy from brands they trust and feel safe with)
- **create positive vibes** – customers develop good feelings towards your brand (people generally prefer to buy from brands they like rather than brands that get on their tits).

Of course, you could build brand awareness by getting naked, painting your brand logo on your bottom and running through the streets of your local town – or you can try these options instead.

Brand awareness principles

Let's talk about what principles should guide you through the brand awareness stage.

Principle 1: Be clear about who you are

Refer back to Chapter 6 and gather your values, personality and unique selling proposition (USP). Make sure they still fit in the context of your Big Little idea and which ADPIP option you've chosen. For example, if you decided you're not really a people person, don't go planning to launch a membership.

You need to keep a consistent voice and vibe across everything you do, regardless of the channel – don't let it all hang out on Instagram then get all serious and strait-laced on LinkedIn.

Remember your values and your personality, and try not to do anything wildly out of character that will confuse your audience. So, if you're having a really bad day, try to stay off socials, and if you have a wild, wacky idea for a post, run it by a business buddy first.

Principle 2: Use consistent branding

Ensure your logos, colours, fonts, photography style and images are consistent across your marketing materials. The goal is that when someone sees your content, they instinctively know it's you before they read a word.

This may mean not using generic Canva graphics to promote your services, but rather, working with a brand designer and building your own custom templates.

> **TOON TIP** I use teal in my Kate Toon branding and wear a lot of teal too. Fantastically, when I spoke at a recent event, an audience member came up to me with a teal clothes peg. She said she saw the peg colour and immediately thought of me! I still have the peg on my desk. That, my friends, is strong branding.

Principle 3: Be confident

Customers can smell fear – if you're tentative with your approach to brand awareness, it won't hit home. Think back to Chapter 4, and squash those imposter symptoms. Your tips and ideas are just as valid as anyone else's. Yes, it may have been said before, but it can be said again. No one can argue with your lived experience, and if people do disagree *(unlikely)* then that's okay too.

Principle 4: Be a real human

A mistake I see lots of brands making with brand awareness is trying to create a perfectly curated social media appearance, spending a fortune on brand photography and trying to make their Instagram feed all matchy-matchy. Now, of course, you want to put your best foot forward, but here's the thing: when I have two brands to compare and they line up in experience, skills and approach, it's often their human side, those quirks and fails and honest moments, that make me pick one over the other.

As I've said before, you don't need to be sharing pictures of your kids, or snapshots from the bath *(unless you have an OnlyFans account)*, but behind-the-scenes snippets can really add warmth and depth to your brand awareness efforts.

Principle 5: Share your face and voice

I know that many people are worried about sharing their face and opinions, about putting themselves out there. Many of us have body issues and wish we looked hotter, younger, plumper or glossier. But we only have one face, and if people don't like it, there's not much we can do.

It's hard to build a brand people trust without letting them see the whites of your eyes, without them hearing your voice and your thoughts and opinions. You can't hide behind polished Canva graphics all your business life.

Principle 6: Be contrary

Now, by contrary I don't mean you need to go out today and start sharing your political and religious views. Rather, I mean that you should try to find something in the industry or area in which you're going to exist that you don't like and want to change.

Perhaps you're launching a crocheting membership, and you want to move away from making cute doilies and coasters and instead make wacky modern creatures. That's a platform; that's something to stand out for.

In the world of SEO, I wanted to stand up (and stand out) against the predominately male status quo and the over-technicalisation of the topic. That gave me an interesting platform to be contrary on, and I've become known for this.

The only thing with being contrary is being aware that some people won't like it, and that's okay. Great marketing is as much about people not liking you as liking you. Divisive marketing will get you a few haters, sure, but it will also generate true loyal fans.

🦉 Ingrid Fernandez wants to stand out in the legal space by rejecting the incomprehensible legalese and jargon and by making the topic more accessible.

🦉 Tony Cosentino wants to be a friendly support in the WordPress space, which can often be dominated by big, arrogant personalities. He also wants to stand against the idea that there's one good theme or one good plugin and provide different pathways.

TOON TIP I've been accused a few times of posting polarising content; some folks really don't like it. But you know what? It's not my job to manage my audience's reactions or emotions. While I would never aim to be pointlessly provocative, aimlessly rude or unpleasant, if I want to post a daft Reel about how I don't like Facebook ads, that's my prerogative. Those who don't like it can scroll on.

Principle 7: Don't hard-sell

Remember, the brand awareness stage is not about asking for money, participation or loyalty. (That comes later.)

Imagine you're at a networking do and you race up to Alan, who is quietly eating a tepid sausage roll, and thrust your Square device in his face and ask him to buy your latest thing. Alan is likely to spit that sausage roll on the floor. Instead, get to know Alan, find out if he's the right customer for you, explain what you do and how you help, give him some free advice and tell him the next step.

Principle 8: Finish strong

While the brand awareness stage is not about the hard sell, it's still important to give people a possible next action. This doesn't have to always be a call to action to sign up to your thing (see Chapter 18) – it could be an invitation to add a comment, send you a message or share your content.

TOON TIP I generally use a clear call to action to sign up to my 'thing' in about 20% of my brand awareness content.

Brand awareness tactics

Let's get into some specific tactics to build your brand awareness as quickly and as easily as possible.

Tactic 1: Set yourself up for SEO success

Yes, I'm starting with SEO as that's obviously one of my superpowers. Here's the thing: it's so much easier to be found for who you are than what you do.

If I search for 'digital marketing coach', Google will shoot back hundreds of results, but if I search for 'Kate Toon', it will only send back me *(and a dental nurse in Ipswich)*. If you're unfortunate enough to share your name with someone famous, or a porn star, then think about the word you could append to your name – for example, 'Brad Pitt Accountant'. If people want to find you, they'll find you.

While right now no one knows who you are, soon they will, so set yourself up for SEO success.

Here are a few tactics to start with:

- **Use personal branding.** If possible, set up a website in your own name (like katetoon.com) and use this as the hub site from which you sell your ADPIPs. If you already have a website with a business name, create a strong 'About' page which details everything about you. I recommend having a good clear headshot with a file name of your name and an alt tag of your name. Also use your own name in the:
  - title tag (which will become the blue underlined link in the search engine results)
  - meta description (the short description that shows under the title link in the results)
  - headline
  - body copy (don't overdo it – once or twice will help)
  - URL (for example, www.yourdomain.com/kate-toon).

- **Use ADPIP branding.** I talked in Chapter 10 about how it's important to brand your products and services in an unusual and relevant way. This is because as your brand awareness grows, so will your product awareness, and people may remember your product names before your name. As I mentioned before, ensure you google your ADPIP name **before** you get carried away with it.

- **Use backlinks.** I cover social media, podcasts and guest posts in just a minute. All of these are great ways to build brand awareness, but they also give you opportunities to build backlinks. Backlinks are links from one website to another, and many SEO experts believe they pass authority or 'SEO juice' to your site.

So, if you get interviewed by *The New York Times* and they link back to your site, it could give your rankings a boost. Make sure you always ask for a backlink.

TOON TIP Most SEO experts believe that backlinks from social media don't provide the same level of authority as backlinks from websites. So, while social media backlinks are great for traffic, they won't build your SEO juice.

Obviously, there's a lot more to SEO than this, so if you want to learn more, google 'the 10 Day SEO Challenge' and dive into that Google pond. Or, you can Google 'Kate Toon' and see if I'm good at SEO ☺.

Tactic 2: Use social media

Now, of course, I could write a whole book on how to use social media to build brand awareness – and hey, maybe I will *(note to publisher ☺)* – but to keep things reasonable, let me give you my top tips:

· **Be somewhere.** The usual advice is to be everywhere, but that's hard when you're going it alone. Instead, think about where your primary audience hangs out and focus your social media efforts there.
· **Get over yourself.** If your primary audience is on LinkedIn and you're not a fan, you'll need to get over yourself and get stuck in, learn the ropes and post quality content as frequently as you can.
· **Set a schedule.** Create a simple schedule of posts you'd like to share each month – have a nice mix of tips, thoughts, testimonials, personal bits and bobs, tools and case studies. But don't beat yourself up if you miss a day or can't plan 30 days in advance – few people can. Just do your best.

Tactic 3: Identify your content pillars

Now that you know what your main ADPIP product is going to be, you should be clear on what problems you're solving and what space you want to fill. Think about what topics you can talk about that will lure customers in. What five or six topics can you talk about every month for a long, long time? ☺

Stephanie's content pillars might be:

- advice and tips
- real-life case studies
- mythbusting
- reports and facts
- community discussions.

TOON TIP I use Agorapulse to share my socials. I tend to use it to post on social media about 20 or so times a month on my Kate Toon–related channels, but I leave room for me to post random stuff as and when I can.

I also post the same content on all channels, obviously allowing for text and image restrictions. And I love recycling old posts – the algorithms mean that few people see the post the first time around, so I like to share a few times just in case.

I talk about launch-specific socials in the next part of the book.

Tactic 4: Guest blog

My brand awareness grew hugely when I started guest blogging. Sure, I was posting blogs on my own site, which only my mum probably read, but then I tried posting content on a site called Flying Solo. The impact was immediate – more followers, more lead sign-ups, more contact form submissions.

This was where I experimented with my tone of voice and really found my writing flow. Here are my tips when it comes to guest posting:

- **Be brave.** You'd be surprised how many digital media sites are desperate for content. Check through their website or connect with someone who works there on social media. Then, get in touch to share ideas. Don't get too emotionally invested in the outcome; just keep trying.
- **Write a strong pitch.** Make sure you make the editor's life easier by writing a strong headline, a good short paragraph that describes the context of the article and why it's important, and some key take-outs the reader will get from your article. You do not need to

write the whole article and send it; rather, get them excited with an outline and the idea, and then wait for the go-ahead before you work through the whole thing.

- **Provide a bio and background.** Write a strong personal bio that shows why you're the right person to be creating this article, and include links to some previous blogs (even if they're just on your own site) so the editor can see your writing style.

TOON TIP As you get featured in publications, start creating a little file of logos. These will look great on your ADPIP sales page in the 'as featured in' panel. The same applies for podcasts you guest on. Generally, I just google '[brand name] logo', but I recommend you check with the publication or podcast first regarding usage.

Tactic 5: Guest podcast

I've appeared on literally hundreds of podcasts, big and small. It's been an excellent way to build brand awareness but also to build relationships with other entrepreneurs and business owners. Generally, it's only an hour out of your day, and it's an amazing way to get confident talking about your skills and services (and ADPIP offering).

The same tips that apply to guest blogging apply to guest podcasting. While the big pods might not be so easy to get onto, there are hundreds of smaller pods out there you can approach. Don't worry about their audience size. Even if your episode gets 20 listeners, that's 20 people who have spent an hour with you in their ears – powerful stuff.

Here are some additional tips:

- **Listen.** Be sure to listen to a few episodes first to get the gist of the podcast's style and vibe, and review the previous episodes to see what's been covered.
- **Fluff.** I get dozens of emails a week from complete strangers asking to be on my podcast. They often get my name wrong, pitch irrelevant topics and generally make no effort to show they give a poo. (They go straight in my email bin – I rarely take guests from unsolicited emails.) Take some time to follow the podcast host, comment on their stuff and share their content so that when you do make contact, they know who you are already.

Tactic 6: Podcast

I love podcasting. I mean, I have three podcasts at the moment and had several before this. But while I think podcasting is a great way to build brand awareness, it's a big time investment.

Each episode of my podcast takes around eight hours to produce, covering finding guests and arranging interviews, preparing episode notes, recording, editing, coding into the site and promotion on social media.

It's a powerful way to build authority, but not the quickest, so I'm not going to cover it in depth here. Instead, I'd say make guest appearances on at least 20 podcasts before you start your own, and when you're ready to learn all my mad podcasting skills, come join the Digital Marketing Collective.

Tactic 7: Piggyback

No one knows who you are, but there are people who are well known. How can you work that to your advantage – not in a creepy, sucky-uppy way but in a way that benefits both you and the more famous person?

I get people reaching out to me every single day asking for a shout-out or some free promo. Often, these people have never interacted with me before, never bought even my cheapest product and never given me a shout-out. Now, sometimes I'll just help because, hey, it's a nice thing to do, but a bit of pre-love helps.

If there's someone you think you could work with and it would be mutually beneficial, help them first! Fluff them a little. Get on their radar before you make any request of them.

> **TOON TIP** I quite literally started my podcast because I was desperate to talk to Rand Fishkin. At the time, he was heading up an SEO company called Moz and did these excellent Whiteboard Fridays that really helped me learn SEO. I asked him to come on my podcast, totally thinking he'd say no, and he said yes! He was my first guest and has since been on several times, and I've now met him in real life (we spoke on the same stage in the Netherlands). He helped me not because it benefitted him but because he's a nice human. Do not underestimate the nice human factor.

Tactic 8: Speak at events

Speaking at events can be scary, but it's an amazingly fast track to build brand awareness, as people physically meeting you creates far firmer connections. It's no coincidence that my biggest revenue year coincided with the year I spoke at 37 events. It was exhausting, but it paid off.

Start small with local business events, but then go big (using some of those guest blog pitches you've written). You might not get paid the big bucks straight away, but the opportunity to speak in front of your ideal audience is invaluable.

Tactic 9: Run giveaways

Running competitions and giveaways can be a great way to build rapid brand awareness, but be careful – often those who are interested in a freebie do not make the best customers, and they'll fade away when it comes time to get their credit card out. You also need to be aware of any applicable laws and the rules of the platforms you're using to promote a competition.

What about Facebook and Google ads?

You'll notice that throughout this book I don't talk about paid advertising. Why? I don't like it and I've struggled to make it work for my offering. Also, I'm not in any way a Facebook or Google ads expert and don't like talking about things I don't have experience in. (We have some great Facebook and Google ads people in the Digital Marketing Collective if you want a recommendation.)

I do believe Facebook and Google ads can be powerful for ecommerce stores, and if you have the money, they can be great for ADPIPs to help build warmish lists of potential leads. I've had some success using ads to promote my SEO checklist, for example, at around $5 to $10 a lead. But I do find that leads from ads do not convert as well as leads from organic content. I also feel that some of the platforms are a little overeager to take credit for a sale I'd likely have gotten anyway through my nurture sequences. For Google ads, the cost per click for my term 'SEO Course' was just too damn high.

I also see many entrepreneurs celebrating their six-figure launches only to reveal that they spent $70K of that $100K on ads. I want to keep as much of my money as possible.

Ultimately, I think Facebook ads can work, especially if you're new and have absolutely no one on your list, but personally I resent giving money to these platforms. And I get a sweet pleasure from achieving sales without them.

Bonus brand awareness quick tips

Here are some quick-fire brand awareness tips to finish off the chapter:

1. **Create your own suite of branded hashtags.** Include your name, your ADPIP name and some quirky ones; for example, #KATETOON, #DMC, #SEONIBBLES, #BUMPRENEUR. (Be aware that others may also use these hashtags, and there's not much you can do about it.)

2. **Build a lexicon of phrases and words.** Create a document with all the words you like using in your posts – not catchphrases as such, but words and idioms that you love – and don't be afraid of using them frequently. For example, two of my most used phrases are 'shitgibbon' and 'willy waivers'. I also sign off my emails with 'hugs and hamsters'.

3. **Get merch.** Don't go crazy like I did and order hundreds of SEO-branded tea towels, but a few cute notepads and pens with your brand on them can be great for giveaways at events and on socials.

4. **Don't focus on 'going viral'.** You might dream of your Instagram Reel being seen by millions, but often viral content doesn't deliver great leads. Remember, smaller, more engaged, loyal followers are far more likely to buy.

Of course, there are dozens more brand awareness strategies out there – you could become a YouTube influencer or a TikTok sensation, for example – but the tactics I mention here worked relatively quickly for me.

If you want to read examples of what worked for others, head to the success stories at the back of this book.

The main thing is to just keep swimming – it may take a while.

TOON TIP Now look, I get it, I'm an introvert too (although you may not think it). Sometimes leaving my cosy little Toon Cave to interact with other humans takes a huge amount of energy, and turning up online is **not** my favourite thing to do. But honestly, it's hard to build an ADPIP if you're a wallflower and want to stay invisible.

But it does get easier. You don't need to start big; start small and build up. You **can** do it.

TL;DR

Building brand awareness is the first step in creating a successful slippery funnel – you need to become known by as many people as possible. But you still need to focus on quality, not quantity, and to do this you need consistent branding and messaging across everything you do.

OVER TO YOU

- Where do you think your audience hangs out the most?
- Which five content pillars are you going to talk about?
- Find one podcast you'd love to be a guest on.
- Write one pitch.

Chapter 17

Interest (and leads)

The interest stage of our slippery funnel is about turning the casual viewers we attracted in the brand awareness stage into actively engaged people and turning absent-minded browsers into keen leads.

Lead generation sounds cold and unemotional, but it's just the process of sparking genuine interest in potential customers, helping them and showing them the possibilities. We want to create good quality 'stuff' that makes them feel happy to hear from us – and be delighted about slipping even further down our funnel.

What is a lead? A lead is a human who has actively indicated that they're interested in your products or service. They haven't just liked a post or commented with a gif – they've taken the next step and given you some personal information.

In the olden days *(back when I was a girl)*, driving leads was all about making chilly cold calls to complete strangers, but thankfully we don't have to do that now – unless we want to.

Rather, we can capture their interest by getting them to complete some kind of small action, such as:

- providing their email address in return for a sexy downloadable
- completing a survey
- entering a competition
- joining your community
- signing up to a webinar.

At this stage, the customer isn't ready to fill out your contact form or buy anything, but they're keen to take the next step, and obviously, we hope that this will ultimately lead to a sale.

Remember the awareness model from Chapter 15? Well, you can use this to map out what kind of lead generation action you should offer:

- **Unaware** – leave them alone. They are not your people.
- **Problem aware** – they want information. Invite them to sign up to your blog, your podcast or your email newsletter.
- **Solution aware** – they want proof that you know what you're talking about. Invite them to sign up to your lead magnet.
- **Product aware** – they want a taster. Invite them to sign up to your free trial or mini course (your trip-wire product).
- **Brand aware** – they are ready to purchase. Now it's time for them to sign up to the real thing.

In the previous chapter I talked about how people become aware of you via your social media channels, your podcast or a guest blog. They then see a call to action to take the next step, encouraging them to visit your landing page, where they're asked to provide some information (name and email) in return for an offer.

The offer must be something of perceived value. In ecommerce land, this is often something like a 10% discount or free shipping. In ADPIP land, it's more likely to be a lead magnet.

Outbound lead generation requires proactive attempts to reach audiences, such as purchasing lead lists, cold calling or direct mail. Inbound lead generation, on the other hand, often uses entertainment and education to lure customers in, building awareness, trust and a degree of connection, then inviting them to move forward. It can cost less than outbound generation but can take a lot more time.

Why is lead generation important?

Let's use a dating analogy. If you stay in brand awareness land, you're just relentlessly flirting with your audience – giggling, flicking your hair and passing notes. At some point, someone (you) needs to make the first move. You need to ask your customer for their number (or email address). If they give it to you, then there's at least a modicum of keenness; if not, you know it was all fluff and nonsense.

Now, a customer giving you their email address doesn't mean they'll go all the way down your funnel to buy, but it's at least the start of you being able to have a more intimate relationship with them.

Brand awareness land is noisy. Yes, you're shouting about your products and services, but so is everyone else, often right next to you. It's like being at a market in London's East End, with two fruit sellers yelling about their apples and pears – do you choose the seller with the best fruit or the seller who shouts loudest?

Lead generation tactics quiet the market – it's just you and your lead doing the do. But how do you get them to do the do with you?

Lead generation principles

Let's talk about what principles should guide you through the lead generation stage.

Principle 1: Consider different lead types

Of course, not all leads are created equally – you may get dozens of people signing up for your freebie and then crickets when it comes to buy. Often that's because you miss the next stage (see Chapter 18).

Back in Chapter 7 we talked about the factors of budget, time, level and connection for your customers. Another way to think about this is the BANT framework, which is a commonly used sales term – do they have the budget, authority, need and timeframe to buy from you?

- Does the prospect have the **budget** for your product or service? I know a lot of people would love to do my big SEO course but can't afford it (yet).
- Does your customer have the decision-making **authority**? This might seem like more of a big business question but it's not. Often, small business humans have to talk to their partner about making big purchases, and it's your job to give them the information and evidence to do that confidently.
- When does the customer **need** the solution? Is it an immediate need or a future need? Again, if you're selling a crocheting membership, the need might not be as urgent as, say, if you're selling a tax return course. This is why it's often necessary to create urgency with your launch model – more on this in Chapter 22.
- What is the customer's **timing** for their decision? Is it days, weeks or months? Some will slip down your funnel in a matter of weeks, but others may take much longer. Remember Sue and her seven years in my funnel? Don't give up.

Leads that don't meet the BANT criteria are still valuable – they may just require a bit more love and nurturing before moving them further along in the sales process.

TOON TIP This is one of the reasons I don't hide the pricing on my offerings or make people jump through dreadful discovery calls to find out the cost of my course. I know my course is a big investment, and I know many people will have to work towards affording my pricing.

Principle 2: Offer value

A lead magnet is a low-commitment freebie, gift or piece of content that potential customers can easily grab in exchange for their contact info (usually just their first name and email). Examples include ebooks, checklists, guides and webinars. I cover some of these later in this chapter.

It has to be free – if there's a fee it would be deemed a 'trip-wire product' (see Chapter 19).

It should provide real value, build trust, establish credibility and offer genuinely helpful content without asking for anything substantial from the customer. After they've accessed the lead magnet, they then move into your email nurture sequence (Chapter 18) where you can work towards them becoming a customer.

Don't be stingy with your lead magnets or feel like you're giving too much away. Aim to provide useful, relevant content that really shows your expertise, experience and authority, and builds trust.

I like to think of lead generation as focusing on the 'what' and the 'why' with a just little bit of 'how':

- **The 'what'** – what problem am I solving?
- **The 'why'** – why is it important?
- **The 'how'** – while I'm not going to give away all my tips for free, I am going to help you move forward by giving you some small solutions so you feel empowered and excited to take the next step.

For example, one of the lead magnets for my SEO course is a checklist. It gives around 30 tips on how to fix up SEO issues, with tools, examples and advice. It represents about 1% of my SEO knowledge.

My trip-wire product for SEO, on the other hand, is the 10 Day SEO Challenge, which provides more detail on bigger problems. It represents about 10% of my SEO knowledge.

The big course is comprehensive, but of course I can't cover everything I know, so it's around 70% of my SEO knowledge.

The rest I share via my ongoing membership the Digital Marketing Collective. Obviously, I'm acquiring new knowledge all the time, but I'm selective about what I add to the course – just because I'm more advanced doesn't mean my audience is.

Principle 3: Go beyond the obvious

One common fear when producing any kind of lead magnet material is worrying about people not wanting to download it because they can just google it. To combat this, you need to go beyond the obvious and provide some personal insights, tips and experience.

Principle 4: Keep it simple

When you're starting out, it can be tempting to launch dozens of lead generation ideas, and of course it's always good to test different ideas and see which generate the best results.

I now have several lead generation tactics for my SEO course, including:

- an SEO checklist
- a mini course
- a free Facebook community
- a free SEO SOS challenge.

But I started with just the checklist, and truth be told, it's still the most successful of them all.

Principle 5: Keep your landing page simple

For lead magnets, you don't need a monster sales page (I cover these in Chapter 19) as a simple landing page will suffice, with a bit of info, a few testimonials and some sign-up fields. You also don't need any fancy software; you can build a lead magnet landing page on your WordPress site in a few clicks.

I use the Gravity Forms plugin that's linked to my email platform (ActiveCampaign), which then sends the nurture sequence (see chapter 18).

The more fields you include on your lead generation landing page, the less likely customers will be to fill it in, but also the more commitment they're showing if they do:

- First name and email address – low commitment, low level of keenness
- First name, email address, mobile number, 'How did you find us?', website address and problem – high commitment, high level of keenness.

Principle 6: Measure everything

Ensure you keep a track of how many leads you generate each month and which of your brand awareness tactics is most effective. Remember, if

10,000 people see your brand awareness content and 1000 then sign up to your lead generation tactic, that gives you a conversion rate of 10%. Keep track of your conversion rate – I have a little spreadsheet where I track all this.

Lead generation tactics

There are dozens of lead generation tactics out there, including events, ebooks, paid ads, influencer marketing and conferences, but I'm going to focus on the four that worked best for me to sell ADPIP products.

Tactic 1: Webinars

A webinar is generally a free one-hour session where people turn up to be educated and, obviously, sold to. It can be live or pre-recorded.

There are dozens of bespoke platforms you can use to run webinars. I used Webinar Ninja for many years, which comes with all the bells and whistles, including pre-made landing pages, email sequences and video conferencing ability. But these days I just use Zoom, and build my own landing page on my WordPress site and create my own funnels in ActiveCampaign.

> **TOON TIP** If you want to see an example of a webinar, head to therecipeforseosuccess.com and look for 'Workshop' in the main navigation.

Webinars provide an opportunity to connect with your audience (although most webinar platforms don't allow you to see their faces, which is why I like Zoom instead). You can use Zoom Webinars, but I just use regular Zoom (large meeting) so I can see people and interact with them more. Webinars also provide a great way for your audience to try before they buy, and get to know you and your offering.

However, they come with some powerful downsides:

- Webinars have a bad reputation for being 45 minutes of the host showing off and promoting, and then two minutes of useful advice. This is why I call mine a 'workshop' instead of a 'webinar'.

- Although pre-recorded webinars allow people to watch in their own time zone, I feel they lose their dynamism. What's worse is when hosts pretend they're live and they're not. *(You can always tell.)*
- Getting people to turn up on a certain day and at a certain time is hard. My show-up rates aren't great – I average about 30% of people showing up on the day, with a trickle of people watching the replay.
- For me, the move from webinar to signing up for my low-cost offer isn't always great. I give a lot (possibly too much) value in my webinar, and I think for many that's enough.

In summary, I do use webinars in my model for Recipe, but they're not the most powerful lead generation tactic.

Tactic 2: Facebook groups

I have two big free Facebook groups:

1. The Misfit Entrepreneurs – for more generalised marketing and business advice
2. I Love SEO – a dedicated space to share SEO advice.

These are private groups where I can talk directly to my audience, and of course, to gain access I ask for the user's email address and send them my lead magnet.

The positives of Facebook groups include the following:

- They provide a great space to talk directly to your audience.
- Visibility of content seems to be higher in Facebook groups than for Facebook pages.
- You have the ability to control the membership and guide the conversations where you want them to go.
- You have the chance to really show your expertise, build relationships through content, Facebook Live sessions, tips and ideas.

The negatives include the following:

- You need to be a strong leader, to have rules and be willing to enforce them, even if it's difficult.

- Time is involved to keep the group vibe going, provide content and answer comments. (I set aside around 20 minutes a day for this.)
- Even though content visibility is higher, it's still not amazing.
- There's always the risk that Facebook will remove group functionality at some stage, which is why it's vital to collect email addresses.

Building community is one of my superpowers, and I hope it will be the topic of my next book.

Tactic 3: Mini courses

I have a free mini course for my SEO funnel called SEO Nibbles. It introduces customers to some core concepts in SEO and whets their appetite to take the next step.

Surprisingly, despite it being comprehensive, it's far less popular than my checklist.

Tactic 4: Checklists

My most popular lead magnet by far is my SEO checklist – it's been downloaded over 17,000 times.

(Psst: It's so successful that I've created a checklist on how to create a checklist. You can find it by googling 'Kate Toon How to create a lead magnet checklist'.)

Here's how to create your own checklist:

1. Remind yourself of your target audience.
2. Identify what problem you are trying to solve, and then identify what 1% of that problem looks like.
3. Identify your customer's number-one pain point.
4. Think of ten tips and points you could offer to help them solve that pain point.
5. Create a structure for your checklist, including an intro (explain how you're helping), middle (help), outro (explain how you helped) and call to action (invite them to take the next step).
6. List out your points, but not as questions that require 'yes' or 'no' answers.
7. Provide links to useful tools and content on your site that will help.

8. Get the checklist well proofread.
9. Include strong branding, a picture of you, your copyright statement and your URL.
10. Ideally, get it turned into an editable PDF by a graphic designer, or do it yourself in Canva.

TOON TIP You can also refer to the advice in the digital downloads chapter (Chapter 10).

Stephanie Holdsworth wants to create a free lead magnet that will drive parents of kids with eczema and allergies into her funnel and towards her health educational videos. She thinks the biggest pain point she can address is the fact that it takes so long to see a specialist.

She thinks about what she can create that helps these people but also positions her as an expert. She decides on a checklist resource.

She decides on the rough title '10 practical steps to take **before** you see a specialist'. She can use Magai to come up with something sexier later.

She starts with an intro, introducing herself and explaining what she's going to cover. Then, she lists out her points, which could include things like the following:

- Keep a trigger diary – what causes reactions? Where are you? What's the weather like?
- Keep a food diary – which foods cause reactions?
- Make a note of all toiletries used.
- Note which washing powders and conditioners you use.
- Make list of all fabrics worn and what impact they have.
- Create a list of questions.
- What solutions have you already tried?

She also includes ideas of things **not** to do, such as 'Don't google symptoms' and 'Don't look at images online', and she includes links to useful factsheets on hospital websites.

She finishes with an outro and an encouragement to take the next step and watch her low-cost trip-wire video tutorial.

She writes the checklist in Word, then gets a designer to create an editable PDF. For now, she uses the Digital Downloads app on Shopify to add her download to the site, following the guidelines in the Shopify help centre.

What about ebooks?

There are heaps of other lead magnet options, but my least favourite is ebooks, or books for that matter – which is ironic since you're reading mine right now.

I think books make great lead magnets, but they do also give the customer a problem (a massive book to read) rather than a quick solution (like the checklist does).

Also, books take a long time to write.

This book is essentially a lead magnet into my memberships and programs, but I wouldn't recommend a book to everyone! It's blooming hard work.

I also love a boot camp or challenge, but I cover them in Part V as they are more of a launch tactic than a year-round lead generation tactic.

TL;DR

Lead generation isn't about sleazy sales calls or trickery – it's about offering your customer a low-commitment way to access valuable content and to start their journey down your funnel. Some lead magnets are more powerful than others, and some take a lot of time and effort. I recommend starting with a simple checklist and going from there.

OVER TO YOU

Create your own lead magnet checklist using the tips in this chapter, save it as an editable PDF and upload it to your website.

＞木 ＞木

Chapter 18

Desire (and nurture)

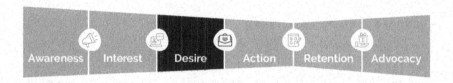

The desire stage is all about creating desire in your customer, making them burn with lust for your ADPIP. You do that by nurturing them – turning that tepid lead into a loving customer.

Your customer has requested your lead magnet, and now you must deliver it, generally via email. In simple terms, you need to create an automation in your email marketing platform and craft a series of emails to deliver that lead magnet and then move your lead further into your funnel.

An email nurture sequence is a series of scheduled, automated emails sent to your customers over a set period. The goal is to nurture relationships and gradually provide value, ultimately leading them to buy from you.

Why is email nurturing important?

Your customer has a problem, and you have the solution, but you need to persuade them that your solution is the best available.

Your email nurture sequence allows you to do this by:

- establishing you as an authority in your niche by sharing advice and tips
- building trust by sharing case studies and proof
- showing the value in what you offer by providing results from previous customers
- building a relationship with your customer by sharing personal stories
- showcasing your products and services by detailing their features, benefits and advantages.

Ideally, your email sequence is working for your business all the time and **selling your services** while you walk the dog or take a bath. It's also totally scalable – the same sequence works for 10 people or 10,000.

Email nurturing principles

Before we run through the actual format of the sequence, let's consider what principles should guide us.

Principle 1: Get the timing right

Your email nurture sequence should usually consist of between five and ten emails, sent one after another at daily, weekly or monthly intervals. The ideal frequency is a topic of debate – too many in a short period and it feels pushy, and people may get annoyed and unsubscribe; on the flip side, if they are too spaced out, people will lose the flow and get lost.

The main thing is that the emails are automated and prescheduled based on triggers, such as signing up to your lead magnet or when the customer opened the previous email.

Principle 2: Use progressive messaging

Each email should build upon the previous one by diving deeper into the topics provided and coming at the topic from different angles, such as via tips, stories and proof points. The goal is not just to disseminate facts but to build a relationship with relevant and useful content.

Principle 3: Personalise and segment

Likely all you'll have to begin with is your customer's first name and email address, but over time you can learn more about your customers, measuring what they click on and asking them what they're interested in. This data can then be incorporated to personalise the content and experience.

Remember, everyone loves the sound of their own name. Including the customer's name in your subject line can warm them up, but don't overdo it in the body of the email as it can quickly become cheesy.

Also, if you do know more about the customer, be wary about sharing that with them. A line saying, 'We noticed you purchased incontinence pads last week and wondered how your bladder feels today?' could be received with horror rather than appreciation.

Principle 4: Cover off consent and legals

When you collect data in any format, you must comply with the legal requirements in your country and the country of the subscriber. So, if you're collecting someone's email address to give them a lead magnet, you must also get their express permission to send them marketing material.

When I send emails, I like to add a sentence explaining why they're receiving the email; for example: 'You're receiving this email because you signed up to receive my SEO checklist'.

You also need to have a clear privacy policy and terms and conditions policy on your website. (Guinea pig Ingrid Fernandez can help with this.)

For more information on this, google 'GDPR' or 'email spam obligations'.

TOON TIP Dodgy marketers may encourage you to scrape emails from platforms or buy lists, but this is a bad idea – it will ruin your reputation and will not provide you with quality leads. It could even get you blacklisted by certain email platforms.

Principle 5: Allow customers to unsubscribe

It's vital to have a clear and easy 'unsubscribe' link on every email you send; don't make customers jump through hoops to leave your list.

The key is to create an engaging experience through emails spaced appropriately over time to nurture leads into customers. It's about delivering value first before overtly selling to build long-term loyalty.

Principle 6: Be more bread

While you can never expect your emails to be received as positively as a message from your favourite child or auntie, you don't want to be seen as spam. The best you can hope for is 'bread' – emails that people accept and may want to read one day but aren't champing at the bit to receive.

To stop your emails being judged as spammy, it's best not to write terrible subject lines. Here are a few tips on this:

- Don't use words that create unnecessary urgency, such as 'do it now' or 'last chance'.
- Don't use words that make exaggerated claims or promises, such as 'double your income', 'incredible deal' or 'once in a lifetime'.
- Avoid junk mail trigger words such as 'weight loss' or 'Viagra'.
- Don't say things like 'this isn't spam' or 'not junk'.
- Avoid money-related words such as 'free', 'discount' and 'bargain'.

Also, don't use all caps, exclamation points, coloured fonts or emojis, and don't add attachments to your email. (Instead, add links to where readers can get your lead magnet from your website – you'll save it in the media files on your site and use the URL in your email.)

Email deliverability is a big topic, but suffice it to say that not all emails will make it to their destination. Most good email tools these days (I use ActiveCampaign) allow you to run a spam check, which will check your content for any potential triggers.

You may also want to consider having a double opt-in email, which requires new subscribers to verify their email address via a confirmation email before they get their lead magnet. This ensures that the people on your list genuinely want to be there.

Obviously, I know you don't want to send spam on purpose, but it can still happen, so be cautious.

Email nurturing tactics

Here are some tactics to use when you're emailing.

Tactic 1: Use simple formatting

Stick with plain text for at least your first email. Plain-text emails may look ugly, but they get the message across faster, and they have a much higher chance of good deliverability. Remove **all** graphics – yes, even that pretty branded header. Once your customer has received a few emails, it's safe to say they're making it to the right spot, and you can start adding in graphics then. I know this impacts the brand experience, but there isn't going to be any experience if the customer doesn't receive your email.

Tactic 2: Keep subject lines short and sweet

If your subject lines are too long, they will truncate – especially on mobiles. I recommend that you use fewer than 50 characters and ensure your important words are at the start of the subject line. Again, don't use all caps in your subject line, not just because of spam but because sentence case is much friendlier.

For standard admin-related emails, clarity and simplicity are best. For email sequences, it's good to create a sense of mystery and pique the reader's natural curiosity.

TOON TIP There are dozens of subject-line generator tools out there, and AI tools such as ChatGPT and Magai can also help you.

Tactic 3: Clarify your message in the preheader text

Most email platforms allow you to include a short sentence of preheader text to further explain the information in the email. Ensure you don't just repeat the subject line.

Tactic 4: Get your sender/reply address right

Your 'From' address (and alias) should ideally be a person's name, as it's more friendly and inviting – for example, Kate@katetoon.com. If this feels too familiar for your liking, try to go with something warmer than 'info' or 'admin', such as 'hello' – for example, hello@katetoon.com.

Don't change the 'From' address on each email – keep it consistent. This will give you more chance of your email getting through to the reader and not ending up in the promo or junk folder. Remember that many of your customers will hopefully add your email address to their address book if they like what you're sending.

Finally, ensure your sender email and reply email are the same. Having different sender and reply emails can trigger spam filters.

TOON TIP Never use 'noreply@company.com'. It's not friendly. No one is going to add it to their address book, and you should never deny readers the option to come back to you.

Tactic 5: Consider your salutation and sign-off

Don't be cute. Start your email with a simple 'Hi/Hello [First name]'. And remember, this is not a formal letter, so avoid finishing with 'Kind regards' and go with a friendlier option, like 'Talk soon', or 'Hugs and Hamsters' (my personal sign-off).

Tactic 6: Include a call to action

Include a call to action on every email. What is the next step you want people to take? It doesn't have to be a big, fat button – even a simple URL will work, or perhaps a question that encourages the reader to email you back. You **want** people to email you back, because then you know they're really interested.

Crafting an email nurture sequence – a basic framework

Okay, so you have your lead magnet ready to go, you've created a simple landing page which collects first name and email address (and has a privacy check box so that you have permission to email the person), and you've hooked up this form to your email platform (or asked your developer to do this for you). Now it's time to create a series of automated emails to build that desire.

Table 18.1, overleaf, shows what a standard email nurture sequence could look like.

Table 18.1: A standard email nurture sequence

Email	Purpose	Send time	Subject line examples	Description
1	Welcomes and delivers lead magnet	Immediately	Steph: 'Does your child have eczema?' Tony: 'Have you ever built a WordPress website?' Ingrid: 'Do you have a terms and conditions policy on your website right now?'	Thank them for requesting your lead magnet, and provide a link for them to download it. Ensure the copy is warm and friendly and personality-filled. Tell them there's more good stuff coming, and perhaps ask them a question directly related to your ADPIP – getting replies is an awesome way to really start the relationship positively. (I find that those who take five minutes to reply are much more likely to become customers.)
2	Identifies major pain point	Day 1 (24 hours after email 1)	'Have you ever worried about X?' 'Most people think X, but if only they knew Y.' 'Do you know the number-one issue relating to [your business]?'	Write about a key issue your audience has, the number-one pain point. Perhaps tell a story of how you once had that problem and overcame it.

Email	Purpose	Send time	Subject line examples	Description
3	Provides case study or social proof	Day 2 (24 hours after email 2)	'Bob was struggling with [issue that relates to your business].'	Show your reader what life will be like after they become a customer. Perhaps write a case study about someone who has already experienced your ADPIP, sharing their challenges and results.
4	Offers help	Day 4 (48 hours after email 3)	'Are you making these mistakes?'	Provide some tips and advice that are genuinely useful to the reader and help them solve even more of the problem than your lead magnet did.
5	Provides call to action	Day 5 (24 hours after email 4)	'Do you need help with [thing that relates to your business]?'	Share your trip-wire product, a mini version of your big thing at a lower cost.
6	Encourages re-engagement	Day 7 (48 hours after email 5)	'Don't miss out on [offer].'	Try to create some urgency to buy your trip-wire product, even if it's evergreen. Use your 'paint the future' line here: 'Imagine when you've solved your problem'.
7	Encourages re-engagement again	Day 10 (72 hours after email 6)	'Are you still interested in [offer]?'	Encourage the reader one last time to sign up.

Now, this is quite an aggressive timeline. I like to allow more like three to four days between emails. Also, I obviously don't send emails 6 and 7 to anyone who has signed up for my trip-wire product.

Your email nurture sequence could continue after this, with more tips and advice, ultimately leading to your big offer. After around ten emails I generally put people back into my general list, where they receive my newsletter.

Here's an example of how I used an email nurture sequence for my Clever Copywriting School site. The subject lines follow the sequence shown in Table 18.1 and explain what each email is about:

1. 'Here's your download – The Ultimate Guide to Copywriting Pricing' (lead magnet)
2. 'Do you know the biggest fear most copywriters face?' (pain point)
3. '10 easy-peasy copywriting tips for new copywriters' (tips)
4. 'Do you use these essential copywriting tools?' (tips)
5. 'Isn't it time you looked a little more professional?' (first sell – digital downloads)
6. 'Become a better copywriter – using just your ears' (free content)
7. 'Feel like you need a little support on your copywriting journey?' (second sell – the Clever Copywriting School membership)

After this, they're added to the general email list, and those who've taken action in email 7 join the waitlist for The Clever Copywriting School.

When it comes to measuring results, here are the metrics you want to look at:

- How many people are **opening** your emails? (Note: You can't measure open rates for plain-text emails, which is a shame, but I'd still stick with plain text for the first email.)
- How many people are **clicking** through to your content?
- How many **conversions** are you getting for your trip-wire product?
- How many people **make it to the end** of your automation without unsubscribing?
- How many leave your list and **unsubscribe**?

For my little sequence above, the click-through and unsubscribe rates are shown in Table 18.2.

Table 18.2: Click-through and unsubscribe rates for my
Clever Copywriting School email nurture sequence

Email	Click-through rate	Unsubscribe rate
1	Unknown	0.99%
2	14.5%	1.15%
3	11.1%	0.63%
4	9.1%	0.73%
5	17.7%	1.22%
6	2.7%	0.23%
7	14.8%	0%

This means that approximately 95% of people make it through the
entire sequence, which is pretty dang good. I put this down to the fact
that I offer constant value and don't send the emails too frequently.

If your results aren't strong, you can make changes to the email
subject lines, content and the timing gaps. I'll be honest and say it's
largely trial and error.

Bonus email nurturing quick tips

Here are some quick-fire email nurturing tips to finish off the chapter:

1. **Use social proof in your emails.** I like to include a quote or
    testimonial after my sign-off.
2. **Use animated gifs.** Once you've sent your first new emails,
    consider adding animated gifs to your emails – they can be fun
    and engaging. I use a tool called GIPHY to create mine.
3. **Keep it short.** Use an informal, conversational style and an active
    voice, and keep the messages short and sweet.
4. **Proofread.** Ensure you check thoroughly for errors and typos
    before you send, and consider using a professional proofreader.
    Although, it's kind of the law of emails that you'll only spot those
    typos after you've sent the email ☺.

TL;DR

Creating an email nurture sequence for your ADPIP is the best way to build trust and create a loyal audience in a less noisy space than social media. Don't rush to sell in the first email; take your time and offer genuine, valuable content before you ask them to buy.

OVER TO YOU

Consider what you'll include in your seven emails and what the subject lines will be.

Chapter 19

Action

Action can mean many different things, and in our slippery little funnels there are several actions we want people to take. We want them to:

1. sign up to our lead magnet
2. buy our trip-wire product
3. buy our ADPIP
4. buy a second ADPIP
5. buy a third ADPIP (and more!)
6. sign up to our affiliate program.

Figure 19.1 (overleaf) shows what this can look like.

I spoke about lead magnets in Chapter 17, but what is a **trip-wire product**? I'm not a fan of daft marketing terms but this is good because it's visual. Imagine a lush forest. We, the customers, are sniffing around in the undergrowth, trying to find that perfect nut or worm (course or membership), and then we spot a tasty morsel. Sure, it's not huge, just a bite-sized chunk, but still we want it. We race towards it, and suddenly we stumble across a trip-wire. Bam! The cage descends and we're trapped.

Figure 19.1: An example sequence of customer actions

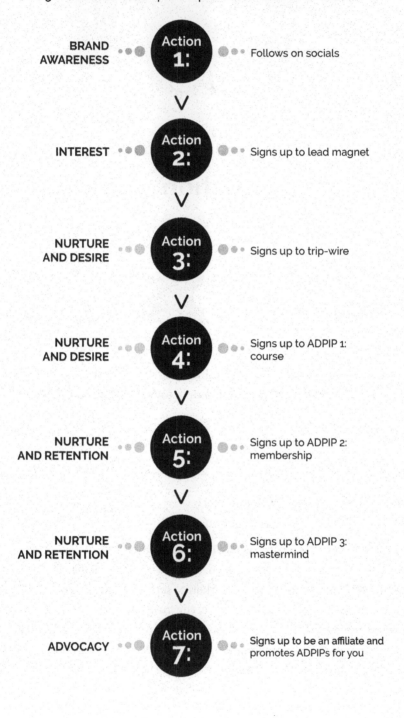

BRAND AWARENESS	Action 1:	Follows on socials
INTEREST	Action 2:	Signs up to lead magnet
NURTURE AND DESIRE	Action 3:	Signs up to trip-wire
NURTURE AND DESIRE	Action 4:	Signs up to ADPIP 1: course
NURTURE AND RETENTION	Action 5:	Signs up to ADPIP 2: membership
NURTURE AND RETENTION	Action 6:	Signs up to ADPIP 3: mastermind
ADVOCACY	Action 7:	Signs up to be an affiliate and promotes ADPIPs for you

Well, a trip-wire product is a bit like this. It's a low-cost product designed to start a relationship with our customer, to lure them further into our funnel and increase the likelihood of them making future purchases. Trip-wire products aren't really sold for their own value but as a means to an end – they are intended to familiarise customers with us and make them feel comfortable spending more in the future.

Unlike a lead magnet, it's a paid product, but so inexpensive that customers will purchase it without much thought. The trip-wire does a few jobs:

- It warms up our relationship with the customers – they get to know us more.
- It allows us to show our authority and expertise, establishing our credibility and building trust.
- It gives a taster of what's to come in our bigger ADPIP.
- It encourages people to get their credit card out and go through our purchase process, and therefore creates familiarity (and logins). This makes the next purchase easier.

The low price (ideally under $100) creates a low barrier to entry and a low commitment, making it easy for customers to take a chance on an unfamiliar brand.

Once someone has purchased our trip-wire, it's easier to upsell them to our big ADPIP and cross-sell them to other small offerings.

> **TOON TIP** Often, trip-wire products are sold at near cost or a slight loss, as their real purpose is customer acquisition. Immediate profit is secondary to lifetime value.

To upsell customers to our big ADPIP, we need to put effort into our conversion copywriting. Conversion is just another fancy word for action. Conversion copywriting narrows the focus to a single goal – to get people to act. As discussed, this could mean downloading a lead magnet, signing up to our newsletter or some other action. But for the purposes of this chapter, it's all about encouraging the customer to buy our ADPIP. We do this by creating a well-written sales page.

A **sales page** is created to sell one thing – just one. It's a web page that sells our ADPIP while we sleep, explaining our ADPIP and reassuring customers of the benefits, and focusing only on closing the deal and collecting payment.

It's not a landing page. Landing pages gather leads, and although they contain elements of a sales page, they are much shorter and simpler. Some of my landing pages are merely an intro paragraph and a couple of data collection fields.

It's not a home page. Our website home page gives an overview of what we do, introduces our brands, offers multiple jumping-off points and acts as a 'magazine cover', teasing the content within our site.

Sales pages are single-minded. They sell one thing and one thing only, and will be the last page a customer sees before handing over their money.

What if I feel icky about sales?

Many of us associate sales with white-toothed, shiny-suited, smooth-talking gits – with door-to-door salesmen, cheesy infomercials and tediously long sales letters. Sales feels like it's about trying to trick people into purchasing, but it isn't. I mean, I know I just described it as trapping cute little animals, but let's imagine those little animals want to be trapped.

We have something that people need in their lives, something that's going to help them solve a problem, fulfil a need or sate a desire, and we should not be ashamed of that. They have a problem, and we have the solution.

And here's a big surprise for you: **people like buying stuff**.

Remember our funnel? We're not trying to sell to the unaware, or even the problem aware – we're selling to the solution aware. These people want to make a purchase but are looking for the right evidence and information to feel they're making a good purchase choice. If you don't sell to them, someone else will (possibly with an inferior product).

Sales page principles

In just a second, I'm going to tell you exactly how to write your sales page. Cool, huh? But before I do, let's run through some core principles.

Principle 1: Get the length right

Your sales page should be as long as it needs to be. There should be enough information to sell your product and enough proof to break down any barriers to purchase (see Figure 19.2).

Figure 19.2: Sales page conversion chart

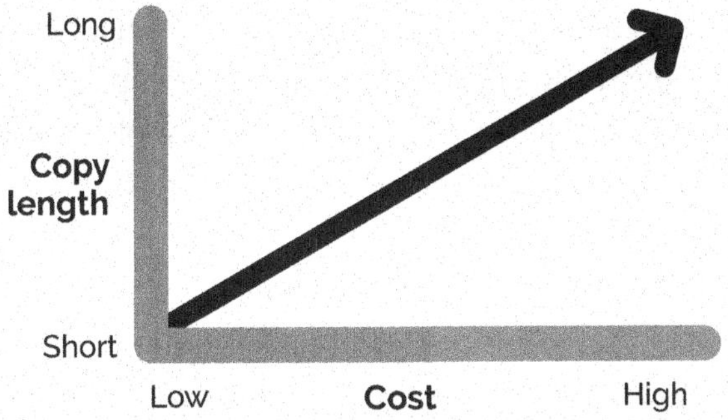

If your ADPIP has a higher price and is a more complex offering, then you'll need more copy (around 5000 words). If your ADPIP has a lower price and a simple structure, then short copy will suffice (around 2000 words). Longer pages also give you more SEO power as there's more opportunity to use (and rank for) multiple keyword phrases, but of course, long sales pages do lead to 'endless scroll' and information overload, so you have to strike a fine balance.

Principle 2: Make it part of your primary navigation

Your sales page should live in your primary navigation – don't hide it away. Google considers pages with no links to them 'orphan' pages and is not a fan of them. Also, if someone finds their way to your sales page in some obscure way, they might not be able to find their way back.

Principle 3: Use the right structure

Although sales pages look complex, they all follow a simple structure, and when you understand this structure you can see it in every sales page you read:

1. the problem the product solves

2. an explanation of the product
3. proof the product works
4. action to buy the product.

I run through what goes into each of these sections later in this chapter.

Principle 4: Be specific

Rather than bombastically claiming to have trained thousands of people, give an actual number. At the time of writing, I have the figure '1505 students' on The Recipe for SEO Success sales page. *(It's more than that now.)* Specificity is more credible and believable than big abstract phrases like 'lots of students' or 'hundreds of worksheets'.

Principle 5: Include clear calls to action

A call to action is a button or text that encourages the customer to act – in this case, to make a purchase. There are often multiple calls to action on a sales page, all leading to the same conclusion. A good sales page can live or die by the quality of its call-to-action buttons. Ideally, a call to action should finish the sentence 'I want to…' *(I think I learned this tactic from conversion copywriter Joanna Wiebe.)* Keep your call-to-action buttons to just a few words.

Here are some bad examples – they're all cold, non-specific and dull verbs:

- 'Click here'
- 'Download'
- 'Submit'
- 'Enter'
- 'Subscribe'.

Here are some better examples:

- 'Try [name of ADPIP]'
- 'Buy now' *(simple but effective)*
- 'Get [name of ADPIP]'
- 'Grab your spot'
- 'Join the community'
- 'Join today'

- 'Join the fun'
- 'Join thousands of others'
- 'Start right now'.

Principle 6: Use imagery

Often, sales pages feel hard to digest because they're so text-heavy. Remember, many people are visual creatures. Try to use photography to break up text.

Use icons to explain simple concepts visually, and use video to show your face and demonstrate how the product works. Keep demos short and sweet – don't give the game away like a bad movie trailer.

Sales page tactics

To make your life easier, I'm now going to take you through a short, snappy, step-by-step guide to writing your sales page.

(By the way, I offer a full sales-page-writing course on my site katetoon.com, and it's included free as a bonus in the Six Figures While You Sleep Program.)

Step 1: Consider the purpose of your sales page

You need to review your work so far and be able to confidently answer these questions:

- What is the (single) purpose of your sales page? What one thing do you want to sell?
- How would you describe your product or service? Describe what you want to sell in a few words. Will the buyer understand your description?
- Why would someone buy your product or service? What problem are you solving?
- How will they feel after buying your product or service? Happy? Relieved? Confident? Brave? Sexy?
- What would stop them buying your product? Tackle the big objections head-on.

TOON TIP The whole way through writing your sales page, keep thinking, 'WIIFM?' (What's in it for me?) I keep a Post-it note on my computer that says, 'So what?', which forces me to move beyond the obvious.

For example, 'The course has 12 modules'. 'SO WHAT?' Well, this means it's super comprehensive and no question is left unanswered.

Don't focus just on the literal features – explain the benefits and the advantages of your ADPIP.

Step 2: Include SEO elements

Although you're likely to drive most of your traffic to this page via your lead generation pieces and funnel, some people may still stumble across you through search engine results pages, so give them a reason to click. You'll need:

- **a focus keyword** – the phrase you really want to rank for (likely your strong product name)
- **synonyms** – additional, similar phrases to use throughout the page
- **a title tag** – A 60-character description of your phrase (with your focus keyword phrase at the start), such as, 'The Recipe for SEO Success Course | learn DIY SEO today'
- **a meta description** – a compelling two-line (150-character) snippet that truly sells the course, such as, 'Drive more traffic and conversions with the ultimate search engine optimisation course for small business and ecommerce. Easy, affordable and fun'. It's seriously up there for the most overlooked but critical piece of copy – it's the first piece of sales content web users will see from you.

Step 3: Write an attention-grabbing headline (and sub)

This is where you grab their attention. If you know your audience well, you should be able to write a headline that truly speaks to them. Advertising guru David Ogilvy said, 'On the average, five times as many people read the headline as read the body copy. When you have written your headline, you have spent eighty cents out of your dollar'.

I love a headline that addresses a pain point or makes a promise, such as 'Wish your website ranked higher on Google?' or 'Get more traffic and sales from Google'.

Then it's time to introduce your subheadline. I like to think of your headline and sub as Batman and Robin – Batman comes in with a strong, high-impact one-liner, and Robin comes in and expands on that and backs it up. Then you have a little call to action for those who are super keen. Figure 19.3 shows how this looks on my most powerful sales page.

> **TOON TIP** You will end up with multiple call-to-action buttons on your page. Why? Because people view your page in 'chunks', scrolling down. They could decide to act at any time, so they should always be able to see a button that helps them take that action.

Figure 19.3: A headline, sub and call to action from my website

Step 4: Write your opener

Here's where you break down what you're offering and how it's going to solve the customer's problem and change their lives. Keep it friendly and chatty. You can refer to the unique selling proposition (USP) you wrote in Chapter 6. A neat way of doing this is to list a few questions that the customer is likely asking themselves.

Here's my opener from my SEO course sales page:

*Wish your site ranked **higher in search engine results?***

Confused by Google tech speak and jargon?

Been burned by dodgy SEO companies?

YES? Well, you need The Recipe for SEO Success course.

The most comprehensive DIY search engine optimisation course ever.

With 1,505 graduates so far, this is the most popular SEO course worldwide.

Follow this with a call-to-action button that says either 'Join now' or, when the course is closed, 'Join waitlist'.

Another option here is to use the PASO copywriting formula:

- **Problem** – the problem the customer currently faces
- **Agitate** – what will happen if they don't solve the problem
- **Solution** – positioning your product as the solution
- **Outcome** – what will happen after they buy your product.

 For Tony Cosentino, this could read as follows:

- **Problem** – 'Struggling to get your WordPress business off the ground?'
- **Agitation** – 'Finding clients, sorting out processes and deciding how to price your services are a real struggle for most WordPress developers, and if you don't get it right, you'll be stuck in a feast-and-famine cycle.'
- **Solution** – 'I can help. My [name of membership] community can help you price for profit, streamline processes, understand best practice, win clients and stay up to date with the latest WordPress news and tools.'
- **Outcome** – 'Finally, a safe space to ask all your questions, build a network, and get expert advice and all the support and coaching you need.'

Step 5: Include a video

I like to include a little two-minute video next, which is essentially of me reading out the copy above. It puts a face and a voice to the brand and lets people decide if they like the vibe.

Step 6: Create urgency

You might want to create a little urgency in this opening section above the fold (the area of content viewable before scrolling) – perhaps a countdown clock, talk of limited spots or some kind of early sign-up offer. This can be a smart way to drive sales. Essentially, the goal is to create FOMO.

 Don't create false urgency and scarcity on your page. I remember signing up to some webinar software that had an offer for the next 12 hours only. I frantically signed up, not wanting to miss out. The next day, when I visited the site, the same offer was there with the clock reset. Yuck! It totally broke my trust and made me instantly dislike the brand.

I use a countdown clock on my sales page to let people know when the course is going to launch and to manage expectations. I only reset it when I relaunch the course.

Step 7: Explain your offering

All the steps so far address the problem the product solves. Now, you flesh out your offering. Explain how it works, who it's for, what's included and more. The more complex your product or service, the more content you'll need. This is where you can break down exactly what's in your ADPIP – the specifics around course modules, number of calls, degree of one-on-one attention, digital downloadables and whatever else you're including.

Remember not to just sit in features land, but instead tell the whole story:

- **Features** – what a thing has
- **Benefits** – how those things help
- **Advantages** – how this is going to change your life.

For Stephanie Holdsworth, this could read as follows:

Our 60-minute short training sessions will help you understand all the complexities of allergies and eczema, comparing treatments, demystifying terminology and busting common myths. *These clear, practical videos will help you feel calmer and more confident about the road ahead (and stop that late-night symptom googling).*

Step 8: Specify your audience

Now you can deal with who the product or service is for. For example:

This nutrition course is for you if:
- *you've tried all those fad diets and they're not working for you*
- *you want to learn simple ways to prepare healthier meals*
- *you don't have time to buy a million obscure ingredients.*

It can also be helpful to clarify who your product or service is not for – it's better than having dissatisfied customers. For example:

This nutrition course is not for you if:
- *you're not ready to live a healthier life*
- *you're not willing to learn new tactics and adopt new habits*
- *you can't commit to a six-week program.*

Often, these who-it's-not-for bits can come across as a bit passive aggressive, so don't include them unless there are some definite and genuine exclusions. For example, my course really isn't suitable for those who already have an advanced understanding of SEO.

Step 9: Tell a story

There are likely to be other people out there selling what you're selling, so give them a reason to buy from **you**. Why are you selling this? What makes you different? How did you get here? Make a connection with the reader and show you care.

It's helpful to follow this formula:

1. I was here with the same problem as you.
2. I took these steps and overcame these challenges.
3. Now I'm here, and these are the results and benefits I've found.

TOON TIP Don't forget to add your headshot – people want to see who is offering them this ADPIP.

Step 10: Provide proof

Okay, now it's time to provide proof that your ADPIP works. This can be hard if it's brand new, but you can use testimonials and feedback from your lead magnet and trip-wire here too. Grab all the results, testimonials, case studies and logos you can and show them off. It's much easier to let someone else toot your horn than try to do it yourself – that's why we love testimonials.

Proof falls into four broad categories:

1. **Results.** These are specific results from previous customers showing how you solved their problem. They can be anecdotal ('I feel more confident') or, preferably, statistical ('I made 27% more sales').

2. **Testimonials.** According to a 2024 survey by BrightLocal, 50% of people trust online reviews as much as those from friends,[4] so it's good to have a decent number of testimonials on your sales page. It's tempting to dot them throughout the page, but I prefer to move them towards the end – people need to know what you're selling before they want to know why it's awesome.

3. **Case studies.** Case studies are longer stories detailing the transformation your ADPIP created for a customer. I like to include shortened versions on my sales page, then link to a separate page (in a new window) where people can read further if they want to (without losing my sales page).

4. **Logos.** Next, you can include logos of businesses you've worked with, media you've been featured in, memberships and associations you're a member of, or awards you have won. Or all four. Of course, get permission to use logos before you pop them on your site.

TOON TIP As I'm teaching SEO, I love to use charts showing how much my students' traffic has increased or how much more money they have made.

---

4 brightlocal.com/research/local-consumer-review-survey

If you're going to use testimonials, make sure you:

- **keep them short** – one line only (you can have a separate page for fully fleshed-out testimonials)
- ensure they **cover a range of topics** so they're not all talking about just value but also support, content, community and more
- **include the person's full name and business, as well as a link to that business,** so people know they're real (there is NEVER a case for including false testimonials)
- ideally **include a headshot**, often grabbable off LinkedIn
- use a mix of **video and written** testimonials.

Obviously, if someone gives you their testimonial, they are giving you permission to use it. I sweeten the deal by giving them a backlink, which in turn helps their SEO. Remember, even if people are raving fans of your course, not everyone will be comfy giving a testimonial – don't take it personally.

> **TOON TIP** If you're brand new to ADPIPs, it can be a good idea to offer free or heavily discounted spots to a few people at the start in return for the promise of testimonials.

Step 11: Provide guarantees

Guarantees make customers feel safe and, therefore, encourage conversion. It sounds crazy, but if you have a clear refund policy, you're more likely to make sales. Giving people an out shows that you're confident about what you're selling. What can you offer your customers?

> **TOON TIP** I offer my SEO course students a full refund within the first two weeks of the course. There are no hoops to jump through to get this. I do not want to keep someone's money if they're not happy. Over the years, only a few people have taken me up on it – all because of illness or a life crisis.

Step 12: Display pricing

Now the customer should be ready to act.

Keep your pricing panel clear and clean. Consider using the headline 'Your investment' for this section as it sounds more solid than 'The price'.

Be sure to:

- make it clear what currency your pricing is in (many entrepreneur types go with US dollars, but that strikes me as foolish if your audience is primarily in the UK or Australia; you can add a currency conversion tool to help people who are not in your country work out their price, and some platforms, such as WooCommerce, allow you to sell in multiple currencies)
- be transparent about whether your pricing includes tax (and if you're unsure on this, check with your accountant)
- add credit card icons to show which payment methods you take.

You can also pimp your pricing a little using some well-worn psychology tactics:

- **The power of three.** Often it's good idea to take the three bears approach to pricing – a lower-cost price (Baby Bear), a middle price (Daddy Bear) and a top-level price (Mummy Bear). Then, you can highlight the 'most popular' option (the one you really want to sell). It's a good idea for this to be your middle option.
- **The magic number seven.** Numbers that end with a seven seem a lot smaller than numbers that end with a zero.
- **Removing commas.** Commas make numbers feel bigger, so try to avoid using them.
- **Longer is more.** If you have three pricing levels, make the biggest, most expensive package the longest visually on the page – include more bullets.

If you offer pay-as-you-go (PAYG) options, be sure to make obvious the frequency and the amount to be paid (and cover in your terms and conditions what happens if a payment is missed).

Step 13: Finish with FAQs

Finish the page with a selection of questions and answers that you think will help the customer make their final decision. What's holding the customer back? For example:

Can I get a refund?
Do payments automatically renew?

Address any final objections with straightforward answers.

A common question is, 'If I don't buy now, will there be another opportunity?' Don't give them a limited time to buy only to start a new offer the day after. Keep it real or you'll lose trust. An FAQ panel is a fast way to disseminate boring information without distracting your customer from the conversion.

I like to have a PRICING – FAQ – PRICING sandwich at the bottom of my sales page.

As I've mentioned, I have a whole course on writing sales pages, with proven tactics. My Recipe for SEO Success page is also a good example to check out when you're writing yours, as it's my real big money earner.

Bonus sales page quick tips

Just because I love sales pages, here are some quick-fire tips to finish off the chapter:

- **Give permission.** It sounds odd, right, that people need permission to buy something they want to buy? But often, customers need to be reminded that it's okay to make this decision, that they're doing the right thing and that they won't regret it. For example, 'If you're wondering if now's the right time for you to take a step toward SEO success, I'm going to ask you a question: if not now, when? The sooner you bite the Google bullet, the sooner you'll be soaring to SEO success'.

- **Paint the future.** Give the reader a little sniff of what the future might hold. Remember the advantage from earlier – what would it feel like to have that advantage? For example, 'Imagine what it will feel like to finally get to grips with Google and have fresh leads flowing in every single week',

- **Remove distraction.** Don't include a sidebar on your sales page, and remove all pop-ups and fiddly bits. If you do need to link to other pages in your site, ensure they open in a new tab or window so customers don't lose the sales page altogether.

- **Make sharing easy.** Consider adding social share buttons that slide down the page as you scroll so people can tell their friends about your amazing ADPIP.
- **Check on mobile.** Sales pages can look great on desktop but be torture on mobile devices. Consider turning off some chunks of your page on a mobile. It can be hard to choose which chunks to remove, so you can do some A/B testing or use trial and error.
- **Be consistent in how you use case:**
  - ALL CAPS is great for headlines and call-to-action buttons.
  - Title Case is odd – I don't like it!
  - Sentence case is great for general copy and subheadlines.
  - lowercase is odd and confuses the reader – don't use it.

TOON TIP You can use heat-mapping software to see which parts of your page get the most 'eyeballs'. This makes choosing what to remove less subjective. There are several apps and plugins that do this – my favourite is HotJar.

There is so much more I could say about sales pages, but this chapter must end at some point, so I hope this has given you a good start.

TL;DR

You're now able to pull together a schmick sales page that has all the elements necessary to convert a casual potential customer into a raving, paying fan. Go forth and sell without sleaze. You got this.

OVER TO YOU

It's time to map out your sales page. I recommend grabbing my sales page checklist and course from the Kate Toon shop to stress test your ideas and ensure you haven't missed anything.

✎ ✎

Chapter 20

Retention

Awareness   Interest   Desire   Action   Retention   Advocacy

It might seem a little premature to be thinking about customer retention strategies when you don't even have any ADPIP customers yet. But, as always, we must start with the end in mind, and often it's a lack of planning ways to keep customers happy that means an ADPIP dies after a few launches.

Customer retention is all about keeping existing customers happy and buying your products for the long term rather than losing them to your competitors. Retention rates measure how many customers you keep over a given period, and obviously, the higher the rate, the better.

Businesses often spend a great deal of time nurturing customers to get the sale but then utterly abandon them after they've handed over their money, which is sucky and not the way forward.

I could have lumped retention together with advocacy, as I think the tactics that encourage people to stay often also encourage people to become advocates. So, bear that in mind as you read through this chapter.

Why is customer retention important?

It's commonly believed that it's cheaper to keep an existing customer than to acquire a new customer. While these articles have mostly been debunked, I would argue while it may not be cheaper, it is easier. Another positive is that loyal and happy customers are far more likely to promote your brand and products through word of mouth, which is a very inexpensive form of advertising.

Strong retention rates also mean financial stability and predictability. You can look ahead over several months and feel confident that you'll still have the customers you have today.

Retention principles

With all the tactics outlined, the goal is to keep customers happy by giving them ongoing value, convenience and reasons to stay loyal for the long term.

A big warning here.

No matter how hard you try to keep your members happy, some won't be. The internet is a strange place, and people can be offended by the smallest thing. One comment, one meme, can be enough to piss someone off and undo all your hard work.

Over the years I've been accused of rudeness, favouritism and so many other isms you would not believe. I've met people in person who have told me 'I thought you didn't like me' because I missed a comment on a particular post.

As your membership grows, it will get harder and harder to give people that personalised feel. All your members will feel they have a connection to you, but it's hard for you to have a connection with all of them. It's super important to monitor your moods and not get online if you're having a bad day. I've made the 'mistake' of oversharing in my groups over the years, but I'm much more restrained these days. I must remember I'm the leader of the group, not just a member.

Something my good friend Mel Leyshon told me really soothed me: 'It's not your job to remember everyone; it's their job to be memorable.'

This brings me to this chapter's sole principle, which is to just do your best – it's all you can do.

Retention tactics

It's unlikely that anyone is going to become an advocate for you right off the bat. Rather, advocacy grows organically over time. Sometimes it even shrinks as time goes on and people get a little disenfranchised. Generally, someone who stays in your world and buys repeatedly is more likely to become an advocate than a one-time wonder.

So, here are some effective retention strategies that have worked for me and you might want to try.

Tactic 1: Use launches for your ADPIPs

I know launches seem like a hassle (we'll make them less of a hassle in Chapter 22), but over and above the pain of admin, launching provides a great user experience. There's a sense of excitement in people joining your thing; it also creates a little community of people who are joining together with the same hopes, dreams and fears.

Tactic 2: Provide an excellent onboarding experience

Whether it's a $27 digital download or $27,000 mastermind, try to create a great first experience.

Even with a simple digital download, you can send a speedy email with a receipt, and follow up with a 'thank you for purchasing' and possibly a little guide on how to access and use the download.

For courses, memberships and masterminds, your new-member onboarding experience is a crucial tool for cultivating long-term love, as it sets the tone for the entire experience. You want to be as genuinely welcoming and informative as you can, which in turn makes it easy for new customers to feel comfy and get involved.

Here are a few tactics I've tried:

· **Mapping out the onboarding process.** Try to get into your new customers' slippers and imagine what challenges they'll have when they first purchase
· **Turning the onboarding process into useful and actionable content.** I have an email onboarding automation (which steps members through the first actions they could take with the course, membership or mastermind), an introduction video

(where I outline the mission, values and content of the ADPIP) and an introduction module (where I detail all the ways to use the membership, how to contact me, how to deal with potential tech issues and more)

- **New member orientation.** A live session after each launch where I can meet all new members and talk about their pain points
- **An introduction post in the groups.** I provide a post where people can introduce themselves to new members and older members can say hi.

Don't forget to reach out to newbie members when they're settled in to ask for feedback on their onboarding experience so you can improve it every time.

Tactic 3: Provide fantastic customer service

Give your customers a clear way to contact you and aim for 24- to 48-hour responses. Be responsive and resolve issues quickly, both in the early days and many months later.

Create FAQ pages and tutorials to deal with common issues, and consider creating a chatbot to handle regular questions.

Tactic 4: Make it personal

While it can be tempting to see each new sale and sign-up as just another row on your spreadsheet, try to make the experience as personal as possible. Gather information about your customers, take note of their individual pain points, then tailor content and communication to them. But don't be creepy. One of my Digital Marketing Collective members, Lauren Moxey, told me this:

> I once signed up to something (I can't remember what the product was, just that it was a bad experience!). I got an email that was a personalised welcome video from one of their team. Sweet, right?
>
> Wrong. It was uber creepy. It came through a third-party email platform, so I had no idea who was sending it. And the video was taken in some random dark room of their house.
>
> I never quite got over those initial feelings and moved on from the product quickly.

TOON TIP Even though I have hundreds of members now, I remember so many of them. This might be a Toon superpower, but I don't think so. It's because I work hard to connect the dots, to make a connection – Stephanie, who ate bananas on our Recipe call; Lucy, who had cool aeroplane wallpaper; Jodie and her dog, Wally. It's not just about their business – it's about them as people.

Tactic 5: Create community

Joining a new community (for a course, membership or mastermind) can be daunting, so encourage connection however you can. Giving your members a strong sense of community makes them feel included, safe and happy, which makes them want to join in more.

Here are some ways I foster community:

- **Facebook groups** – I use Facebook groups for all my ADPIPs; these groups make it easy and convenient for members to connect, share information and ask questions (as I've mentioned, I've tried alternatives, but my audience can't be bothered to learn a new platform when they're already using FB regularly)
- **Buddies** – I have a buddy system set up whereby older members 'adopt' newer members and guide them through the first few months
- **Chats** – I have regular 'ask me anything' sessions where everyone can get to know each other
- **Friday Lives** – each Friday I encourage members to go live and talk about something happening in their business
- **Subcommunities** – since I have a broad selection of humans in my courses and memberships, I try to create sub 'gangs' to make the larger group less intimidating, just by using tags and regular connection posts.

Tactic 6: Reinforce your awesomeness often

Remind customers why they chose you and how you continue to solve their problems better than others. Share any good feedback you get within your community, and add testimonials to the sales page.

Take time to regularly highlight key features of your ADPIP that existing members might have forgotten about. As business owners, our products are burned into our brains and souls, but to our customers they're just a small part of their busy lives. Also, this demonstrates you're committed to helping people get the maximum bang for their buck.

> **TOON TIP** I have dozens of amazing free templates in my membership, but members often forget about them after they join, so I post regular content in the Facebook group promoting all the freebies, masterclasses and courses.

Tactic 7: Show up

If you're heading up your ADPIP, don't fob people off onto minions as soon as they've paid. I remember joining a course a long time ago, and I went to the Facebook group and had a scroll but couldn't see a single post from the actual course leader. Instead, I saw that my only touchpoint with him would be that once a week, he'd pick a few questions from the group at random and do a ten-minute live video. Everything else was handled by his team.

This would have been fine if the expectation had been set upfront, but it hadn't. I immediately asked for a refund – and, after being made to jump through many hoops, was begrudgingly granted it.

Tactic 8: Make payment renewals easy

Streamline payment to reduce friction so it's a no-brainer for customers to stay. If your ADPIP has a rolling subscription, be aware that this will cause headaches. People lose cards and get phished, and their cards eventually expire – this means bounced payments and chasing people up.

Try to set some business rules around payment, always with kindness and good grace. For example, someone who is struggling could have an extra week to pay.

Also, send reminders about payment. I send a seven-day notice and a three-day notice, giving people ample warning and preventing a nasty surprise when the payment comes out.

Tactic 9: Ask for feedback and implement changes

Yes, you may have created your ADPIP with a clear plan, but you're finding that it isn't connecting quite as you'd like. Ask your customers for feedback, and show them that their voice matters. If you get feedback and make the changes requested, you'll build trust, showing your customers that they're appreciated.

Don't see making changes to your ADPIP as a sign of weakness – it shows great strength and leadership to be able to adapt to meet customer needs.

I've tried out so many different ideas in my groups, but before I do, I always seek the opinion of the existing members via:

- simple **polls** in the group
- **idea posts** asking members what they want next or what they feel is missing
- **contentment surveys** to find out if members are generally satisfied, asking specifically what they think needs improvement
- anonymous **exit surveys** when members leave explaining why they chose to leave.

Also, as my groups have scaled, some solutions no longer fit, and I have needed to come up with new strategies. Be open to evolving, and don't stick rigidly to your plan.

I'll be honest and say that I save reading exit surveys for 'strong mind days', because of course, even though I'm an absolute wonder beast, there are parts of my business that aren't perfect. When people leave, it's easy to take it personally, especially if you're a strong force in your product, but remember – it's not all about you.

Alternatively, get someone else in your business (such as a virtual assistant) to read the surveys and summarise the necessary changes for you. They're one step away and will likely be much less emotional.

Tactic 10: Share success stories

Share customer success stories and testimonials – social proof from others boosts trust and confidence in your solution.

We love to hero members of the group, celebrating their wins both in the community, on socials and via our regular newsletters.

Tactic 11: Provide opportunities

I like to reward people who have invested in me by offering them:

- **discounts** – I offer discounts to customers who purchase one ADPIP and then another
- **promotion** – I invite members onto my podcasts and offer them opportunities to write blog posts and email introductions
- **speaking opportunities** – I generally pick all my speakers for my conferences and events from among members of my Digital Marketing Collective
- **expert status** – I elevate loyal members to experts within my course and communities (provided, of course, they are experts in their field!)
- **affiliates** – I join my members' affiliate programs and promote their products and programs
- **referrals** – I regularly connect people, drop their names in other groups and recommend them for job and PR opportunities.

I even create the odd Reel on behalf of some of my ecommerce members to promote their products, just for fun as I love a good silly Reel.

Tactic 12: Keep members engaged

It's easy to focus on getting just more and more people into your ADPIP (and living in TOFU land), but I find greater satisfaction and reward in working with my BOFU humans.

If all your attention is on the newbies, the oldbies can end up feeling a little unloved. To ensure I keep both old and new people happy, I:

- **keep content fresh** – I add new training modules, resources and digital downloads to the membership each month based on member feedback
- **meet changing needs** – as the world changes, I adapt, such as by offering longer payment plans or discounts in tough times
- **communicate regularly** – I send weekly email updates for my courses and monthly updates for my memberships
- **provide valuable content** – I continually look for fresh ways to deliver content, such as articles, resources, videos, webinars, mini courses, conferences, meet-ups, 'do it days' and more.

It's also nice to reward long-term members with extra bits and bobs. I do this in my membership by:

- **sending lovely gifts** each year a member renews (all sourced from my members)
- **celebrating renewals** in the group and on socials
- **offering perks** to members who pay annually, such as the chance to post a listing in my directory.

> **TOON TIP** I have debated over the years whether the annual gifts are a good use of my time and money. I did have one member who was so annoyed that I'd sent them a cheese board that they took time to post it back to me with a nasty note, which was wild! But 99% of my members appreciate them. Who doesn't love nice packages in the mail?

Tactic 13: Create diversity

I foster an inclusive and safe environment and encourage openness and diversity. Many courses, memberships and masterminds focus on a particular gender, industry, niche or business level – but I don't. Not that being niched is a bad thing, but I just like to welcome everyone. It makes marketing a little harder but the group much better.

My membership includes all genders and races across a huge variety of industries. I don't require people to be at a certain 'income' level to join – I try to keep pricing affordable for small business.

The range of humans in my ADPIPs – having people from all walks of life, and allowing people to fully be themselves and feel like they are welcome – makes them much more enjoyable. The diversity helps bring together different perspectives and ideas, and gets people out of their 'bubble'.

Tactic 14: Don't force participation

Whatever you do to make people feel at home, you'll find some course, membership and mastermind humans never show up at all. Ever. This can be a worry as you rack your brains thinking of ways to get them involved. But there are only so many things you can do. I'd say that around 40% of my membership are lurkers who never post, comment or show up to calls but continue to pay year after year.

With my courses, I'd say a solid 30% make it to all the calls, and some never make it to a single one. Do your best to foster engagement, but don't force people to participate, and remember that just because they're not showing up doesn't mean they're not happy.

Tactic 15: Track retention results

I'm not hugely data driven and go on vibe more than anything else, but if you want to carefully measure your retention results, this is what I'd look at:

- **Retention rate** – the percentage of your members who stay for a set period (a year usually)
- **Churn rate** – the percentage of members who leave over a year
- **Average membership length** – how long a member stays
- **Renewal rate** – what percentage of members renew their memberships
- **Member engagement** – which you can measure through group engagement, turn-up rate for live sessions and logins to your membership area.

What about offering different levels?

So far, I haven't tried this tactic. Many courses, masterminds and memberships offer tiers, which can help keep members engaged because you've segmented them out and are better able to meet their needs. So, for example:

- **Basic membership** might include access to the community and membership portal and a few calls a month
- **Standard membership** might include everything above, and also the opportunity to join online workshops and co-working sessions
- **Premium membership** might include the bits and bobs in basic and standard, and also some one-on-one sessions.

You may also want to consider student, senior, charity and lifetime memberships. (I offer discounts to not-for-profits and scholarships to people from minority groups.)

The reason I haven't offered different levels is because I don't want to create 'otherism' in my groups. I don't want those of the basic tier to feel lesser, or alienate them because they can't afford the higher tiers. I'd rather launch a separate product (a mastermind) than divide my lovely membership into camps.

TL;DR

Don't spend your entire life living in TOFU land, waving your hand around to get new customers. After you've launched your ADPIP and have some customers, love them hard. Even if there are just a few of them. They are your OG and will become your advocates in future if you treat them well.

OVER TO YOU

Creating retention starts from the very first post you share about your ADPIPs, because it's like maintaining a relationship. Of course, not everyone is going to like you or your products, but if you're truly yourself and lead by example, then I believe you will create raving fans.

So, the one big thing for this chapter is to remember to be yourself, no matter what.

>ᴎᴄ́ >ᴎᴄ́

Chapter 21

Advocacy

Awareness | Interest | Desire | Action | Retention | Advocacy

Advocacy is funny – what makes a customer love you so much that they start to advocate on your behalf? It's like asking why someone becomes your friend. There are so many intangible factors at play, and I do wonder if it's something you can engineer or if it's more of a natural phenomenon. But I do benefit from lovely advocacy from my customers, so let me explain my thinking.

Advocacy is all about having customers who genuinely support your brand and your ADPIPs through positive word-of-mouth. Generally, these are humans who:

· are enthusiastic and loyal customers
· believe in your brand so strongly that they would recommend it to others without incentive
· feel invested in your success and part of your story
· serve as informal and unofficial brand ambassadors who grow awareness and trust of your brand through their influence.

Why is advocacy important?

We learned in the previous chapter that people trust testimonials from strangers, often more than from friends and more than sales copy from you. I can sit here and tell you I'm the best thing since buttered crumpets, but if someone else says it, it's much more powerful. I'm at the stage now with my SEO course where the word-of-mouth recommendations are so strong that Figure 21.1 happens.

If someone mentions an SEO course in a large Facebook group, dozens of my ex-students flock to mention my name positively. Often, people who haven't even done my course will recommend me because they have heard of me from others.

Now, of course, we want people to advocate for us just because they love us, but there are ways to chivvy them along too.

Advocacy principles

As I said, I think advocacy is less easy to 'engineer' than other stages in the funnel, but I think the right attitude and approach can help. Here are some principles to guide you.

Principle 1: Be positive

While I'm not a fan of false positivity, I do think you need to genuinely enjoy interacting with your customers and want to help them, rather than going into the ADPIP arena simply to make money. While you may think it's all about planning the perfect content outline, it's more about intentionally creating positive experience for your customers.

Principle 2: Be generous

I've talked already about having good, solid boundaries, but I also think that as an ADPIP creator you must be willing to go the extra mile. Doing the bare minimum will only get you so far. Being generous with your time, your ideas and your advice goes a long way – it's noticed not just by the individual you help but by everyone else watching.

Principle 3: Be authentic and honest

I know authenticity has become a little bit of a buzzword in marketing these days, but there's a reason for that. People can sniff out fakers so

Figure 21.1: Advocacy for my SEO course

8 hrs · 🌐

You know, after I did a course on SEO, I felt a little defeated. I thought there was no way I'd be able to find keywords that my website could compete against the bigger, more established players. But I didn't give up, and really focused on keyword research. And guess what, it works. Here's traffic to my website in the last six months. I wrote a couple of optimised posts back in October ... and it's great to see traffic, email sign ups and sales continuing to flow! If you're on the fence about SEO, check out Kate Toon and her incredible courses ... the 10 day SEO nibbles is a great place to start!

How are your active users trending over time?

Active Users

5K		
4K	● Monthly	4.3K
3K	● Weekly	1.4K
2K		
1K	◢ Daily	238
0		

Q1 Oct Q1 Nov Q1 Dec Q1 Jan Q1 Feb Q1 Mar

▶ Digital Masterchefs with Kate Toon
(Members area) · 😊
17 mins · 😊

#thankyou

I just wanted to say thank you Kate - I may not have finished the course yet, but I have still implemented several steps and keep updating the website to the better.

Here is a screenshot of the lovely green numbers -the last 28 days compared with the previous 28 days 💚

These numbers are amazing and definitely encourages me to keep doing the changes as taught in the big SEO course.

Is it too much to ask to keep seeing this increase month by month. I will work for it I promise 😊

Users	Revenue	Conversion Rate	Sessions
3.9K		2.43%	5.1K
↑19.2%	↑61.0%	↑41.3%	↑22.9%

Hi Kate,

Just thought you might like to know - I finished putting all my new SEO knowledge from the course into place mid-April.

I use the 'measure up' worksheet every month, and I just checked my Google Analytics stats. From April to May, my traffic has TRIPLED in one month!!

insert happy SEO dancing

243

much more easily these days. You might be able to keep up the ever-grinning chirpy façade on your Instagram wall, but it's less easy when you're showing up day in and day out for your course students or members. This may require you to share your good days and bad days and be vulnerable, but that vulnerability will build connection.

This also ties into being honest about how things are going, and owning and apologising for mistakes. For example I recently considered changing the way I price my Recipe course, adding an annual fee for the original course sign-up peoples. While this was a reversal of a previous promise I'd made, I felt I had good enough reasons to do this.

I didn't. My customers were unhappy and told me so. And so, I went back to plan A and apologised. I don't feel I lost face; I don't think it undermined me. I think it showed that I'm human, I make mistakes and I own them.

I got many emails after this praising my honesty and willingness to take feedback.

Principle 4: Embrace the cult of personality

Here's the weird thing about humans – we love to follow people. Most of us are hardwired to want to belong to a tribe or gang. And every good gang must have a leader. Whether you lead from in front, from behind or from under a duvet, you do have to lead.

Also, to make people love your personality, you need to have one. You need to go beyond 'professional and knowledgeable' and show your quirks (as discussed in Chapter 6). You're going to need to share a little of what makes you laugh, cry, get angry or get excited.

Principle 5: Reach back and sideways

I favour leading by example. I naturally enjoy advocating for others, I've been called a 'people pimp' more than once. I love connecting people, name-dropping in a connecting kinda way.

But my big message here is to reach downwards or across rather than upwards. Too many people think that the way to become well-known is to suck up to some big, famous person, someone known in your niche – to buy their course, rave about them on socials and desperately hope they notice you.

It's not. Or, it hasn't been for me. Rather, I like to reach across to like-minded peers who will benefit from a relationship or advocacy as much as I will, or to reach back to people who are at the start of their journey, advocating for them when no one else will.

Principle 6: Create connection

Honestly, I'm a deeply introverted person – I can do people, but only for short periods, and then I need time to recover. And that's why I love operating in the online space. I can come in, share some banter, chat to members, offer help and advice, and then retreat.

I do feel a genuine connection with my members. I could list their names in my sleep, and I remember odd little things about them.

It's my natural state to consider everyone a friend first (and then be proven wrong). I think this helps people feel deeply and genuinely connected to me. I do consider my members my friends, and I think the same is true for them.

Of course, there are risks here that need to be managed when the line between customer and friend gets blurry. I do sometimes feel stressed that I'm not giving everyone enough attention. But I'm honest about that too.

Advocacy tactics

Here are a few tactics I've tried to create advocacy.

Tactic 1: Provide proof of purchase, membership or completion

I provide my customers with badges and social media graphics so they can share with others that they've joined my ADPIP, graduated from my course or are a proud long-term member of my ADPIP.

Tactic 2: Ask for testimonials

I ask my members for testimonials (both written and video), which I use on sales pages and social media. Even the act of writing a testimonial reminds my customers how much they enjoy and value my products.

Tactic 3: Solicit user-generated content

Occasionally, I'll run a challenge to share something on socials in return for a goodie. Most recently, I asked my Digital Marketing Collective members to share pictures of their pets reading my books – just fun and light and minimal effort.

Tactic 4: Invite customers to be podcast guests

I invite my members to be guests on my various podcasts. *(At last count I have four, I'm a podcast addict.)*

Tactic 5: Set up an affiliate program

While most of my customers recommend me just via word of mouth for no reward, I've recently set up an affiliate program for my ADPIPs, which offers a 20% ongoing slice of anyone they bring into my world. I feel this is good enough to make it a nice thank you, but not so excessive that it's going to make someone recommend something they didn't like.

Tactic 6: Maintain an open-door policy

As mentioned in the previous chapter, inviting your customers to give feedback on your products and services also creates advocacy – it's hard to advocate for someone who is closed and rigid. Doing research, arranging focus groups and running polls with your customers builds connection and trust.

*

I honestly don't do more than this. I think advocacy is much more organic than retention, and requires you to continuously deliver exceptional customer experience and just generally be a good human. It's about having a gang of customers who feel strongly invested in you because you are strongly invested in them. And often, they're motivated to sing your praises without any reward or backhanders.

TL;DR

Advocacy is a combination of being your genuine self *(warts, burps and all)*, having the best intentions, being friendly, and offering great value and thoughtful customer service, as well as taking feedback on board and recognising your mistakes.

OVER TO YOU

For this chapter, there's no task list to tick off, but I would like you to do a little more navel-gazing:

- Do you think you're coming into the world of ADPIP with good intentions? What are your intentions?
- Do you think you're an honest and genuine person who's willing to share? What are your boundaries here?
- Can you be humble and occasionally foolish, as well as smart and efficient? Can you think of a funny 'fail' story to share?

PART V:
THE NEXT STEPS

Chapter 22

Lovely launches

Now look, I know you're excited. I know you want to make your ADPIP and launch it tomorrow, and you are more than welcome to. (As long as you're happy for it to flop like an overweight seal sliding off a rock. Brutal, I know, but it needed to be said.) Seriously, though, it would be **such** a shame for you to make this sexy little ADPIP thing and then find that no one buys it.

You need to set yourself up for success, and you need to learn the biggest lesson about launching ADPIPs. Here it is *(drum roll)*:

Launching is not about what you do in the few weeks before you put your ADPIP out there – it's about what you do all year round.

Do I need to launch at all?

Well, yes and no. Let's deal with the no first.

Many ADPIPs are sold on an 'evergreen' model, meaning they're available all the time. Generally, these evergreen courses are sold without support, as it's too hard to support people joining at different times and at different stages.

But here's why I don't like the evergreen model:

- **There's no urgency to join.** If it's always there, well, I'll just join tomorrow.

- **There's no group experience.** I don't get the excitement of the launch; I don't get a cohort of other people joining with me. I just join and quietly do the thing. Yawn.
- **For supported things like memberships, it's hard to scale.** The admin to onboard one human is often as much as to onboard ten, so having randoms trickle in here and there is more of a pain than just launching.

As I noted in Part IV, the personal touch is everything in the ADPIP world. Just because we're selling digital products doesn't mean we can forego the human connection – in fact, it's even more important. Also, the personal touch and support is something that small business humans can offer that big anonymous brands can't. We must remember this at all stages – think of it as our superpower.

> **TOON TIP** When I started my 10 Day SEO Challenge course, there were no big SEO companies offering courses. Since then, dozens have popped up offering amazing, sexy SEO courses free of charge. Yet mine still sells. Why? I think it's because people want to learn from me. The only thing I have to sell here is me and my personality. Scary, right?

I do have some low-cost courses that are evergreen, but really, they plug the gaps in my funnel between launches, and most are there as trip-wires, not end-goal ADPIPs.

Here's a true story for you. When I launched the Clever Copywriting School membership, I set it up as an evergreen model, so anyone could join whenever they liked. In the early days, this was nice – I only got a member once every few weeks, so it wasn't a hassle. But the membership grew so slowly. After three years, I only had just over 100 members.

Then I decided to shut the doors, create a waitlist and launch.

That first launch, I got 55 people in a week. This proved to me that people love a bit of excitement (genuine excitement, not hype) and respond to FOMO. Since then, I've launched it three times a year. This makes the admin side of things much more predictable and manageable too. The Clever Copywriting School has now merged into my main membership, the Digital Marketing Collective.

Launch lies

The thought of launching anything probably makes you feel queasy – it's so loud and so vulnerable. It's like standing in the street shouting 'Buy my thing' while people bustle past trying not to make eye contact.

Launching is also fraught with disaster – website crashes, emails going astray, broken payment systems. It's all too stressful and terrifying, so instead we'll just make this fabulous ADPIP, release it to the universe and hope for the best. Sure, we'll do a few social posts, but that's it. Because if people don't know about our ADPIP, then they can't reject it, and if they can't reject it, we can pretend everything is okay. Right?

Let me convert you into launching by dispelling some myths:

- **Launching is scary.** No, you're not shouting on a street corner – you're chatting over coffee with an interested friend. Launches are about education, not balloons and champagne. They're about sharing how great your product is without overselling it – you don't need to make bombastic claims or use 700 exclamation marks. And if you've created a slippery little funnel, your audience is genuinely keen to hear more from you.
- **If it's good, it should sell itself.** There are many amazing products out there that nobody buys, and on the flip side, there are many dreadful products that sell well simply because the brand is good at marketing. Your product will not sell unless – guess what? – you sell it.
- **No one is buying in this economy.** I know that sounds like a legitimate reason not to try, but people are always investing in good solutions. Lack of money doesn't necessarily mean people won't buy – it just means they're more judicious about their purchasing choices. So, rather than putting less effort into selling, it's time to work harder and be more thoughtful.
- **If I fail, the world will end.** You will fail. You will likely launch several times and fail miserably. I know a super successful entrpreneur who launched, went through all the things, ticked all the boxes and sold only one spot. That's okay – success favours the persistent. The truth is, if you do fail, no one will notice – in fact, no one will ever know unless you choose to tell them. Rather, you

can put the failure aside, lick your wounds, make some tweaks and try again in a few months.

- **Launching is exhausting.** It can be, for sure, which is why I only launch three times a year. It can be intense, but it can also be easy and stress-free if you plan well and don't let your adrenaline rise. You don't need to be everywhere, you don't need to do everything, but you must manage your expectations about how many people you will get initially and not compare yourself to the famous entrepreneurs.

Preparing to launch

Okay, so I think we might need a little recap of where we're up to. By now, hopefully, you have:

- gotten over your fears (at least enough to get started)
- defined your audience
- defined yourself – your brand values and personality
- chosen your ADPIP end goal
- started building brand awareness
- created a lead magnet
- created an email nurture funnel
- set up your trip-wire product
- designed your sales page(s).

It's important to note that I do **not** expect you to have completely built your ADPIP by this point. In fact, I encourage you not to. As I mention frequently in this book, a huge problem I see in this space is the belief that you need to have everything built before you can launch. You don't, and you shouldn't. Rather, you should have a rough plan for your ADPIP, then sell some spots, then work it out in conjunction with your early buyers. This might sound terrifying, like trying to build a bicycle while you're riding it, but it is honestly the best way. Remember back in Chapter 11 I talked about how I sold my course to 20 people and then built it? Yes, it was a little hectic, but it meant I didn't waste time building a course people didn't want, or wait for months to launch something because I wanted it to be perfect first.

Now, obviously, I'm not suggesting you be dishonest and sell something you have no capability to make. You should at least have your content planned out and perhaps the first few modules created. Rather, I'm saying you don't need to have it 100% perfect before you sell.

But let's get back to launching. Here are the steps involved.

Step 1: Work out your launch dates

First up, pick the date you want to start your ADPIP.

I'd be trying to find a clear week that's not in the middle of school holidays and not close to any public holidays. You want to choose a time when both you and your customers can clear the decks and focus.

Now, work backwards from this date to create a plan. It might look something like this:

- **As early as possible** – waitlist page open
- **Week 5** – social media starts
- **Week 4** – waitlist sequence starts
- **Week 3** – challenge or webinar
- **Weeks 1 and 2** – doors open, sales email sequence starts
- **Week 0** – ADPIP starts.

Now, as I've said, you're going to be working on promoting your ADPIP all year round, getting people into your funnel and selling your tripwires. But focused launch activity should start around six weeks out from the start date – long enough for everyone in your following to know about it, but not so long that you (and they) get sick of it.

You also need to understand the phases:

- **Prelaunch** – the period before anything is on sale
- **Launch event** – either before or during sale
- **Open cart** – when the ADPIP is buyable
- **Close cart** – when you shut the doors and go back to waitlist mode.

> **TOON TIP** I like to keep my launch doors open for two weeks. I did try one week, but it wasn't long enough for people to become aware of the launch. Three weeks makes it a bit frustrating for those who sign up on day one and have to wait around for the course materials to start.

Step 2: Create a waitlist page

I don't like to have separate waitlist and sales pages – rather, I change all the buttons on my sales page from 'JOIN NOW' to 'JOIN THE WAITLIST'. These then click through to a page where I collect people's first names and email addresses and shoot them through to my email platform to launch the waitlist sequence.

I do this because I like to manage my customers' expectations and be transparent. My sales page includes everything people need to know about my ADPIP, including the pricing. This allows people to visit the page several times before they purchase to plan and budget. My courses, memberships and masterminds are an investment – something that even a successful business owner would have to financially plan for.

I don't want to hide inclusions or pricing and force my potential customer to go through the horror of a 'discovery call' *(read 'glorified sales pitch')*.

Why a waitlist? Creating a waitlist allows you to talk directly to people who are genuinely keen for your product, rather than just vaguely keen. They've shown real and absolute interest. Sales of my big course from my waitlist average around 10% to 15%, whereas from my big list it's more like 1%. Creating a waitlist also allows you to communicate with these customers more frequently and with more confidence. You're not annoying them – they asked to be here.

> **TOON TIP** I allow people to opt out of waitlist communications at any stage via a special unsubscribe button that simply removes the 'waitlist' tag in my email software.

Step 3: Create a waitlist sequence

After a user has signed up to my waitlist, they receive a simple confirmation email (plain text, just in case this is the first email they've ever received from me).

After that, they receive around five waitlist emails prior to launch. The content of these varies depending on the ADPIP, but generally, I use them to:

· overcome any final objections

- provide more specific detail about how the ADPIP works, actual call times and more detail on inclusions
- provide results from previous students
- provide testimonials and proof.

TOON TIP You might not have a stack of testimonials when you start out, but if you've followed my flow outline in Part IV you should be able to gather some about your lead magnet and trip-wire that you can use. Also, you could get some guinea pigs to test your product and give feedback.

Throughout the email sequence, I invite people to email me back directly if they have any deeper questions or just want a little affirmation.

My waitlist is there to comfort my customers by providing answers and proof, and to comfort me. Seeing the numbers on the waitlist grow gives me confidence. When I hit 300 or so people in the waitlist, I can be fairly confident it's going to be a good launch.

(Psst: Be aware that 300 on your waitlist is a lot and something that's taken me a while to get to.)

Step 4: Decide on your early-bird discount

An early-bird offer is a time-sensitive promotional discount that is designed to encourage early or advance purchases. It rewards your customers for committing to purchase before a certain deadline – usually with a price discount – and creates a feeling of urgency or FOMO.

I've always found early-bird offers a little odd. Yes, they're a great way to get bums on seats and help you feel comfy about your launch, but you're usually giving away 10% or 20% of your sales price to your keenest customers, who were going to buy anyway.

I've only used them once so far, and yes, they did get people across the line faster, but they reduced my profitability. I prefer to use bonuses to reward early sign-ups.

Step 5: Decide on your bonuses

Plan a few sexy little things that make your offer more enticing. Some add yet more content as bonuses, but I prefer to offer a personal touch.

In my time, I've used:

- little goodie bags posted out to early sign-ups
- ten-minute website reviews for the first ten people in the course
- an additional face-to-face workshop with early sign-ups
- a free 15-minute chat with me.

Remember, bonuses need to be valuable, but they shouldn't take lots of time to build and deliver. They should also be scalable, so don't include an hour of coaching for every new student – that's fine when you have three people sign up, but if you get 30 people it will ruin your life.

Step 6: Create your pre-launch socials

Now, obviously, I'm sharing socials all year round to improve brand awareness and generate leads, but I do have special social media posts that are related to upcoming launches. I start posting these around five or six weeks out. They cover:

- course inclusions
- testimonials
- results
- pain points
- desires.

All of them include a call to action to sign up to the waitlist. I also go live on Facebook, Instagram, LinkedIn and other platforms and talk about the upcoming course.

Step 7: Plan your launch event

It's nice to do something special around your launch – something to build excitement, gather your potential leads in one spot and help them get to know you better.

I've tried a few **boot camps** over the years. Boot camps are free mini experiences that happen in the run up to your launch – the goal is to give people a taste of the bigger ADPIP experience before they buy. It also allows you to show yourself as an expert, build relationships and help empower your customers.

Recently, I ran the SEO SOS challenge. The format was simple; it consisted of:

- a free Facebook group that people could join
- a daily small challenge that they could complete
- emails sent to them each day with the challenge and tools
- live videos in the group each day where I talked about the challenge.

I also gave away five free ten-minute website reviews.

I was lucky enough to get around 900 sign-ups, mostly through organic marketing, and around 100 from a short-lived Facebook campaign for around $10 a lead. (I shut it off quite early – I've already mentioned my dislike of Facebook ads.)

Of the people who signed up to that round of the big SEO course, 100% had done the SEO SOS challenge. The conversion rate from challenge to big course was around 6%, but I suspect more will sign up later in the year.

As I mentioned in Chapter 17, I do also use **webinars** here and there, but I find they really aren't as powerful as they used to be. I think people are webinared out. They should not be the only arrow in your quiver. If your webinar goes well, it will warm up your customers even more than your email nurture sequence and move them to the next step with more confidence. The difficulty is getting people to sign up and show up.

Step 8: Write your sales emails

I don't overwhelm people with my sales emails – usually, I send around five in the two-week period:

1. **Day 1** – launch
2. **Day 3** – update on number of spots left, FAQs and proof
3. **Day 7** – update on number of spots left and reminder of bonuses
4. **Day 13** – course is about to close, it's now or never, painting the future
5. **Day 14** – course is closed, and questionnaire.

The questionnaire is a simple three-question form which asks the wait-listed humans why they decided not to join. It's so useful in planning future launches.

If someone buys at any point during this flow, they are removed from the flow.

> **TOON TIP** Some people email a few days after launch to ask to be allowed in, and if I'm under my number limit, I let them. If they are any more than a few days late, I ask them to wait until the next round.

The launch

By launch day you should be feeling you've done everything possible to drive customers, and you should be able to roughly guess how many people are going to sign up.

As I've now launched my large SEO course 27 times, it's easy for me to predict this number. I can measure waitlist-to-big-course conversion rates – and I also know that I'll get a lot of sign-ups on day one, then a trickle for two weeks, then a blob on the final day.

The night before launch day, I:

- change the buttons on the sales page from 'JOIN WAITLIST' to 'JOIN NOW'
- test-buy each product to ensure the flow works and the sales go through
- mark my products as 'out of stock'.

On the morning of the launch, I

- set a launch time – usually 8 a.m. as it works well for Australian, American and British customers
- mark products 'in stock'
- turn the chat function on so I'm ready to help people sign up
- send my first sales email
- promote on social media
- go live in the relevant Facebook groups
- onboard my first customers.

My launches run for two weeks, and the first few hours can be a little fraught. In the old days, my site used to regularly collapse! But now I'm organised.

Optimise your next launch

After each launch, I sit and work out what went well and what didn't. Also, while it's all fresh in my mind, I'm swift to reset for the next launch and will complete such tasks as:

- resetting the countdown clock and launch dates on sales pages
- updating any relevant FAQs about launch dates
- resetting the waitlist tags and emails
- setting up new groups for future boot camps
- rescheduling the webinar (if I have one).

I launch my ADPIPs three times a year, usually in February, June and September. This suits my lifestyle, gives me a good income and means I'm not launching all year around.

How small is too small?

You might want to know what happens if you only get one or two people on your launch. Do you still go ahead? Honestly, I would. I know it feels like a lot of work for just one person, but imagine how great an experience they'll have and what an advocate they'll become.

I would just drastically reduce the amount of support you give – so, rather than have, say, eight one-hour group coaching calls, offer them two dedicated one-hour calls.

TL;DR

Launching doesn't have to be scary, especially if you work through it logically and take the emotion out of it. The key is to manage your expectations and not see a small launch as unsuccessful. Every launch is practice, and you will improve.

OVER TO YOU

Think about your launch date. Grab a pen and paper or the *Six Figures While You Sleep* workbook and work out a schedule for your launch activities:

- What will you include in your waitlist emails (even if it's just one or two points)?
- What social media posts do you want to share?
- What bonuses might you include?
- Do you want to do any extra events or boot camps to promote your launch?

Also, set aside time to 'reset' your launch when it's done so people can join the waitlist for the next launch immediately.

Chapter 23

Managing your time and money

Managing your money is a hugely important part of being an ADPIPer. Your goal may be to fully replace your service-based income, but that's going to take some time and patience.

I've talked throughout the book about money and pricing, but I wanted to draw it all together in this chapter to manage your expectations.

ADPIP is not a get-rich-quick scheme

Despite what you read online, digital downloads, courses, memberships and masterminds are not going to make you an overnight millionaire, and often those sharing their miraculous success stories are either stretching the truth or have done a lot behind the scenes to get there.

I have made millions from my courses, but it's been over years, not months. Table 23.1 (overleaf) shows my real combined revenue figures from my days as a copywriter through to moving into a 100% ADPIP business *(I know, how vulnerable)* so you can see how it's all panned out. From 2018, I had no new copywriting clients.

Table 23.1: My real revenue

Financial year	Pre-tax income	Change from previous year
2013	$146K	
2014	$153K	+5%
2015	$202K	+32%
2016	$247K	+22%
2017	$265K	+7%
2018	$550K	+108%
2019	$670K	+22%
2020	$820K	+22%
2021	$1.1M	+34%
2022	$894K	-19%
2023	$907K	+1.5%

I wondered where to put this, but here seems as good a place as any. A few things to note about this:

- I was ticking along fine as a freelance copywriter, making around $150K a year with minimal expenses.
- I kept things steady when I created The Clever Copywriting School and my Recipe course in 2015, but it wasn't easy.
- Back in 2016 I didn't have any extra hours as I had a five-year-old, so instead I had to reduce my workload, and it had a big impact on my revenue.
- It took a while for my passive income projects to take over, and it wasn't until two years later, around 2018, I really saw the rewards. My revenue jumped up by over 100%, and I was able to stop taking on copywriting clients altogether.
- My revenue hit an all-time high in 2021, but this is partly because one launch of Recipe went into 2021, rather than the 2022 financial year.

- The next year, 2022, wasn't quite as profitable. This was partly due to COVID-19 but also because when I hit $1 million, I intentionally set my budget for $100K less the following year so I could work less and travel more.

My business, and most businesses, are not always rapidly increasing lines upwards. There will be quieter years, hard years, investment years. My goal is a reliable, consistent income and longevity without burning out, and I set revenue goals that help me achieve this.

Figure 23.1 shows the breakdown of my income now from my various ADPIPs – 'Kate Toon' covers my Digital Marketing Collective membership and related products on that website.

Figure 23.1: My 2023 income breakdown

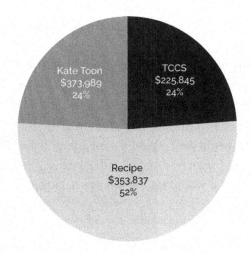

As you can see, my big Recipe for SEO Success course generated 52% of my overall income last year.

As a revenue stream, courses can either give you regular income (if evergreen) – a nice trickle of cash here and there – or big globs of income. I use the launch model for my Recipe course, so I can earn up to $150K in a matter of a few days.

The other globs are digital downloads, memberships and a mastermind. The benefit of these is more regular, predictable income spread out through the year. This year (2024), I decided to merge

The Clever Copywriting School with the Digital Marketing Collective as there was a lot of crossover and several members in both. That will impact my revenue, as not all members will move across, but it will also allow me to focus.

Now, it's hard to know how these figures will land. No one really shares their revenue. Perhaps it looks like a lot; perhaps it doesn't. But the thing to remember here is that I only work 20 hours a week and only have a small team of part-time humans helping me.

Managing your money

Now, it's all very well and good to make this money, but how do you manage it?

If you think feast and famine is problem now, wait until you start ADPIPs. When I started my Recipe course, suddenly I was making $100K in a few days – but then that $100K had to last me for months on end.

Also, it made life incredibly stressful for 90% of my income to depend on three launches a year. I created memberships to have more consistent and regular income between these big course launches.

But the truth is, I would not have survived the world of ADPIP if I hadn't adopted a **profit first** strategy – meaning that even if I received a huge blob of cash, I was clear that not all of it was mine, and I carefully squirreled it away so it would last me for the next three months.

> **TOON TIP** I talk a lot about financials, revenue and financial literacy in my previous book, *Six Figures in School Hours*, so check that out if this is all new to you.

Profit First, the book by Mike Michalowicz, espouses a methodology much like the envelope system (where you stuff money in different envelopes for different purposes). The idea has been around for yonks but gained popularity through Mike's book. It requires you to separate your money into different accounts and pay yourself a 'profit' first.

The idea is that thinking of your business in terms of 'profit first' enables you to manage cash better, relieve financial stress and have a more resilient business.

This book has been hugely influential in my business, and I credit it for my ability to pay off all my debts and get myself to the strong financial position I'm in today.

For me, the key to having a financially healthy business hasn't just been about spending less than I make. It's been about spending money wisely and finding enjoyment in saving it, rather than wasting it on non-essentials.

Here's how to implement profit first (the quick version).

Step 1: Work out your percentages

Your percentages will vary depending on the stage and structure of your business. Generally, for up to around $250K, you're probably going to go with something like the figures in table 23.2 *(although you can buy* Profit First *to get more detail)*.

Table 23.2: *Profit First* percentages for a sub-$250K business

Profit	5%
Your pay	50%
Tax	15%
Operating expenses	30%

Now, these percentages are from the book, but I'll be honest and say that in my experience:

- they don't account for GST, which likely should come off before you do anything else
- I think the tax is a little low – I'd aim for 20% at least
- I think that 30% operating expenses is too high – I'd aim for 25%
- I started out with 1% profit while I got used to things.

I would say, though, that you should read the book, work out your own figures and then stick with them for the first six months. After that, fiddle with them based on your experience.

Step 2: Set up multiple bank accounts

Every business is different, and the accounts you'll need will depend on whether you're a sole trader or a company, and a service-based or ecommerce business, but at the least I think you'll need accounts for:

- incoming (where all the money is paid into)
- profit
- owner's salary and superannuation
- tax (and GST)
- expenses.

Be sure you chat to your accountant about all this first.

Step 3: Pick a payment duration and stick to it

I started doing my *Profit First* transfers after each invoice was paid. Then I moved to daily, then weekly, and now I do it once a month. Yes, this means I'm paying myself a profit monthly. Of course, if there's nothing in there then I can't divvy anything up.

Step 4: Always pay the money into the separate accounts in the order I mentioned earlier

It took me three months to implement the process properly and nearly six months to really get into the flow of it. At first, I found myself paying money into 'profit' and immediately having to transfer it to 'expenses' as I didn't have enough money to keep going. If this had continued to be a problem, I'd have clearly needed to cut costs. Over time, it got easier as I built up buffers.

What is net profit?

Net profit – sometimes known as net income – is the amount of money your business earns after deducting **all** expenses. That includes all costs of goods sold (COGS), fixed costs, interest, salaries, taxes – the whole kit and kaboodle:

> *Revenue – (COGS + operating expenses) = net profit*

Net profit helps you see the true financial health of your business and whether you're making more than you spend. You'll see two net profits on financial reports:

1. net profit before tax
2. net profit after tax.

My net profit percentage is really the only figure I care about. It will vary depending on the ADPIP and the quality, but as a rough rule of thumb I'd aim for:

- 80% net profit for digital downloads
- 70% net profit for courses
- 50% net profit for memberships
- 50% net profit for masterminds.

The reason the percentage for memberships and masterminds is lower is because they require more hands-on input (both from you and, potentially, your team).

Figure 23.2 shows how my profit has changed over the last few years.

Figure 23.2: My net profit to total income

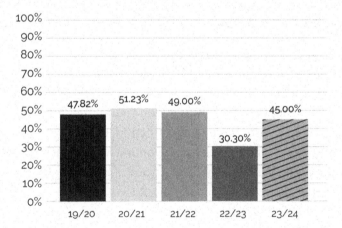

Why isn't it higher, you might ask? Well, because I like to play in my business. I run events which have terrible profit margins and drag the figures down; I experiment with new marketing tactics; I wasted a lot of money on Facebook ads.

And last year I wrote a book *(Six Figures in School Hours)*, and I gallivanted around the country, and I took a month off to travel around Europe with my son. I also decided not to run one round of the Recipe course *(I was tired)*, and that had a huge impact on my profit margin. I had the freedom to do life and business on my terms, and that is priceless.

This year, it's more of a bum-on-seat year – no Facebook ads, no big fancy events, no book-tour parties *(well, maybe one)*. And already (the financial year is not yet over at the time of writing), my profit margin is creeping back to 45%.

Don't count your chickens

Even if you do work out your numbers as suggested throughout this book, thinking about conversion rates and the number of people in your funnel, remember that things can go wrong. The world changes; business changes.

Make sure you have a buffer, and don't throw in your day job immediately. I built my ADPIPs over three years, then finally gave up my copywriting business.

Figure 23.3 shows a timeline of my financial ups and downs and how I approached each year.

What does 'six figures' mean, then?

How you define six figures is up to you. Many people talk about having six-figure launches ($100K) but then don't admit that they spent $75K on Facebook ads. Also, these figures often include tax (GST or VAT). So, take the showy-offy figures you see online with a pinch of pfft!

Here's one final table. Table 23.3 (overleaf) shows my earnings for each iteration of my main course, The Recipe for SEO Success – just literally the big course earnings, not the additional earnings from the smaller courses, events, podcast sponsorship, speaker gigs and more.

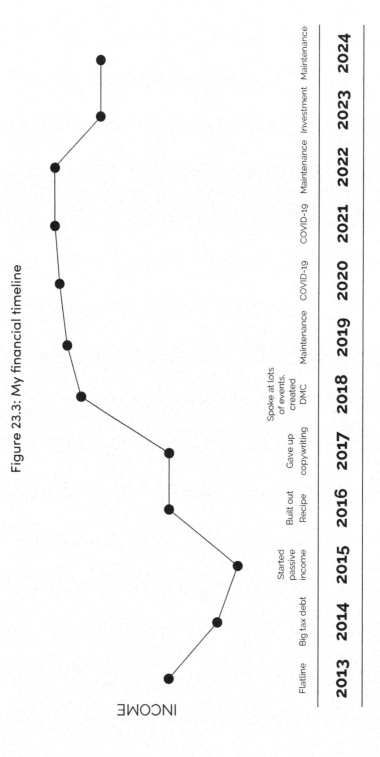

Figure 23.3: My financial timeline

Table 23.3: Earnings from The Recipe for SEO Success

Course number	Date	Earnings
1	February 2015	$9,900
2	July 2015	$19,680
3	August 2015	$58,035
4	October 2015	$32,850
5	May 2016	$48,180
6	January 2017	$26,290
7	February 2017	$59,892
8	July 2017	$98,944
9	October 2017	$122,040
10	June 2018	$116,955
11	February 2018	$108,480
12	October 2018	$125,430
13	June 2019	$142,270
14	March 2019	$144,005
15	October 2019	$153,200
16	April 2020	$151,920
17	July 2020	$146,223
18	September 2020	$108,243
19	February 2021	$129,132
20	July 2021	$121,536
21	September 2021	$103,104
22	February 2022	$95,746
23	June 2022	$125,885
24	October 2022	$94,788
25	February 2023	$100,784
26	June 2023	$117,528
27	February 2024	$115,068

Do the math

When you're thinking about ADPIPs, it's important to decide whether you want them to be your entire thing or just a part of your thing, and if just a part, what percentage.

So, say right now your service-based business brings in $100K a year. In Australia, you'd be taxed around $25K, but obviously you're going to have expenses as well at, say, $25K, bringing your taxable amount to $75K. At the time of writing, that would leave you with around $59K-ish a year in your pocket.

Perhaps you're working 40 hours a week to achieve this and taking a month off a year. This means every hour you're working, you're making about $52.

How do you want to replace this?

If you sell a template for $52, you're saving yourself one hour a week. Sell a course for $520, you're saving ten hours a week.

Sell 20 people that course and you make $5200, and you could take a couple of weeks off.

But of course, we must plan the time to make the thing. Back in Chapter 9, I mentioned that it takes me eight hours to create one template. So, I need to invest that time first. This means I need to invest $416 of my time into my template before I start earning anything. Courses, memberships and masterminds will need more.

You will need to invest time before you make money. And you will need to consider how much time. Can you afford to take five hours a week from your regular income? Over a year (48 weeks) that would be 240 hours, meaning you'd lose out on $12,480. Can you replace that with ADPIPs? Absolutely! I believe you could make ten times that amount in a couple of years if you follow the advice in this book.

But be clear on all of this **before** you take the plunge.

Value every dollar that comes into your business

Remember that every dollar you earn came from someone else's pocket. Appreciate that your success is built on other people choosing to invest in you. Despite what Gordon Gekko might say, greed is not good.

Strong finances mean you have the freedom to make life choices that suit you. But never get smug. Stay humble, people!

TL;DR

It's important to manage your expectations when it comes to ADPIPs – yes, you can make six figures in a year or even a day, as I have done, but it is unlikely to happen overnight.

OVER TO YOU

- Wrap your head around *Profit First* and set yourself up for success. What are some strategies you could implement?
- Make some realistic decisions about the time you can afford to invest in ADPIPs and what return you'll need to make to justify that.

Chapter 24

The final word

How are you feeling after reading all this? Excited? Energised? Overwhelmed?

I know you will have questions, and some of you may want some support on your ADPIP journey. As mentioned at the start of the book I have a few options to help you here (which you can find through my website, katetoon.com):

- my free Facebook group – The Misfit Entrepreneurs
- my paid membership group – the Digital Marketing Collective
- my mastermind specifically created to help you set up your ADPIPs from start to finish – Six Figures While You Sleep: The Program.

As I've mentioned throughout the book, creating passive income through digital products is an amazing way to earn a living. It's given me the freedom to work around my family, travel the world, pay off all my debts and create some generational wealth. It's given me freedom, community, a creative outlet and a nice lifestyle.

But I am not an overnight success, and it does take work and patience.

As I reflect on my ADPIP journey, I'm genuinely amazed. I did not have a big, earth-shattering idea; I am not a super genius; I did not have huge financial resources to pull on. Rather, like you, I had a busy life and a few small ideas. The key for me has been not giving up. It has been turning up each day, whether the previous day was a raving success or a miserable failure. It has been not listening to the naysayers. It has been not listening to the negative thoughts. It has been enjoying the journey, not just the destination.

I wish you huge luck with your ADPIP, with the fat caveat that your future success is not about luck – it's about doing the do and being a brave beast.

I'd love to hear more about your ADPIP adventure; just email me at ADPIP@katetoon.com.

PART VI:
SUCCESS STORIES

Success isn't always about greatness.
It's about consistency. Consistent hard work
leads to success. Greatness will come.

Dwayne 'The Rock' Johnson

>ᴛᴊᴋ >ᴛᴊᴋ

Chapter 25

Coral Wilkinson

Coral Wilkinson is a long-term member of the Digital Marketing Collective who is well on her way with her ADPIP adventures.

She's a registered nurse, advocate and author who supports people to understand Australia's aged care system. With 30 years of experience in health and aged care, Coral assists families in ensuring the well-being of their loved ones in their own home.

Prior to launching her ADPIPs Coral was servicing clients one to one:

> *I was working hard – long hours, very time-intensive, one-on-one, and I couldn't stretch myself any further. More and more people wanted our services, so I realised I had to work smarter and not harder because I didn't have any extra hours in my day. That's where the idea for a more passive income meeting the needs of more people became a reality for my business at that time.*

So, Coral's Big Little Idea was to set up a community to support those trying to navigate the aged care system. She was a little fearful at first:

> *My biggest fear was, 'God, what if no one buys it?' This is that weird imposter syndrome that I think most of us can't escape from. But repeatedly, my community and my clients told and showed us that they wanted to come back; that they wanted more.*

I also felt that I was just an RN who had worked in a hospital. Why would anyone listen to me? But my approach is to always be genuine and perhaps overdeliver, but really caring about what we do. I also have so much experience dealing with this personally for my dad and now my mum.

So, Coral forged ahead. Her goal was to support those in the sandwich generation – people who are running their businesses, raising their families and have ageing parents:

They want to support their parents and do the right thing for them, but they're really time-poor. They want great advice, accurate advice, and support, and so they come to us and say, 'Help!'

As well as creating various digital downloads, including a roadmap and a checklist, Coral started with a paid online masterclass for $47. And now she's launching her membership:

It will be a one-off offer of $997 for 12 months. After that, the price will go up. We're creating, I guess, that tension of 'get in early, this price will not be repeated. It will be going up'.

Coral has worked hard to build awareness, teasing the launch via her newsletter and social media. She's also setting up a waitlist page so she can segment her audience. She believes her most powerful brand awareness tactic has been speaking, as well as her popular book, *My Parents Are Ageing, What the Heck Do I Do?*.

Right now, ADPIPs represent around 15% of Coral's overall income, but she hopes to increase this to 80% over the next few years.

Her advice for those at the start of their ADPIP adventure is this:

Look, absolutely do it, and do it sooner rather than later. It took me some time to understand this and to have the courage to do it. Absolutely do it. If people are on your website, checking you out, seeing what you offer, they're interested. Give them that service, that product that will make you a little bit of money easier. Just do it.

Find out more about Coral at See Me Aged Care Navigators: seemeacn. com.au.

Chapter 26

Fi Johnston

Fi is a member of the Digital Marketing Collective and a successful ADPIPer. Originally a chartered accountant, Fi is the founder of Peach Business, an investor and multiple business owner, a money and business educator, a speaker, a strategist and a coach.

Her ADPIP adventure started during COVID-19:

So, during COVID I noticed I had a lot of businesses reaching out to me saying, 'I don't know how to work out my finances myself'. They were talking to their accountants, but not getting the support they needed. And I realised there's a huge gap in the market for people who want to learn how to do their own finances. And that's where my digital products started.

Fi launched her first online program, 'I'm a scrappy business owner', quickly in May 2020:

I wrote the content as I went. So, it was a very participatory experience for the first round of participants. My biggest fear at this time was, How will I get all this done? I wasn't afraid people wouldn't buy it; I was afraid I might not be able to create the content while delivering to my one-to-one clients.

Now, Fiona has created a six-month membership so members can spend the first three months educating themselves and the second three months implementing what they've learned.

Her ideal client is a woman in business who wants to feel good about the money she's making and wants to make more of it.

As far as her sales funnel goes, Fi explains:

I've built brand awareness using campaigns, so I run one or two big campaigns a year. My most recent one was a documentary, so that's helped me become better known. I then use email to convert people. I have probably too many lead magnets at the moment.

Fi feels a bit ick about the word 'funnels': 'These kinds of terms really sort of trigger me as an ethical business owner'. I suggested she change to calling it a 'slippery tube of joy'!

Fi encourages retention in her membership by delivering transformation for them:

We have weekly sessions; we talk about different topics. We have a Facebook group which is developing into a valuable space. I will also be running lots of other events through that time. Every three months we run a challenge. Once somebody reaches the end of the six months of initial membership, they get to stay for as long as they like for half the monthly price.

Right now, Fi's ADPIPs represent roughly a third of her income, and she wants to reduce her one-on-one time over the next couple of years.

Her advice to newbie ADPIPers? 'Create a sales page with a button on it that says "Join the waitlist".'

I wholeheartedly agree!

Find out more about Fi Johnston at Peach Business Management: peachbm.com.au.

Chapter 27

Jade Warne

Jade is a member of the Digital Marketing Collective and a bit of an Instagram legend, with more followers (around 120,000) than you could shake a stick at *(if stick-shaking is your thing)*. She's also a successful ADPIPer.

Prior to starting her ADPIP, she was the social media manager for Shoes of Prey and is now focusing on helping small business owners achieve 'icon status' online through her photography, videography and coaching. As well as having various courses and digital downloads, Jade runs a membership called InstaGrowth Club.

Jade got her Big Little Idea during COVID-19 and told me:

The membership, like all my best ideas, was born out of the depths of despair. I'm only ever motivated to do things when I'm on the kitchen floor and I'm crying my eyes out. I really was just doomscrolling on my phone. And I had no money, no website and no email list – nothing. I just had the phone in front of me, and I just looked at it and I was like, 'Well, holy shit, this is all I've got. Why don't I fucking just go all in on this thing and see if I can make some money out of it?' Right?

She has built brand awareness for her ADPIPs mainly through social media, providing high-impact, easy-to-digest snippets of action that get results.

Jade told me that one of her biggest issues is time:

Time is a factor that we don't talk about in terms of learning and growth, and business success. You just can't get around it. Business just takes time. Brand awareness takes time. People having their success takes time.

Jade uses Instagram DMs to build relationships with her prospects and her members. In fact, until recently she didn't have a sales page at all, but simply DMed people a PayPal link to purchase. She does this largely through ManyChat.

ManyChat is free to use and a godsend. It takes about literally eight minutes to set up because I have tutorials on it, and that's how long they go for. And then, within the next ten minutes, you can be just reaping emails. So, I can get, like, 2000 emails a night if I have a good ADPIP that people really want.

Now that Jade has a large platform and more budget, she's able to create a proper landing page, which was six months in the making.

Jade is all about proof of concept:

The proof of concept costs nothing. And once you get the money coming in, you can invest in those platforms that you need if you want to scale, which is the next point that you are heading toward out of this: making money in your sleep. You're not going to do that if you're not scalable, if you haven't got the systems. But you need the money first. And I think they both work together beautifully.

Now, her income from ADPIPs represents about 50% of her overall revenue, but she hopes to increase that.

Jade's tip for her fellow ADPIPers is to use what comes naturally:

Don't think that you have to do business a certain way using certain tools and spend a certain amount of money. Use what you're good at, whether it's LinkedIn or it's YouTube or it's whatever. There's a plethora of different tools that you can use. If you're a digital ADPIP person, one of them you're going to be good at – go hard in that one, get revenue back from it, and then use that to expand and to build. Don't wait.

Find out more about Jade Warne at smallbusinessgrowthclub.co.

☽ ☽

Chapter 28
Nic Kastner

Nic is a member of the Digital Marketing Collective, but she is also the founder of Australian School Mums, the largest community of like-minded school mums inspiring each other with easy access to everything needed during the school years.

Her ADPIP empire includes an online directory, free and paid digital downloads, affiliate deals and advertising in her twice-yearly product guides.

Nic's journey started when she was looking for resources for her eldest son, and she told me:

I didn't know anything about the school journey. I didn't know where to go, didn't know who to ask. Within a couple of months of starting school, COVID-19 hit, and we all went down into lockdown. So, it was all a bit chaotic, and what started as a small Facebook group between a couple of mums at school grew to about 1000 members within 10 days. We've just reached over 32,000.

While she didn't start the community with the intention of making money, as time went on and she was spending more and more time on it, she realised monetising was a great idea. But she was also worried:

I had to be creative and think about what I could actually offer and present to businesses to make sure that there was an offering there, without that dreaded feeling of taking advantage of mums in a safe space that had been created.

With such a large community, Nic already had the brand awareness, so it was time to turn that warm audience into genuine leads. She does this in a few ways:

We have free digital downloads that lead to paid 'packs' of resources. We also have a directory with three different tiers of membership.

Nic also has what I call ADPIP-adjacent offerings, like advertising and affiliate deals. But she's very strict about who she works with:

If it doesn't come into our house or if I don't use it, I don't promote it. I don't work with many, but the ones I do I absolutely love. And I do get paid a small percentage of commission for that. But I also love sharing products and services directly from our ASM partners.

At the moment her ADPIPs represent about 30% of her income, with the rest coming from her family business:

I went through a bit of a juggle there as well, along with the pricing pressure. But I read this amazing book: Six Figures in School Hours. *It allowed me to re-juggle and rethink the way I was doing things. It made a huge difference to how I was working, so I'm forever grateful for that.*

Nic offered the following advice for future ADPIPers:

Pinpoint a niche that you already have a keen interest in and create a community around it. Surrounding yourself with like-minded people will help you understand their needs, wants and pain points, and in turn give you a natural ability to cater to them. As the community gains momentum, brands catering to your community will want to get on board.

Learn more about Nic Kastner at Australian School Mums: australianschoolmums.com.

Glossary

Above the fold: In the olden days, this term was used to describe the top portion of a newspaper. In email or web marketing it means the area of content viewable before scrolling.

Advocacy: When your customer becomes a mini brand ambassador and tells their friends, family and pets about your amazing stuff.

Affiliate marketing: A performance-based marketing strategy where a business rewards affiliates for each customer they deliver.

AIDA: The AIDA model outlines the way consumers move through each stage of their purchase decision-making. It stands for Awareness, Interest, Desire and Action.

Automated Digital Passive Income Product (ADPIP): A digital product that can be packaged to provide a passive business income.

Backlinks: Links from one website to another. Many SEOs believe they pass authority or 'SEO juice' to your site.

BANT framework: A framework for determining whether your customer has the budget, authority, need and timeframe to buy from you.

BDF: Beliefs, Desires, Feelings – when marketing your service or product, it's important to know the customer's beliefs, desires and feelings revolving around the service or product to better appeal to them.

Big Little Idea: A small idea that already kind of works but which you can make better. It's about looking at something you already offer and finding a new way to deliver it.

Body copy: The main copy of your web page.

Brand awareness: How familiar your target audience is with your brand.

Brand personality: How your brand comes across; how people describe you.

Brand values: The way your brand behaves or how it comes across in the world – what you stand for, and what you won't stand for.

Call to action: The next step you want the audience or reader to take. Common calls to action on websites are those little buttons that say 'Buy now', 'Read more' or 'Add to cart'. I like to write calls to action that keep the conversation going without the ick of sales pressure or FOMO.

Click-through rate: The percentage of people who click from your thing to the next thing.

Clive Google Factor (CGF): What your ideal customer is googling at 3 a.m. (See also *Pain point.*)

Conversion: Another way to describe an action, most likely a sale.

Copy deck: A fancy way to describe the document containing all the copy and supporting materials for your copy project. It's usually in Microsoft Word or Google Docs and covers the copy, SEO keywords and calls to action. This is useful to have to send to designers and developers once filled out.

Course: An educational experience delivered through the internet through videos, text and, potentially, online meet-ups.

Customer journey: A sales funnel model that includes what happens after a customer makes a purchase. The customer journey considers all their interactions with your brand and all the little touchpoints. It encompasses awareness, interest, desire, action, retention and advocacy.

Demographics: The study of a population based on such information as gender, race, jobs and location (where people live). Knowing who you're selling to is crucial to setting up successful marketing strategies.

Digital downloads: These come in many different forms, including ebooks, worksheets, checklists and templates. Essentially, they all serve the same purpose: to solve a customer problem and help them do something quickly.

Digital Marketing Collective: My membership community, which pro-vides exclusive access to digital marketing learning content, supported by a Facebook community offering ongoing accountability and support to members.

Directory: A website (or part of a website) where businesses can list their products and services into logical categories. They usually include images, a description, contact details and a description of products and services.

EEAT: Like a digital footprint, encompassing your Experience, Expertise, Authority and Trust.

Email funnel: How a subscriber goes from prospect to customer through strategic email communications. Copywriters write the emails and can get involved in planning data-driven email campaigns, so customers get the right email at just the right time.

Email nurture sequence: A short series of emails that addresses customer pain points and helps with advice and offers.

FAQs: Frequently asked questions. On a sales page, they provide a fast way to disseminate boring information without distracting your customer. They build transparency and trust and address any final objections with straightforward answers.

Features: The parts of your offer that are noticeable because they seem important, interesting or typical.

Fixed costs: Costs that remain the same in your business no matter how much you sell.

FOMO: The fear of missing out.

GDPR: General Data Protection Regulation, The European Union privacy and human rights regulation.

GST: Goods and services tax, an indirect tax levied on the supply of goods and services in Australia.

Home page: The first page of your website, which gives an overview of what you do, introduces your brands, offers multiple jumping-off points and acts as a 'magazine cover', teasing the content within your site.

Kevin Bacon Factor: Another name for six degrees of separation.

Landing page: Landing pages gather leads. They contain elements of a sales page but are much shorter and simpler.

Launch: A product or course campaign that creates excitement and urgency.

Lead generation: In marketing, lead generation is the initiation of consumer interest or enquiry into products or services of a business. You are trying to generate interest. Leads can be created for purposes such as list building, e-newsletter list acquisition or sales.

Lead magnet: A freebie to promote to your audience, provided in exchange for their email address. My favourite kind of lead magnet is a checklist.

Learning management systems (LMS): Tools that enable you to set up course content quickly and easily, but which can be a little restrictive.

Mastermind: A business mastermind is a private group or training program, lasting for a fixed time, where a group of humans come together to help achieve their goals. A leader (an expert in their field) guides discussions and creates a safe space. Members inspire and learn from each other, providing accountability and support.

Membership: An online membership allows exclusive access to learning content, community, accountability and support for an ongoing fee.

Meta description: The HTML tag used to describe the content of a web page. You see it below the title and URL of a page in search engine results.

Mission: The 'why' for your business and the products you want to put out into the world.

Net profit: The amount of money an enterprise makes after subtracting all expenses from total revenue.

One-to-many model: In the context of generating 'passive income', it's all about taking services you currently deliver one-to-one and finding a way to repurpose and repackage them so that you can sell them to many people at once.

Pain point: The customer's problem that your product tries to solve.

Parkinson's law: The idea that a task takes as long as you give it.

PASO: Problem, Agitate, Solution, Outcome – a copywriting formula that helps with sales.

Passive income: Income generated through products that can be sold automatically and repeatedly with relatively little effort.

Personal branding: Using your own values, personality, imagery and tone of voice to market yourself, forging a deeper connection with your readers.

PITA: A client who is a 'pain in the arse'.

Privacy policy: A policy on your website that indicates how you will use customer information.

Profit: Revenue minus costs. (See also *Net profit*.)

Profit margin: Your profit as a percentage of your revenue.

Revenue: The amount of income your business makes.

Return on investment (ROI): The ratio of net profit versus the cost of investment. A high ROI means the investment's gains compare favourably to its cost. As a performance measure, ROI is used to evaluate the efficiency of an investment or compare the efficiencies of several different investments.

Sales funnel: A traditional marketing concept that shows the steps customers take from awareness to purchase (and beyond). The idea is that like an ever-narrowing tube, with a lot of people entering at the top and fewer people making it to the bottom.

Sales page: A web page created to sell one thing. It explains your ADPIP and reassures customers of the benefits. It focuses only on closing the deal and collecting payment.

SEO: Search engine optimisation – optimising a website so it ranks well on Google and other search engines.

SEO elements: Parts of web pages that can be optimised for SEO, such as the title tag, meta description, headline, body copy and URL.

Shag, marry, kill: A method for prioritising your time.

Six figures: A potential financial goal for your business that means different things to different people. You could aim for six figures of revenue, after-tax revenue, gross profit or net profit.

Social media plan: A plan to raise awareness of your ADPIP through social media, incorporating scheduling across platforms.

Social proof: Case studies or testimonials that show your customer what their life will be like after they've purchased from you. See also *Testimonials*.

Templates: Fill-in-the-blanks documents that solve a customer problem and help them to do something quickly. (See also *Digital downloads*.)

Terms and conditions: A policy setting the boundaries of what is and isn't included in your product or service.

Testimonials: Written forms of social proof from customers who have purchased your products.

Title tag: Also known as the 'meta title', it defines the title of each web page. Search engines such as Google use it to display your page name in search results.

Trip-wire product: A low-cost product that paves the way for the customer to buy a more expensive product later.

Unique selling proposition (USP): The major reason that your product or service is different from, and better than, the competition's. It must provide a major advantage AND be strong enough to attract new customers.

URL: The address of your website.

VAT: Value Added Tax – a tax on the sale of goods or services in the United Kingdom.

Virtual assistant (VA): a human who provides administrative support online and remotely.

Waitlist: An email list that customers can sign up to so they can be the first to know about a product or service becoming available.

WIIFM: What's in it for me – a question to ask yourself when writing any kind of sales copy.